HEN DOMEN, MONTGOMERY

'IPSE COMES CONSTRUXIT CASTRUM
MUNTGUMERI VOCATUM'

Domesday Book, I, fol. 254a, i

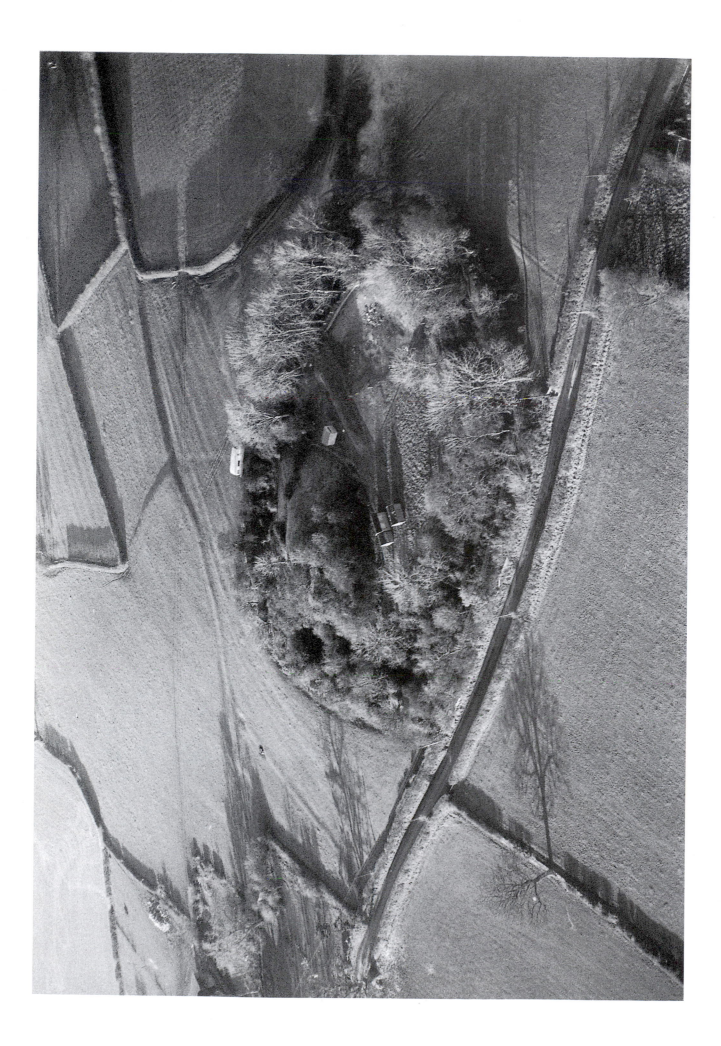

HEN DOMEN, MONTGOMERY
A TIMBER CASTLE ON THE ENGLISH–WELSH BORDER
A FINAL REPORT

Robert Higham and Philip Barker

With contributions by Peter Barker, Sue Browne, Richard Brunning, Jonathan Freeman
Seán Goddard, Linda Hurcombe, Ian and Alison Goodall, Gill Juleff, Valerie Maxfield
Ruth Morgan, Stephanie Ratkai, Sue Rouillard, Mike Rouillard

Illustrations by
Mike Rouillard, Sue Rouillard, Peter Scholefield, Jonathan Freeman
Philip Barker, Sean Hawken, Steve Rigby

UNIVERSITY
of
EXETER
PRESS

in association with
The Royal Archaeological Institute

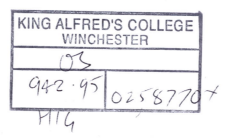
First published in 2000 by University of Exeter Press
Reed Hall, Streatham Drive, Exeter EX4 4QR, UK
www.ex.ac.uk/uep/

British Library Cataloguing in Publication Data
A catalogue record for this book is available from the British Library.

ISBN 0 85989 652 8

Cover design: Bettina Newman; aerial photograph: © Clwyd-Powys
Archaeological Trust; excavation photograph: © Hen Domen Project;
reconstruction drawing: © Peter Scholefield

Typeset in Times New Roman 10.8pt by Mike Rouillard, Department of
Archaeology, University of Exeter

Printed and bound in Great Britain by Short Run Press Ltd, Exeter.

DEDICATED
to the people of Montgomery

Upon this Primrose hill
Where, if Heav'n would distill
A shoure of rain, each severall drop might goe
To his owne primrose, and grow manna so

John Donne, at Montgomery castle

CONTENTS

List of Figures ix

Acknowledgements xiii

Summary xv

Introduction 1

Chapter 1. Background and Earlier Work on the Site 11

Chapter 2. Pre-Castle Phases 25

Chapter 3. The Bailey 35

Chapter 4. The Motte 61

Chapter 5. The Artefactual, Environmental and Survey Evidence

    Pottery from the Motte 83
        Stephanie Ratkai

    Metalwork from the Motte 94
        Ian and Alison Goodall

    Metalwork and Other Material from the Bailey 98
        Robert Higham and Mike Rouillard

    Wooden Objects 111
        Seán Goddard and Sue Rouillard

    Tree-ring Dating 117
        Ruth Morgan

    Metallurgical Slags 121
        Gill Juleff

    Animal Bones 126
        Sue Browne

    Geophysical Survey 135
        Peter Barker

    Survey of the Pre-Castle Plough-Soil Surface 137
        Jonathan Freeman

Chapter 6. Landscape History and Fieldwork around Montgomery 141

Chapter 7. Conclusion

    The Dating Evidence 159

    The Structural Evidence 164

    General Discussion 171

Appendix: A Photographic Memoir 183

References 187

FIGURES

Frontispiece Aerial photograph of Hen Domen from the south, 26 December 1984 (©Clwyd-Powys Archaeological Trust, 84-41-7)

Title Page Detail of (New) Montgomery from John Speed's *Atlas* of 1614

Introduction

0.1 General location map 2
0.2 Areas excavated 1960–1992 5
0.3 Recording grids 6
0.4 Key to conventions used in the illustrations 7

Chapter One

1.1 The immediate context of the site 12
1.2 Northern half of bailey: middle period, phase X 15
1.3 Granary (Building XXXVIII) and lesser hall (Building XLVIII) 16
1.4 Phase X, reconstruction drawing 17
1.5 Northern half of bailey: later period, phase Y 19
1.6 Phase Y, reconstruction drawing 20
1.7 Northern half of bailey: last period, phase Z 22
1.8 Phase Z, reconstruction drawing 23

Chapter Two

2.1 Geophysical and ground survey, west of castle earthworks 25
2.2 Aerial view of castle earthworks and area west of motte 26
2.3 View of (former) ridge and furrow east of castle earthworks 26
2.4 Pre-castle Buildings XXXI and LVII beneath bailey 27
2.5 Pre-castle Building XXXI 28
2.6 Survey of field surface beneath north-west quadrant of bailey 29
2.7 Survey of field surface beneath north-east quadrant of bailey 30
2.8 Computer plot of central area of fig. 2.7 31
2.9 Detail of stone platform (1396) 32
2.10 Pre-castle/early castle features 33

Chapter Three

3.1 Northern half of bailey, phase T/U: the early castle 36
3.2 Building? LVI at bailey entrance 37
3.3 Primary palisade posts of northern rampart 38
3.4 Excavation of the bailey rampart 39
3.5 Fence 17 at tail of rampart 40
3.6 Building XXVI 40
3.7 Carbonized timbers of Building XXVII 41
3.8 Section through rampart and bailey interior 42
3.9 Cistern XLIII during excavation 42
3.10 Excavation of Building LIV 43
3.11 Building LIV 44
3.12 Building XXXVIII 46
3.13 General view of Building XXXVIII 47
3.14 Building LIa 48
3.15 Alterations to bailey defences of early castle: phase U/V/W 50

3.16   Artist's reconstruction of excavated areas of the early castle 52
3.17   Location of excavations: inner ditch of bailey and outer earthwork 53
3.18   Bailey inner ditch (looking southwards) 54
3.19   Bailey inner ditch (looking northwards) 54
3.20   Sections of inner ditch of bailey 55
3.21   Section A, inner ditch of bailey 56
3.22   Plan of cutting D, by bailey entrance 56
3.23   Section of outer earthwork ditch, cutting E 57
3.24   Outer defences, the rampart 58
3.25   Outer defences, the ditch 59

Chapter Four

4.1   Motte contour survey and excavated areas 62
4.2   The motte: the structural evidence, phases T–X 63
4.3   The motte: plan of ?phase X during excavation 64
4.4   Evidence of early/middle period structures at end of excavation 66
4.5   North-east corner of Building LVII 67
4.6   South-east corner of Building LVII 67
4.7   The motte: profiles of building foundations 68
4.8   Profile through ?cistern 68 68
4.9   View of ?cistern 68 68
4.10   Relationship of first motte tower, bridge and Building LIa 69
4.11   Artist's reconstruction of early motte tower 70
4.12   The motte: burned deposits (destruction of phase Y?) 72
4.13   The motte: uppermost surviving evidence (phase Z?) 74
4.14   Artist's reconstruction of last motte tower 75
4.15   Western ends of gullies 6 and 12 75
4.16   Main motte section, looking west 76
4.17   The motte: major section at east end of excavated area 77
4.18   The motte: sections through large gullies 78
4.19   Gullies 24, 5 and 110 79
4.20   Possible structural interpretation of large gullies 79
4.21   The motte: simplified sequence of building development 80
4.22   View of motte excavations in progress (south and east walls) 81
4.23   View of structural evidence at end of excavation 81

Chapter Five

5.1   The pottery (motte) 92
5.2   The pottery (motte) 93
5.3   Ferrous objects (motte) 94–95
5.4   Non-ferrous objects (motte) 95–97
5.5   Ferrous objects (bailey) 98–102
5.6   Copper alloy objects (bailey) 103–106
5.7   Lead objects (bailey) 106
5.8   Bone objects (bailey) 107
5.9   Stone objects (bailey) 107–108
5.10   Leather (bailey) 108
5.11   Worked daub (bailey) 109
5.12   Wooden objects 112–116
5.13   Tub: key sketch 118
5.14   Tree ring analysis of tub: bar chart 119
5.15   Ring-width curves 120
5.16   Geophysical survey of southern half of bailey 136
5.17   Computer-processed data from the pre-castle surface 138

Chapter Six

6.1	The immediate context of the site	141
6.2	The wider landscape setting of Old Montgomery	142
6.3	The environs of Old Montgomery	143
6.4	Aerial view of Montgomery and surrounds	144
6.5	The Montgomery area: OS 1:25,000	152
6.6	Sarkley: location map and profiles of survey area	153
6.7	Sarkley: isometric projection of survey data	154
6.8	Hollow way at Sarkley	155
6.9	Lymore Park: location map and survey area	156
6.10	Lymore Park: section through causeway	157
6.11	Lymore Park: excavations in progress	157

Chapter Seven

7.1	Artist's reconstructions of early and middle periods	168
7.2	Artist's reconstructions of later and last periods	169
7.3	(New) Montgomery castle	172
7.4	The ford across the River Severn at Rhydwhyman	173
7.5	Pit 1/27 during excavation	175
7.6	Pig burial in bailey rampart	175
7.7	Metal-working debris in Building XV	177
7.8	Wooden tub *in situ* in bailey ditch	177
7.9	Reconstructed jug of (developed) Stamford ware	178
7.10	General view of model of Hen Domen	179
7.11	Detail of model of Hen Domen	180
7.12	View from Montgomery towards Wales	181
7.13	View from Montgomery towards England	181

ACKNOWLEDGEMENTS

Without the help of numerous friends and colleagues it would not have been possible to continue the excavation of Hen Domen for so long, and in more than the conventional sense it has been truly a team effort. Due acknowledgement was made in our 1982 report to a great many individuals and bodies who had supported the excavation in its earlier stages. We are grateful, however, first and foremost to the owners, Mr & Mrs J. Wainwright, for permission to excavate and for much encouragement over so many years: without their co-operation the project would literally not have been possible. We are also very grateful to the occupants of Hen Domen Farm in the latter years of the excavation, Sharon and Russell, for their patient tolerance of perennial disruption.

CADW have been supportive throughout in many ways, not simply in granting legal consent to excavate. Mr Richard Avent and Dr Sian Rees have in particular taken much interest in the site. Mr Ivor Tanner, recently retired CADW master-mason in mid-Wales, gave practical assistance in ways too numerous to mention, and other members of the Tanner family of Montgomery gave much valuable help over many years. The health centre at Montgomery and its doctors, John Welton, Peter Ashton and John Wyn-Jones, provided first-class service to the excavation on many occasions. Glyn Pritchard of Hen Domen carried out the machine backfilling with great sensitivity to the site. Many of Montgomery's publicans have sustained the daily needs of the excavation and we are grateful to them all for their hospitality, particularly in the later years Colin and Denise Reece of the Bricklayers' Arms, who also provided a very high standard of evening cuisine. Finally, among the local support, a special expression of thanks goes to the Montgomery Civic Society, whose members supported the excavation with moral and financial help, and at whose headquarters, The Bell visitor centre, valuable storage space was provided over many years.

At the end of the 1992 season, Drs John and Ann Welton organised a farewell lecture in the Town Hall, followed by a garden party at their home where many old friends of the excavation gathered. In October 1999, as preparation of this final report was nearing its conclusion, a reunion party was hosted at The Old Rectory, Llandyssil, by Nicholas, Eva and Susannah Moore.

Second, thanks are due to those who undertook responsibilities on site, as supervisors, draughtspersons, finds assistants and photographers at some point between 1980 and 1992: in particular, Peter and Jeremy Barker, Peter and Pamela Scholefield, Christopher Kelland, Seán Goddard, Mike Rouillard, Lesley Bryant, Jim and Sally Navin and Paul Stamper. It would be impossible to name all those who dug as volunteers, but in a real sense their contribution has been the greatest. They frequently paid us the compliment of returning for several years and often met all expenses themselves.

Third, thanks are due to all those individuals who, either directly, or through open days on site, made contributions to our funds. The principal financial support, however, came (in the years mainly covered by this report) from the following bodies, to whom we are most grateful: Exeter University Department of History and Archaeology Research Fund; the Department of Extra-Mural Studies, University of Birmingham; the Robert Kiln Trust; Tiltridge Ltd, Upton-on-Severn; Barker & Carson Ltd, Droitwich; the British Academy; and the Cambrian Archaeological Association. The final season of excavation, backfilling of the site and subsequent post excavation work was made possible by a generous grant from Exeter University Research Fund.

Fourth, we would like to thank those who have assisted in the production of this report, as specialist contributors, as illustrators or as commentators on parts of the text at draft stage. The technical facilities at Exeter University which have made the production of this report possible were provided first by the Department of History and Archaeology and, in the final stages, by the School of Geography and Archaeology.

The work dealt with in this volume covers a period in which the responsibilities for the excavation evolved. From the late 1970s to the mid-1980s, the annual season was accomplished through a training school in which the Universities of Birmingham and Exeter collaborated. By the later 1980s, as examination of the lowest levels of the bailey proceeded into the pre-castle levels, fewer training experiences were possible and we reverted to a smaller and traditional volunteer work-force (though still largely recruited from a constituency of undergraduates and amateur enthusiasts). This we continued as the excavation moved to the top of the motte. By the end of the decade, one director had retired from his post at Birmingham University. The formerly joint organisation of the annual season was subsequently handled by the other director, from Exeter University, who pursued the excavation to its close in 1992. This report has been written by Robert Higham, with input from Philip Barker at draft and final stages, and with much assistance from Mike Rouillard in the co-ordination of its various components and in refinement of the final text.

The ideas generated during the excavation also benefited from discussions with many archaeological visitors, too numerous to mention. Explaining what we were doing and our interpretation of what we found to this succession of helpful, but critical observers was immensely useful. This valuable dialogue contributed to our own appraisal of methods and observations as well as to our progressive refinement of interpretations in successive seasons.

The Royal Archaeological Institute's association with this volume maintains some continuity with the 1982 report. Publication has been assisted by a subsidy to University of Exeter Press from Exeter University's Research Fund. Finally, we express our thanks to the staff of University of Exeter Press for their support throughout the final stages of this project.

SUMMARY

This second major report of the Hen Domen excavation includes a discussion of the structural and environmental evidence excavated since about 1980 (when the first volume, published in 1982, was completed), together with artefact evidence recovered throughout the excavation, which began in 1960. The reader should refer to the first volume, P.A. Barker & R.A. Higham, *Hen Domen Montgomery: A Timber Castle on the English–Welsh Border* (Royal Archaeological Institute, 1982), for an account of the earlier work, as well as to the *Summary Report* published by the Project in 1988. A brief account of the mid-twelfth-century phase of the castle bailey was also published in *Current Archaeology*, 111, vol. 10, no. 4 (September 1988). Accounts of progress have regularly appeared in the annual round-ups of research published in *Medieval Archaeology*. The total areas excavated during the course of the excavation from 1960 to 1992 are shown on fig. 0.2.

The project has, throughout, embraced an interdisciplinary approach in which many methods of research have been brought to bear upon its subject matter. Fieldwork, excavation, aerial photography, geophysical survey, artefactual and environmental studies have all been amalgamated within an overall historical framework.

Excavations in the bailey revealed further evidence of the use of the site long before the castle was built in the later eleventh century. More of the pre-castle field was exposed, together with evidence of structures beneath the field itself. A fragment of another potentially pre-castle phase was located at the edge of a section of the bailey outer ditch. Residual finds, of prehistoric and Roman date, also attest earlier uses of the landscape in which the castle sits.

The north-east quadrant of the bailey, partly excavated by 1980, was completely removed down to natural boulder clay. This revealed the construction features of the earliest castle and subsequent modifications to it, as well as the pre-castle features referred to above. The former included the first palisade and fighting platform and the first domestic buildings, including a hall, smaller houses and a probable granary. Together with the material discussed in the first volume, this evidence now provides a complete picture of the northern half of the bailey and its rampart from foundation to abandonment.

The ditch of the bailey was sampled, sections being dug in both dry and waterlogged areas. Part of the outer rampart was also excavated, revealing that, like its inner counterpart, it too had carried a timber palisade.

The motte top was excavated so that the area examined was linked to that excavated in the 1960s on the eastern face of the motte, where evidence of a series of bridges had been discovered. On the motte top, an evolving building site was excavated, starting (as in the bailey) with a simple and massive structure whose main posts were deeply buried. This sequence, which seems to last until *circa* 1300, ended with a very different structure which simply sat on the summit. A part-section was also dug in the upper levels of the motte, revealing the crest of the underlying ringbank which was the constructional prelude to the finished motte.

The only part of the site into which we intruded without making detailed record was the western part of the motte ditch, where, throughout almost the whole thirty-two years of the excavation, it was necessary to dig a series of elsan pits as part of the excavation's domestic arrangements.

From time to time, fieldwork has also been pursued in the parish of Montgomery, which is part of a wider landscape of great interest. This has sometimes stimulated separate pieces of research (notably, P.A. Barker, C.R. Musson and Paul Everson, on a field system adjacent to Offa's Dyke). A summary is given of our more general fieldwork and details of work undertaken near Hen Domen, in Lymore Park and at Sarkley. A tentative reconstruction of the environment of the castle at the end of the twelfth century is offered. This discussion extends the range of material included in the 1982 publication, which concentrated on the immediately adjacent landscape context and on the tenurial aspects of the *castellarium* and lordship.

Some of the results of the excavation are presented in an exhibition, created at the end of the excavation, at The Bell, the visitor centre of the Montgomery Civic Centre in Arthur St, Montgomery. The exhibition was funded by the Robert Kiln Trust, the Montgomery Civic

Society and various private donations. The three-dimensional model of the excavated parts of the site was made by Peter Scholefield and the exhibition panels were executed by Richard Rogers.

In one sense, the outcome of work spread over thirty-two years has been the publication of reports in 1982, 1988 and now in 2000, as well as the publication of various interim discussions along the way. We hope that, between them, these have made a solid contribution to castellology and to medieval archaeology in general. But we also hope that our efforts have produced other benefits for the wider world of archaeology, particularly in the development of excavation techniques and in the training of countless volunteers and several site supervisors. Some of those who have spent time at this site have gone on to full-time or part-time employment in archaeology. Last, but certainly not least, is the contribution we hope the excavation has made to the community of Montgomery itself, not simply in visible form, in the exhibition at The Bell, but in less obvious ways over many years. In an age when academic research is too easily measured by speed of execution and quantity of production, we must remember that it is not only the publication of fieldwork which matters, but also its pursuit. Its social, cultural and educational values are too easily overlooked and the total human effort involved is too easily under-estimated once the results are on the published page.

The site itself remains unthreatened and will presumably remain as a well-preserved field monument for many centuries to come, the southern half of its bailey providing a rich potential resource for further research. The re-seeding carried out after backfilling has been very successful. Some erosion of the outer rampart's external face is taking place, especially outside the motte. Within the bailey, the vegetation has restored itself very quickly on the rampart crest and in the motte ditch, where it had been cut back during the excavation. In the interior, the only potential problem is the growth of saplings, particularly where grazing cattle are deterred by thistles. If unchecked, sapling growth could lead to new root damage of archaeological deposits in the southern half of the bailey.

At the time of writing negotiations are in hand with the National Museums and Galleries of Wales regarding the most appropriate museum for deposit of the finds and archives.

INTRODUCTION

In our first major report about the excavations at Hen Domen (Barker & Higham 1982) separate chapters dealt with The Area, The Site and Its Context, The Documentary Evidence, The Organization of the Excavation and The Methods of Excavation. Clearly, what was written there applies also to the contents of this second volume, for, although the excavation has extended over many years and has seen many changes of personnel, it has been pursued within a framework with many threads of continuity in both general strategy and methodology. On the other hand, this single and final report is now offered instead of the series which was anticipated when the first volume was prepared. To assist readers who do not have access to the 1982 or 1988 reports, and to make the present volume as far as possible self-contained, a resumé of the structural evidence published earlier is given below in Chapter 1. We are aware that, in writing this report, we have been putting together materials and ideas created over many years and that in such circumstances the end-product may show some signs of fragmentation. We have done our best to minimize this problem but some of the specialist contributors wrote their reports many years ago (those on bones and dendrochronology, for example, in the mid-1980s) and, were they writing these reports now, they would give them different style and content. To those colleagues we offer our thanks for their patience in awaiting the outcome of their efforts.

Research Issues

When first started in 1960 the excavation had the limited aim of recovering pottery from a site with a documented history, as part of a wider study of the region's medieval ceramics. Very quickly, the potential of the site for illuminating much more was appreciated and for many years the excavation addressed a simple but crucially important issue: what was a timber castle like, in detail, and how did it develop during approximately two centuries of occupation? This issue was explored at length in our 1982 report, but the latter also addressed two other important matters. First, it related the castle to its surrounding landscape, both in its place in a succession of fortified sites, prehistoric to medieval, and in its immediate landscape context containing a mixture of relict, historic and contemporary features. It was felt important to emphasise that no archaeological site ever existed in isolation. This view, already well appreciated by earlier generations of archaeological fieldworkers and historical geographers, was then being adopted by archaeologists and historians in the more acute form which eventually produced the current vogue for 'landscape history'. Second, our 1982 report explored the documentary history of the site, its owners, and the *castellarium* and lordship whose centre it was. In so doing, it tied the archaeological research firmly into the historical dimension of castle studies and made a particular contribution to the latter by illuminating, for the most part, not just the castle of its rich and powerful founding family, but also a (relatively) poorly documented site whose main period of occupation reflected a lesser family of marcher lords.

In producing this final report, we have maintained general continuity of these research aims, while also extending them. First, we have demonstrated further evidence of the structural complexity of this timber castle. This is important not simply in providing the mandatory publication of excavation, but also in reinforcing the thesis of our general exposition of the subject (Higham and Barker 1992): such sites can conceal a complexity of development belied by the superficial simplicity of their surviving earthworks. Although our 1992 study gathered excavated data from numerous excavations, the vast majority of these were small-scale and the demonstration of data recovered from a larger exercise such as that at Hen Domen is as valid today as it was forty years ago. Second, we have extended the range of data considered, so that our general conclusions about the site and the lifestyle of its occupants are based on the full array of historical, structural, artefactual and environmental evidence available to us. Third, we have explored the landscape dimension further in tentative reconstruction of the twelfth-century surroundings of the castle. Although the area examined is fairly small, we believe this has two values. On the one hand, we have reflected the ongoing trend towards holistic landscape history, which is important in the domain of castle studies because so much in this field had been site-orientated for so long. On the other hand, we have not simply concentrated on the nature of the castle's hinterland but also, in a limited way, on the society which occupied this. We have tried not only to publish an excavation report but to make a contribution to medieval social history of a more general nature. The content of this report thus reflects recent and current trends in medieval archaeology while basically retaining the framework of research issues created in earlier years.

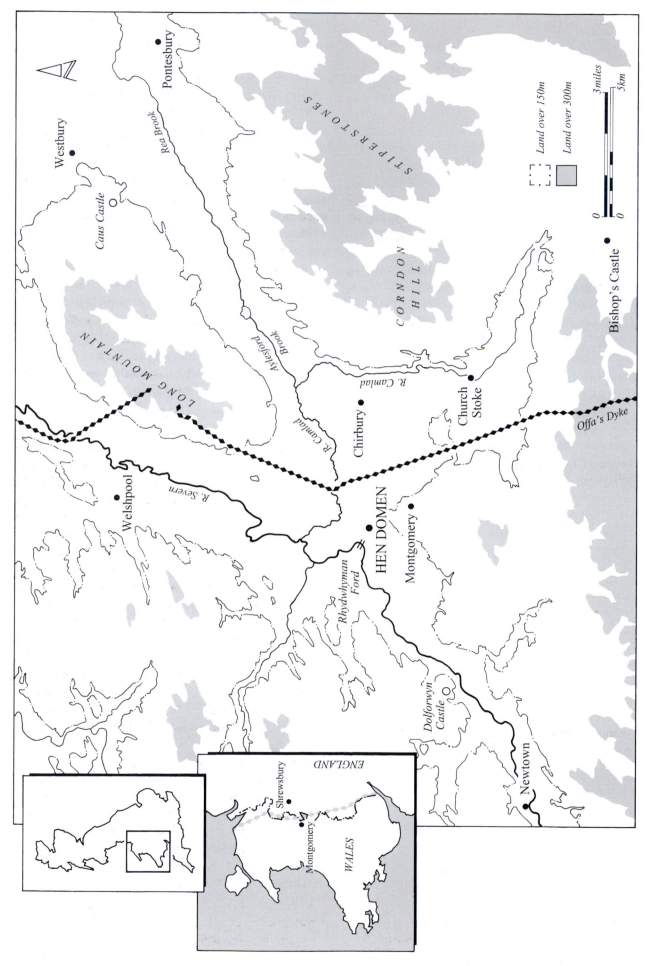

Fig. 0.1: General location map

Strategy

In the Foreword and final chapter of the 1982 report, the hope was expressed that Hen Domen would be excavated completely and would one day be taken into state guardianship to be displayed, as one of a pair, with its successor, New Montgomery Castle. As discussion of the latter idea progressed, the practical difficulties involved became more and more apparent and it seems now unlikely to occur. In 1992, when the excavation was, despite these earlier prognoses, drawn to a close, the general circumstances surrounding British field archaeology had also changed considerably. Some of these changes had a direct effect on our ambitions at Hen Domen. The levels of public funding available had declined and there was greater emphasis on private funding; the universities, from which research excavations such as Hen Domen had generally been organised, were subject to recurrent financial and academic pressures which made them less able to support long-term work whose results might not be published for many years. In addition to or perhaps because of such changes, the archaeological world had adopted much of the conservationist outlook of society as whole: it was noticeable how fewer excavations there were, at least of the traditional 'seasonal' character, by around 1990, the year in which the most famous of all such excavations, Wharram Percy medieval village in Yorkshire, was brought to an end.

The changing archaeological climate was already very obvious by 1987, when excavation of the north-east sector of the bailey at Hen Domen was entering its final phase. By then we also knew that even to define the 'whole site' for excavation was an impossible task—the extended section of the outer bailey ditch contained evidence which appeared to pre-date the castle and perhaps extended far out into the adjacent field to the north. The field west of the motte was also known to contain features of more than one period. Rather than plan for the total excavation of the other half of the bailey and the motte, enormous tasks requiring financial and other resources whose acquisition seemed unlikely, we decided to seek permission from CADW for a more limited excavation of the motte top. Although experience showed that the southern half of the bailey was unlikely to be a mirror image of the excavated (northern) half, it did at least seem likely to contain other domestic buildings. The potential of the motte, on the other hand, was less well understood, and an argument could be made for its examination in order to gain a more balanced picture of the whole castle. The realities of time and resource meant, however, that we proposed an excavation of its summit only, not its total removal and reconstruction as we had, perhaps over-optimistically, imagined years before. Accordingly, excavation of the motte top began in 1988 as that in the north-east sector of the bailey was finishing (1988–90).

In the event, even the modest strategy adopted for the motte top was brought to an end prematurely, in 1992, because of the difficulties of acquiring funding for the excavation for more than a season at a time. Without resources with which to plan a proper strategy of excavation and post-excavation work, it seemed not only very difficult but also unwise to continue. A generous grant from the University of Exeter Research Fund enabled a final season to be mounted and the post-excavation work to begin. Although a great deal of evidence was excavated, examination of some of the earliest structural features discovered in the motte remains unfinished, and any secrets which the depths of the mound may hold await discovery by a future generation. Before general backfilling of the motte top, the surviving features were individually backfilled and some were also lined with polythene. The edge of the excavation was also outlined in a metre-wide strip of drain-through fabric which should enable any future excavator to continue where we left off.

We feel, however, that we have probably understood most of what the motte top can tell us. Any archaeologist who excavates the castle at some future date would be better advised (unless total removal of the motte is an option) to examine the untouched, southern half of the bailey, and the remainder of the inner and outer defences, which can be guaranteed to yield a high return: this is suggested by the excavated evidence from the northern half of the site, by surface features in the southern half (notably a large building hollow in the south-east and a prominent rampart bulb in the south-west) and by the results of geophysical survey. It is nevertheless interesting that very few of the features excavated in the northern half were running southwards into unexcavated ground. This occurred only at the western and eastern extremities. At the west end, the large hall (below, fig. 3.14, Building LIa) continues southwards, and its approximate extent has been measured by a ground-probing radar survey (below, fig. 5.16). At the east end, we felt throughout the excavation that features on the bulb of the rampart were parts of a defended entrance which could have been properly understood only if both sides of the entrance had been excavated simultaneously, a possibility made difficult by the fact that this is also the current entrance to the site. Between these extremities lies the small, central courtyard which separated the buildings excavated to the north from those whose existence can be assumed to the south.

In retrospect, we can see that, by extending, in both fieldwork and publication, from the 1960s to the 1990s, the project transcended an important phase in the development of British archaeology. One culture, in which so much was achieved with strong academic and educational motives and a major voluntary input, was gradually superseded by another culture in which the simplest activities seemed to cost an arm and a leg and (at least in universities) research and its publication seemed driven less by genuine academic strategies than by externally imposed monitoring of published output and success in acquiring finance for it. Though we were happy that, over thirty years, the project had contributed much to knowledge of medieval castles, we were also conscious, by the end, that it had survived this cultural change largely through will-power, but with increasing difficulty. The wrapping up of the excavation was, accordingly, a process in which satisfaction of past achievement was tinged with not a little sadness. Those who saw this excavation through so many years did so very much out of a sense of personal commitment, and this commitment was, despite the funds raised, the project's most important single resource. We therefore make no apology for writing parts of this report in the first person.

Procedures

The excavation was pursued in short summer seasons with volunteer labour and with considerable emphasis on training. We continued to stress dissection of archaeology in the horizontal dimension—which proved so useful in earlier years—and sections were generally used as an aid to excavation of individual features. Apart from ditch sections, only two significant standing sections arose from the years of excavation described here: first, the longitudinal section of the bailey rampart which was the result of total excavation of the north-east sector of the bailey; second, on the eastern face of the motte near the junction of the 1960s excavation and the later work. Indeed, even running sections were abandoned where they were found to obscure the evidence (for example, on the motte top) or to reveal nothing significant (for example, across the bailey rampart). Almost all the digging was done by hand: the lower levels of the bailey rampart and the section on the east face of the motte were dug partly by machine. Backfilling was by machine, finished off by hand.

Recording systems were largely those described for the north-east sector of the bailey in the 1982 report. When excavation of the motte began in 1988, the 5m grid was transferred there from the bailey and the same digging and recording methods applied, except that, given the relatively small area concerned, it was found more convenient to plan the whole motte top together rather than grid square by grid square. Fig. 0.3 is a key plan showing the 5m grid used in the north-eastern part of the bailey and on the motte, as well as the imperial grid used in the 1960s in the north-western part of the

bailey. The latter, laid out on the ground in 10ft squares, was portrayed in the 1982 report as 20ft squares which have also been used in our overall key plan. The plans showing the evidence excavated in the north-east sector also have easting and southing measurements derived from a datum at the top left (north-west) corner of the post-1970 area. Individual features/deposits were given 'context numbers' for recording purposes. Erring on safety's side, sub-divisions of them were sometimes numbered separately, though these numbers might later be subsumed in a single number on the published plan. This, and the re-allocation of discarded numbers, sometimes leads to the occurrence of widely separated numbers for adjacent (and sometimes related) features. The role of context numbers as nothing more than convenient labels should be remembered.

Inevitably, in an excavation which ran for so long, we have had to contend with some inconsistency in the quality and nature of site records and it would be dishonest to pretend that every aspect of digging and recording proceeded equally well all the time. In the early and later seasons of excavation a small group of people was relatively easy to co-ordinate and the recording was channelled through a very limited number of personnel. In the middle years, however, when larger numbers of diggers were taken on and the seasons were organised as an advertised 'training excavation', we faced a dilemma common to all such excavations - how to give everyone attending some experience in as wide an array of digging and recording as possible, while at the same time maintaining 'quality control' of the result. Some aspects of the site record, despite our best efforts, undoubtedly suffered in those years, but never, we can confidently say, to the detriment of our overall understanding of the site. Equally, there can be no regret about the 'training dig' years because so many people gained some benefit from them and they helped us keep the excavation going through a period of financial difficulty. It should also be emphasised that, though difficulties of record control may sometimes arise in the examination of a large open area, these are by far preferable to the constraints on interpretation created by examination of small areas, even though in the latter 'control' is easy and the record satisfyingly tight. This simple methodological point is still worth making, more than twenty years after the debate in the 1970s about excavation techniques, because, at the time of writing, so much excavation in Britain has for various reasons reverted to more or less 'key-hole' exploration.

Our first published volume laid much emphasis on the visual presentation of the detailed structural evidence. This was partly because the evidence encountered in the bailey was unparalleled, and partly because in the 1960s and 1970s excavation and recording techniques were

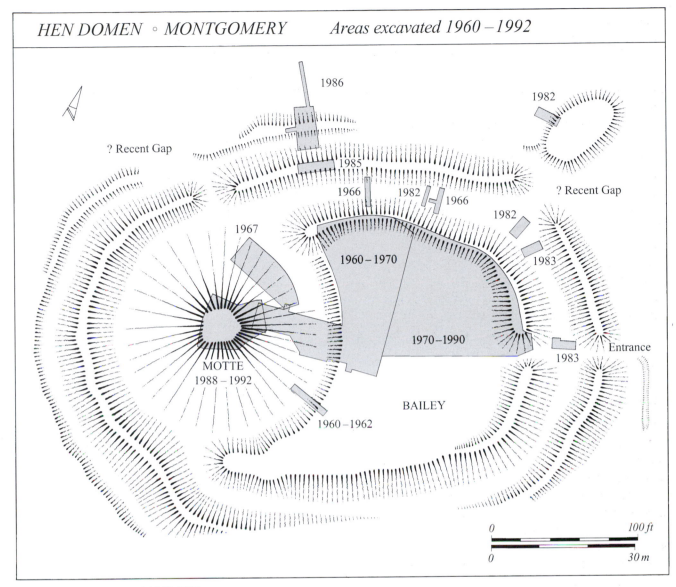

HEN DOMEN ∘ MONTGOMERY   *Areas excavated 1960 – 1992*

1986

1982

? Recent Gap

1985

? Recent Gap

1966   1982   1966

1982

1967

1983

1960 – 1970

1970 – 1990

1983   Entrance

MOTTE
1988 – 1992

BAILEY

1960 – 1962

0   100 ft

0   30 m

Fig. 0.2: Areas excavated 1960–1992

themselves undergoing major changes (to which the work at Hen Domen itself made a significant contribution). In the present volume, we have aimed rather to describe the site's overall development and occupation, as well as its immediate environment, using the full range of structural, artefactual and other data available. Presentation of the structural aspects is accordingly somewhat simpler for the bailey, with more detail shown for the motte top which is a crucial part of the site not dealt with in our earlier publications. Neither is this report consciously written at any particular 'level' (to use the jargon of the post-excavation world). Fuller detail is given where necessary to demonstrate particular matters and less detail elsewhere. We have tried, in a simple sense, to 'tell a story', but with the evidence and its interpretation kept under separate control.

In many respects, the writing of the present report has followed the model of its predecessor in general approach. The text covering the structural archaeology is as brief as possible and we have not given detailed descriptions of layers in the ground or the features in them except where these were very distinctive and of particular importance. During the excavation of the north-east sector of the bailey (since 1970) over 1,500 separate contexts were recorded and subsequently more than 100 were recorded on the motte. Countless individual drawings were made, as both record and aid to excavation, of post-holes great and small and other features. It is not, we feel, the role of an excavation report to translate the minutiae of site records into published form and, as in our 1982 report, these are not presented here except where they relate to structural developments and their interpretation. Nor have we given here a blow-by-blow account of the site's stratigraphy and of every deposit excavated, although the site was dug, wherever humanly possible, according to strict stratigraphic principles. We have provided primarily an account of the structural features encountered, interpreted in the sequence which stratigraphic dissection of the site revealed. There are accordingly some omissions of minor

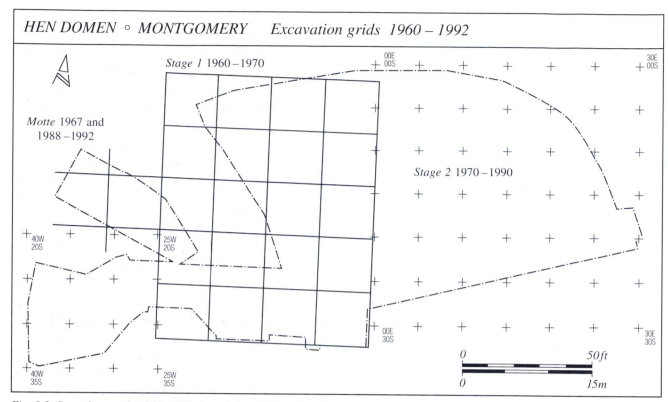

Fig. 0.3: Recording grids 1960–1992: imperial grid (linear) and metric grid (+)

data which were observed and recorded. Occupation of a timber-built site for over two centuries led to the creation of some scrappy ground evidence which, to us at least, was inchoate: minor hollows in surfaces; small, randomly distributed and unconvincing post-holes; deposits which at first appeared to be structural but which, on excavation, made no sense at all; and small, localized deposits of numerous sorts. The reader must trust us that, in our processing of the recorded evidence into publishable form, we have not allowed anything of basic significance to be lost. In our 1982 volume we presented many plans as separate sheets in a folder accompanying the text. In this report we have not felt this to be necessary. The only part of the excavation covering a large area was that concerned with the earliest levels of the site in the north-east part of the bailey. Elsewhere, on the motte, in the bailey ditch and on the outer defences, the areas concerned are much smaller and suitable for presentation in single page format. To depict the early castle we have illustrated the overall pattern of evidence in simplified form and shown a number of individual structures separately.

The site consists of boulder clay and stones, and the layers which were distinguished from each other in excavation, whether by colour, by texture or by the 'feel' of the experienced digger, were essentially variations on a theme. We uncovered successive phases of archaeological evidence by supervising the careful trowelling of this boulder clay and its derivatives, which varied from very clean clay to very dirty (so-called)

'occupation layers'. Sometimes the process involved removing easily identifiable deposits, sometimes it involved the gradual attrition of clay and stones until something different emerged. The steeply sloping ground surface beneath the castle, together with the occupants' need to level up the interior, created widely divergent patterns of stratigraphy. In the centre of the bailey, natural boulder clay lay not far beneath the turf. In the lee of the rampart, however, not only were there more deliberate deposits but the combined results of erosion from the centre of the bailey and from the rampart itself produced a stratigraphic nightmare whose dissection owed a great deal to instinct rather than text-book excavation. On the motte, we were constantly aware that we were digging deposits whose original form may already have been altered by erosion. Whereas the bailey had been a 'collecting' zone, the motte top had been a 'losing' zone, at least until it was consolidated by the growth of turf.

We have tried to distinguish the fairly certain from the more hypothetical. Where the evidence may bear more than one interpretation, in matters of function or of date, we have said so. We have followed, for the most part, the observations and interpretation(s) made in the field, since we believe strongly that the best time to understand an excavation is when it is taking place, not years afterwards. A major contribution to the writing of this report has therefore been from the end-of-season summaries distributed to those who worked on the excavation and to colleagues elsewhere. These arose from on-site analysis of each season's evidence and

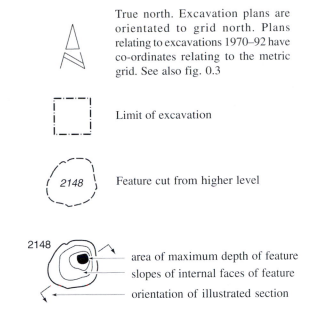

True north. Excavation plans are orientated to grid north. Plans relating to excavations 1970–92 have co-ordinates relating to the metric grid. See also fig. 0.3

Limit of excavation

2148   Feature cut from higher level

2148   area of maximum depth of feature
slopes of internal faces of feature
orientation of illustrated section

Fig. 0.4: Key to conventions used in the illustrations

contained most of the major points which are presented here. Occasionally, however, reflection on our recorded data has led us to change our view on points of interpretation, but such changes have been neither major nor frequent.

We have tried to avoid the temptation, which to excavators is a considerable one, of writing as though every piece of evidence encountered made sense and fitted into a coherent, water-tight scheme of interpretation. The vagaries of survival of the evidence, and its recovery, observation and recording, are, if excavators are honest, very considerable. There is no justification for, or point in, glossing over difficulties and we have pointed these out wherever they present significant issues: for example, the curious contrasts between the surface of the pre-castle plough-soil in the north-west and north-east quadrants of the bailey; the elusive nature of some of the primary bailey palisade post-positions; the baffling interpretation of the large gullies around the top of the motte; the potential dating discrepancies amongst the small number of C^{14} assessments. So, as well as describing and analysing the results of our efforts, we have, where appropriate, tried to draw out important methodological lessons.

We have pointed out in earlier publications, and it is worth repeating here, that some of the contrasts in the archaeology of the bailey coincide with the north-west and north-east quadrants in which it was excavated, before and after 1970. In particular, the last two major phases of structures identified (called Z and Y) contained far more evidence in the north-west than in the north-east, and the character of the pre-castle land surface was different in each area. We can, however, be confident

that this is a product of objective excavation and recording simply because, with the evidence of the north-west quadrant in mind, we were *expecting* to find more evidence in the north-east. We looked very hard for it but there was simply less of it: the contrasts, though coinciding in a somewhat exasperating way with a major division in the excavation's development, were real.

During the backfilling of the north-east sector of the bailey in 1990 a sealed metal container holding a copy of the 1982 report and various other late twentieth-century printed items was buried in the small extension cut into the rampart face in order to expose post-hole 1464/7 belonging to pre-castle building LVII (below, fig. 2.4). In 1991 it was observed that the lower part of the bailey had not drained properly after the rain of winter 1990/1991. This was perhaps because the excavation, particularly the removal of the buried soil from beneath the rampart, had altered the earlier drainage pattern. A drainage channel, filled with stones, was therefore inserted to take water out through the bailey entrance. By 1992, when the excavation finally ended, this device had been successful. Subsequent visits to the site have confirmed this.

When the whole site had been backfilled we were struck by how small its interior and motte top seemed to be. Opening up the bailey in particular and exposing the foundations of numerous buildings had altered our perception of the site over many years. Now, with the site restored to its former contours and freshly grassed, it was difficult to imagine the wealth of structural evidence we had encountered. The point is made not simply as a reflection on how one's appreciation of space can alter. It underlines the most important single message of the whole excavation: that the simplicity and frequently small scale of timber castle earthworks can conceal an extraordinary complexity and quantity of structures. We have elsewhere (Higham and Barker 1992) pursued this crucial point on a wider front.

Personal Philosophy

It is an obvious, but easily forgotten fact that research and its reporting are as much a product of their own time as are the people, places and events which are their subject matter. The excavation and fieldwork at Hen Domen extended over thirty-two years and by the time this report is published it will be forty years since the first season of digging took place. That long period has seen many changes in the organisation and approach of British archaeology. But against a changing background, the project itself was conducted throughout with much of its original spirit intact, a spirit which from the perspective of the late 1990s looks somewhat old-fashioned and, to some eyes, 'amateur'. Nevertheless, what the project often lacked in resources it certainly made up for in its genuine thirst for knowledge and in its provision of an educational experience for countless aspiring excavators. In another sense, too, the project continued to be a product of the circumstances of its foundation, in that it kept solidly to a traditional philosophy of simple archaeological and historical correlation and synthesis. Between the 1960s and 1990s, archaeological thought moved through various phases, as one fashion succeeded another in an effort to look at archaeological data afresh and explore new ways of making it illuminate the past. In writing this report, in the late 1990s, it might have been tempting to re-think our material and imagine how we would have construed it had the project, for example, been established now, rather than nearly forty years ago. But, rather than use our material as the source of an ongoing intellectual game, we have brought the project to a published conclusion in the same traditionalist frame of mind with which we pursued it in the field.

It should, of course, be noted that in the 1990s the project would not have taken the same form: it is not hard to imagine the response from curatorial and funding bodies (not to mention university employers) to a request for several decades of annual, volunteer-based seasons of excavation producing two major reports separated by nearly twenty years. A Hen Domen project of the 1990s, if it had occurred at all (which is perhaps unlikely), would almost certainly have consisted of small, virtually sampling excavations of various parts of the site, not unlike so much archaeology carried out in the early and middle years of this century. We make this point not, we stress, to glorify the length of our project for its own sake: after all, the entire digging time was not great. The total of all the short annual seasons was the equivalent of approximately two years' excavation. It is, however, a relevant observation on the evolving character of British archaeology in general.

The length of the project is also very relevant to the matter of our overall approach to its interpretation. In spending season after season living in the same bailey (and sometimes on the same motte) as the castle's occupants, with the same smell of woodsmoke, from our camp-fire, that must have surrounded them, and seeing at night the same stars at which they gazed, we gained a sense of empathy with them which could not possibly have been acquired in a short time and which makes it almost insulting to regard the buildings and artefacts they left behind as simply disembodied data to be used for contemporary intellectual entertainment. We were, obviously, always conscious that so much of the castle which we struggled every year to understand had completely disappeared. We also knew that while, in one sense, we were re-creating the past, we were in another

sense simply creating it. But, despite these limitations, we also felt a sense of honest communication with the past inhabitants of this place, who, given the small internal area of the site, must have trod exactly where we trod every day. And even on the darkest of nights or in the foulest of weather, it was never a hostile environment—indeed, the security which the ramparts had afforded the castle's occupants seemed, in a curious way, extended to us. The atmosphere provided by the spirits of those who had preceded us was always a benign one, as though, watching our feeble efforts to understand them (and no doubt amused by the grossness of our mistakes!), they knew our intentions were honourable. For many years, during the excavation of the bailey rampart, a succession of red admiral butterflies would settle on the bright boulder clay in the midday sun. So regular were these occurrences that we referred each year to our winged visitor as 'Roger of Montgomery', the castle's founder, and imagined his ghost watching over our labours. It was in one sense a typical 'in-house' joke of the sort which abounds on excavations, but in another sense the point had more significance. Another, somewhat curious product of the excavation's long duration was that the authors' familiarity with the site was as long as that of its founding family, who owned it from *circa* 1070 to 1102. Indeed, given the peripatetic lifestyle of aristocratic families, the personal visits of Roger de Montgomery and his sons were presumably extremely infrequent, so that we (and other long-term members of our team) may have seen more of the place than did the leading members of this illustrious Norman family whose castle it was.

In what follows, therefore, we have approached the matter of social reconstruction from an unashamedly simple and humanistic point of view because this was, throughout the excavation, the philosophy which guided us. We have done our best to build up a picture of the past which we hope the medieval occupants of Hen Domen, were they now with us, would recognise at least in outline. While acknowledging the gulf which separates us from them, we have assumed a continuity of human thought and experience across the centuries which, we hope, gives us at least a chance of understanding something of their lives. To misquote a famous archaeologist, archaeology is about people, even if we have to approach them through things. We have, at the same time, been very mindful of the limitations of our evidence in the knowledge that what archaeology cannot tell us (or anyone) is almost as important as what it can. Finally, we do not subscribe to the view, sometimes argued by medieval archaeologists, that historical sources provide a limitation to the interpretation of archaeological evidence. We are enthusiastically old-fashioned in maintaining the value of documentary frameworks, where they are available. At Hen Domen, not only do the documentary sources (critically discussed at great length elsewhere—see Barker & Higham 1982, Chapter III) provide crucial dating evidence and information on the site's social history, but they also give us the names of individuals and families associated with the castle. To regard such data as anything less than of prime importance seems, to us at least, misguided. The essence of interdisciplinary study is the appreciation of each discipline's strengths and weaknesses and of their potential to complement each other. To put it simply, excavation could never have revealed Roger de Montgomery, or the de Boulers family who were the castle's twelfth-century lords, but equally the documents could never have revealed the multiplicity of structures they built or the varied material culture they enjoyed. But, in order to be fair to the archaeological evidence, we have also assessed it independently as part of the methodological discussion in our concluding chapter. We have also approached the whole excavation and publication of the site on the assumption of its identification with (Old) Montgomery, argued at length, on a combination of documentary and topographic evidence, in our 1982 report. From that identification arise many other assumptions in our interpretation of the site and its archaeology.

CHAPTER 1

BACKGROUND AND EARLIER WORK ON THE SITE

This chapter provides an overview of the evidence previously published about Hen Domen in general, its history and the excavation of those phases of the castle bailey which overlay the early castle. Fuller details (including full references to historical sources and maps) will be found in Barker & Higham 1982, but for readers without access to that out-of-print volume, what follows should help make the present report, as far as possible, a self-contained statement. Some aspects of what follows are discussed further in Chapters 6 and 7, below.

In providing, in one report, both a synopsis of earlier work and full treatment of subsequent work, some compromises have been necessary in the organisation of material. In particular, the following synopsis contains new reconstruction drawings, hitherto unpublished, of the later phases of the castle's development, because this is where they will be initially helpful to the reader. These are repeated later in the report (in Chapter 7) where they can be viewed with the equivalent drawing of the early castle, giving an overall impression of the site's development. It is an inevitable result of this ordering of the material that reconstruction views of some phases of the motte top are included in this synoptic chapter before the evidence of the motte top itself has been described (below, Chapter 4). Cross-reference should be made by the reader between the various related parts of the text and illustrations.

The Site and its Setting (figs 0.1 and 1.1)

Hen Domen, Montgomery, Powys (NGR SO214981) is the site of a medieval timber castle built by the Normans in the 1070s and occupied for slightly over two centuries. Its Welsh name means 'the old mound' and was presumably created after the site's abandonment, but its contemporary name was Montgomery. It is a fine example of a motte and bailey, a very common type of medieval castle. Its motte is 8.0m high, 40.0m in diameter at its base and 6.5m in diameter at its summit. The bailey is quite small, covering just over one-third of an acre, but it is heavily defended with double ramparts and ditches. Excavation of the junction of the motte and the bailey rampart showed that at Hen Domen the motte was a primary feature of the site's design (Barker & Higham 1982, 72). The castle was built on a ridge of boulder clay overlying shale. This clay was an excellent material for the building of the motte, digging of the ditches and piling up of ramparts, as well as being used for the wall-cladding of some of the timber structures. There is no evidence that any part of Hen Domen was rebuilt in stone during its 200-year life.

All archaeological sites are part of a man-made landscape, and at Hen Domen there survives good evidence of the immediate landscape in which the castle was built and occupied (fig. 1.1). The ridge and furrow adjacent to the site in fields c and d represent a field system of pre-Norman date (Barker & Lawson 1971). The evidence of Domesday Book and of pollens preserved in an excavated part of this buried field show that the area had already been abandoned as arable before the Norman Conquest and was being used as a hunting chase. Two hollow ways (g and j) as well as house platforms of unknown date (at b) lie among these fields. Other relict roads are labelled e and i, and h is the course of an ancient road which is still in use. Other fields (marked f) have the curving boundaries suggestive of enclosed strips within originally open fields. Whether these post-date the abandonment of Hen Domen or were contemporary with its occupation we cannot be certain. But the demesne ploughlands of Roger de Montgomery and Roger Corbet, mentioned in Domesday Book, were probably close to the castle (see below, Chapter 6) and it is quite possible that in these curving boundaries we see remnants of some of Old Montgomery's strip fields. Sarkley is documented by the fifteenth century (see Chapter 6). The origins of the present-day farm called Siglen and the hamlet called Hen Domen are not known. The latter may overlie the site of a small borough which the lords of the castle apparently tried to foster in the late twelfth century. Alternatively, it may be of later date. It is, nevertheless, interesting that the castle's main entrance, at its eastern end, did not attract the development of a permanent and substantial roadway—the adjacent hollow way actually swings away from the castle. Were it not for the incontrovertible evidence from historical record and excavation, which shows the site to have been intensively occupied for over two centuries, one might be tempted to conclude, on the basis of field observation alone, that the castle had been dropped into

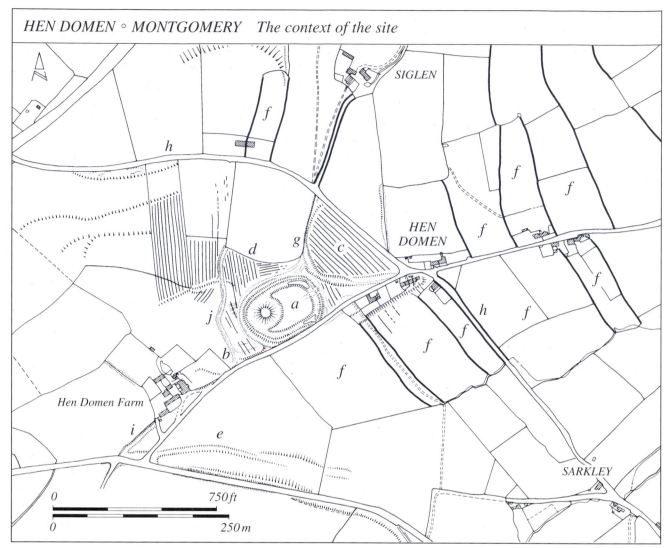

HEN DOMEN ○ MONTGOMERY   The context of the site

SIGLEN

HEN DOMEN

Hen Domen Farm

SARKLEY

0   750 ft

0   250 m

Fig. 1.1: The immediate context of the site (after Barker & Higham 1982)

this landscape and used for only a short period.

The location of the castle was influenced by the nearby crossing of the River Severn at Rhydwhyman. This was a large ford, whose probable Anglo-Saxon name, *Horseforde*, implies its military value. It lay at the end of valley routes which gave access to central England, and had been important for over a thousand years previously. Within a short distance of it are situated an Iron Age hillfort (Ffridd Faldwyn), a Roman fort (Forden Gaer), the Welsh–Mercian frontier of Offa's Dyke, and a new castle and town established in 1223 by Henry III at present-day Montgomery to replace the first Montgomery castle. Two road systems can be seen on the present-day map, one reflecting the importance of Forden Gaer and the first castle, the later one radiating from (New) Montgomery (see fig. 6.5).

The History of the Site

As is the case with many smaller medieval castles, there are few direct documentary references to Hen Domen which are contemporary with its occupation. Domesday

Book (1086) provides the first clear statement of the castle's existence and relates it to Roger of Montgomery, earl of Shrewsbury. Roger, one of William the Conqueror's close supporters, had contributed ships to the invasion fleet of 1066 (van Houts 1987) but seems not to have arrived in England until later. Endowed first with lands in Sussex, Roger was earl of Shrewsbury from *circa* 1070, and Domesday Book states he had built a castle on the western fringe of Shropshire and called it Montgomery. Whether he re-used the name of his Norman home out of nostalgia, or as an aggressive act of defiance against the Welsh, or both, is not clear. It has been noted that about half of all the Shropshire lands which Roger retained in demesne were in the Montgomery area (some twelve out of twenty-five holdings) and that the rest were widely scattered in the shire (Gwynne 1971–72, 101). This may indicate his particular interest in the area, which he otherwise largely entrusted to the Corbet family, and may help explain his choice of name for the castle. Perhaps he intended to establish a town and priory, classic features of Norman colonization in Britain, though he never did so. The castle (which should be referred to as Old Montgomery, to distinguish it from its thirteenth-century successor) certainly became a base for conquest in central Wales: by 1086 considerable tracts of Powys were under Roger's control. In this early phase, the structural evidence, simple and massive, is a good reflection of the military character of the occupation. Since he was an important figure in the Anglo-Norman world, however, Roger may have played little personal part in these developments after the site's foundation. Following the Norman Conquest, many of the estates in the area, wasted in the previous generation, came back into cultivation. Several small timber castles were built by the earl's tenants in the Vale of Montgomery and along the Severn valley as a result of increasing Norman influence.

Shortly before his death in 1094, Roger de Montgomery became a monk of Shrewsbury Abbey, his own foundation. In 1095, the garrison of Hugh, Roger's son, was massacred in a Welsh attack on Old Montgomery castle, so the Norman conquest of the area did not go unchecked. The episode led to a royal military campaign in Wales. This early phase of the castle's history came to an end with the fall of Robert of Bellême, Hugh's brother, in 1102. In rebellion against King Henry I, Robert was defeated and his lands in Shropshire and its border, in west Wales (centred on Pembroke), in Sussex and in Yorkshire were confiscated. The king exploited the situation to his advantage (Davies 1987, 40), retaining most of these lands but installing trusted men, including Baldwin de Boulers, along the western fringe of Shropshire in newly created lordships. Most of the earldom of Shrewsbury itself became a royal shire.

The family of de Boulers (Baldwin I, Stephen, Robert and Baldwin II) held Old Montgomery from around 1102 until 1207. The first Baldwin, who probably came from Flanders (see Warlop 1975–76), was married to one of Henry I's illegitimate daughters, Sybil de Falaise. The de Boulers were far less rich and powerful than the earls of Shrewsbury had been, and this was their only castle and its lordship the limit of their powers, though later in the twelfth century they acquired lands elsewhere through marriage into a Yorkshire family. In this second phase of its existence, however, the castle had important domestic and administrative functions as well as military ones. Sometimes the de Boulers were at war with the Welsh, but not always. Their local tenants provided a garrison and hunting attendants, as well as provisions for the castle. The lord of Hodnet, an outlying manor in Shropshire, was their steward, periodically bringing his family to Old Montgomery and being provided with suitable lodging to carry out his business. The de Boulers never rose to the highest ranks of marcher society, but they were undisputed lords of their own territory, much

of which would be visible from their residence on top of the motte at Hen Domen. It is from the period of their ownership that the fullest archaeological picture of the castle has been recovered. Contrasting with the simpler, massive impression provided by the earlier structures, now its defences and crowded courtyard of domestic buildings well reflect the mixture of military and domestic life that characterized the longest single period in the site's history. The environment of their castle, *circa* 1200, is discussed below (Chapter 6).

By 1207 the family had died out in the male line and their lands passed to the king. Robert de Boulers and Baldwin II de Boulers were outlived by their widows for many years: Hillaria Trussebut lived until 1241 and Gwenllian the Fair until 1243. Whether, in the first instance, residence in the castle had been part of their dower arrangements or whether provision was made for them in another house within the lordship is not known. From 1207, however, the sheriffs of Shropshire maintained the castle, but from 1215 the area around Montgomery was in Welsh control. In 1223, in renewed war against the Welsh, the English king Henry III planned the refortification of Montgomery, but rather than rebuild the old castle he chose a new site nearby for a much larger stone castle. All later references to Montgomery castle are to this new castle, and Hen Domen disappears from history. The archaeological evidence, however, suggests that the site was re-occupied, and the explanation for this probably lies in the local topography. The crossing of the Severn at Rhydwhyman, not visible from New Montgomery, continued to be an important meeting place of Welsh and English down to the 1270s, after which Edward I's conquests in North Wales, completed in the 1280s, reduced the political importance of Montgomery. As a forward control point for the river crossing, the castle probably had a final lease of life of fifty or more years' duration. In this period, however, it was a purely military outpost and had none of the social attributes of the twelfth century. The contraction of the occupied area in the latest structural phase reflects this change of character very well.

Dating and Phasing of the Site

The overall dating of the site rests heavily upon the documentary framework outlined above. It is assumed that the early castle dates from between 1070 and 1086, and that the last castle dates from some time after 1223. Between these two major documentary dating horizons must be fitted a multitude of structural events whose precise dating is not assisted by the documentary or any other evidence. The chronology suggested here, following our earlier publications, is based very much on spreading the archaeological 'phases' through the documented period in question. In addition to the documentary evidence, there is a limited amount of artefactual and scientific dating evidence. The dating and phasing issue is dealt with further below (Chapter 7). It is tempting to relate the middle period plan (called phase X) to the occupancy of the de Boulers, but the rebuilding may not have been embarked upon immediately after their acquisition in the early twelfth century and precise dates are impossible to suggest. Equally it is impossible to be certain whether phase Y, succeeding X, was started within the de Boulers' occupation (in which case it reflects some important social change), whether it reflects the period of royal custody in 1207–15, or whether it post-dates 1223. Between phases Y and Z, a deep silt layer accumulated in the lowest part of the bailey, in its north-east corner, suggesting a period of disuse, at least of this part of the site. It is possible that this coincides with the period of Welsh control of the area from 1215 to 1223 or it may simply reflect diminishing occupation within the bailey. With the exception of the earliest and latest archaeological data, however, the phases as presented here are inherently greatly oversimplified. The buildings separated out into individual plans were probably the product of a more continuous process of repair and replacement. It cannot be proved that all the structures presented in one plan were erected at the same time, nor that they were demolished at the same time, but simply that at some stage in their use they were contemporary with each other. In reality, at any single point in time, the castle may never have looked exactly as presented here in any of our overall plans or reconstructions. We have also preferred, in various places, to interpret particular structural evidence in terms of evolution *in situ* rather than create further discrete 'phases' of building: for example, within the evolution of the motte tower and the bailey palisade structures.

The Pre-Castle and Early Castle Structures

These are dealt with at length below. Evidence for these phases (T/U/V/W) came from the excavations both before and after *circa* 1980 and is amalgamated into one discussion in Chapters 2 and 3.

The Motte

As none of the motte top had been excavated when the 1982 and 1988 reports were published, all the evidence for this part of the site is presented here in Chapter 4.

The Middle Period Castle (figs 1.2, 1.3 and 1.4)

The early castle underwent various modifications, with evidence of a new palisade and other structures dug into the top of the rampart (see Chapter 3). The date of these changes is not known, nor is the date by which the bailey was transformed into the new layout for which we have the fullest plan (phase X, fig. 1.2). It represents the de

Boulers' castle at some stage, or stages, of its development by the end of the twelfth century. Fig. 1.4 is a composite attempt to reconstruct what the bailey looked like in this period, and is based as closely as possible on the excavated evidence. This illustration was first published in our summary report (Barker & Higham 1988) and has also appeared in other publications. Some elements in the middle period plan survived from the earliest castle, notably the granary Building XXXVIII and the site of the cistern XLIII, but in many other respects the plan was different in detail, as well as being generally more built up. Phase X was principally composed of post-hole structures and there was evidence for use of clay as solid walls (Buildings XII and XXII) or as cladding to thicken a skeleton of posts and wattles (the outer and inner palisades and the rooms beneath the inner fighting platform). The reconstruction drawing and plan are here discussed progressively from the motte down to the bailey entrance.

When these illustrations were first published, there was virtually no evidence for the form of bridge x, but the massive supports for the preceding and following bridges t and y suggested that the bridge could be raised in some fashion as an early form of drawbridge. Accordingly, a leaf of the bridge in the reconstruction was shown raised. In later seasons, excavation of the motte top added to our knowledge of the bridges, revealing that at some stage also a narrower bridge had rested on smaller posts (below, Chapter 4). But the difficulty of correlating constructional events in the bailey with those on the motte remains. Similarly, there is little evidence for the palisade and fighting platform, shown encircling the base of the motte, except that when a chord was cut across the motte (Barker & Higham 1982, 72) there were a number of large post-holes which seemed to have no other function, though they made no coherent pattern. It seems highly probable that there was some form of defence here since, if there were not, the motte would be defended only by the outer palisade on the sides facing away from the bailey.

In the early castle there was unequivocal evidence of a very large building at the foot of the motte, probably a hall of two storeys. Building LIb seems to have been a post-hole building of similar dimensions, though extended eastwards, and is here reconstructed with a portico, though a single aisle is an alternative possibility. This building has been shown with its panels clad in clay and with a shingle roof.

Building XIV/XIII is here reconstructed as an apsidal chapel on the grounds that it directly underlay the more convincing chapel of phase Y and because from one of its post-holes came the remains of a limestone vessel, perhaps a stoup for holy water. At the north-western end

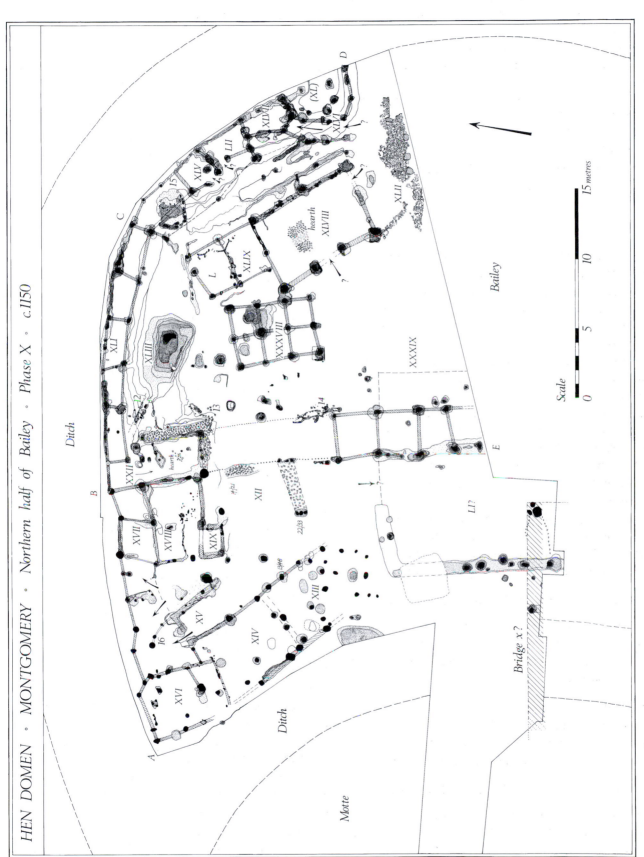

HEN DOMEN · MONTGOMERY · Northern half of Bailey · Phase X · c.1150

Ditch

Motte

Ditch

Bailey

Scale

0   5   10   15 *metres*

Bridge x?

Fig. 1.2: Plan of northern half of bailey: middle period, phase X (from Barker & Higham 1988). Note that LI? on this plan equals LIb in the text

of the chapel is tower XVI on the thickened end of the bailey rampart. It is reconstructed as being of three storeys with a flat roof. It may possibly have had a gabled roof, but its plan is an awkward shape and a flat roof seems more probable.

The palisade which encircled the bailey is presumed to have been of clay, reinforced with a post and wattle skeleton, since the post-holes which make up its evidence are of many sizes, some quite small and dug in a wandering line along the rampart crest. The palisade itself is presumed to have been some 4.0m (14 ft) high, as it must have been in the early castle, to accommodate structures beneath and fighting platform above. In the reconstruction the lower part of the palisade is shown clay-clad, while the upper part is of vertical planking, jettied out over the ditch, with hoardings and, in places, various forms of roofing, chiefly to demonstrate the possibilities rather than be definitive, since there is no evidence for these elaborations. There is, however, independent evidence of jettying from other sources of the period. These include an eleventh-century capital from Caen (France) and a twelfth-century narrative carving fron Modena (Italy). In England, the north tower at Stokesay castle (Shropshire) has a jettied upper storey of *circa* 1300. This, and other evidence for jettied structures, has been discussed in the wider context of timber castles generally (Higham & Barker 1992, where references will be found). The roofing of the fighting platform is again purely conjectural, but in a small castle such as Hen Domen, there would be a real possibility of being hit in the back by an arrow shot from the other side of the castle, so that a roof would be a sensible precaution.

An unexpected discovery was that the bailey itself had been divided into two halves by a continuous series of buildings running south from Building XXII (ironically almost exactly along the line of the balk between the two stages of the excavation). The reconstruction of this line of buildings posed considerable problems, but as it was probably intended for defence as well as a social division, we have incorporated a fighting platform across the whole complex. This fighting platform is suggested not only by the continuous barrier of buildings but also by a change in design from the first hall, to Building LIb on the same plan, with its extra row of outer posts on its eastern side. Building XXII and the other structures to its west formed a group partly domestic, partly industrial in character. Building XXII, with its clay walls and central hearth, must have been a well-insulated lodging and the remains of a similar structure may be represented by XII. The floor of XV was littered with scrap iron, perhaps debris from a workshop and smithy.

Fig. 1.3: Foundations of the granary (XXXVIII, left) and lesser hall (XLVIII, right) from the middle period in the bailey

Fig. 1.4: Artist's reconstruction of excavated areas in middle period, phase X (by Peter Scholefield)

To the east of the central division there are two prominent buildings—a granary, XXXVIII, retained from the earliest castle, and a lesser hall, XLVIII. The granary is reconstructed here as a sort of Dutch barn, with open or semi-open sides. The smaller hall had a hearth and two small attached rooms, L and XLIX, at its northern end. Behind the granary was a cistern or static water tank, XLIII, set in the lowest part of the bailey, and fed from a gutter, 12. This, too, may have been a development of an earlier feature of the castle. Fig. 1.3 is a photograph of this area under excavation, showing the granary to the left and the lesser hall to the right. As well as illustrating these particular structures, the photograph also shows the general character of the bailey excavations.

The tower by the main gate, XLVI, is D-shaped on the plan, but was presumably round, the evidence for its eastern side being lost on the front slope of the rampart. It is reconstructed with a clay-clad lower storey, a jettied upper floor and a conical planked roof, though other variants are of course possible. There is little evidence for the form of the gate. The reconstruction shows a simple gate with a fighting platform forming a bridge above. It is worth noting that the existing earthworks on the other side of the gate passage do not suggest that there was a second, matching tower there. The entrance passage contained a cobbled area with some post-settings. It is not clear whether these represent simply a metalled surface or a building. None is shown on the reconstruction.

The evidence for the outer defences comes from the excavation of a short stretch of the outer rampart which showed clearly that there had been a palisade of small post-holes which presumably strengthened a clay wall, backed by a fighting platform lying on the ground surface, rather than raised above it. This structure, and the ditch lying outside it, is described in full below (Chapter 3). Defenders trying to hold these outer defences would be in a desperate plight if the attackers managed to break through to the inner ditch, so we have tentatively suggested that plank bridges, capable of being quickly withdrawn, might have been provided and we have shown one of these.

Whatever the merits of this reconstruction, which undoubtedly contains errors of detail, it must echo the general realities in a number of ways. The bailey was certainly crowded with buildings, the interior would be claustrophobic, and there would be no view into the surrounding open country except from the motte or the fighting platform and towers of the bailey. In this respect the present earthworks, with their open views, are quite misleading. Inside, there was very little open space except immediately within the entrance; the buildings were

substantial, of two or three storeys in some cases, and, most importantly, the castle was formidably defended. An attacker approaching from the fields to the north would be faced with concentric defences of quite massive proportions, reinforced by deep ditches, in places full of mud or water. We estimate that the distance from the bottom of the inner ditch to the top of the bailey palisade was some 10.0m. Once an attacker got into the bailey, the battle would become like street-fighting—in many ways the most difficult and fearful kind—in which each building has to be taken separately, with the attackers surrounded on all sides. Nevertheless, despite its defensibility, the evidence of this phase also reveals clearly the social character of the castle, with its profusion of domestic buildings of all sizes and functions and its provision of water supply and storage. In this simple sense it was quintessentially a castle, in which domesticity and defence were inextricably linked.

The Later Castle (figs 1.5 and 1.6)

The bailey later underwent radical changes, partly in the structural techniques employed and partly in the general layout of its buildings. The new structures of this period (phase Y) made little use of upright posts set in pits, the evidence of timbers in the ground comprising shallow sockets outlined in stones where uprights stood and shallow gullies in which sill beams rested. In either case the buildings were supported by their own framing. The most striking illustration of the change came from the rampart, where there was little direct evidence of defences. At the north-west corner a pattern of shallow post-sockets and an outline created by intense burning revealed a D-shaped tower (IV) overlying the tower of the preceding phase. Between the bailey and the motte ditch lay a palisade set in normal post-pits (V). Near the bailey entrance the incomplete plan of an oval tower was recovered (XL). Between them no structural evidence in the ground was apparent. But in the adjacent bailey ditch two timbers were recovered from a waterlogged deposit, 1.2m in length with a slot 0.075m cut in them, pegged at intervals of 0.38m. These were probably the base plates of a structure whose upright planks, 0.38m (15in) wide and 0.075m (3in) thick, would have made a formidable wall. These timbers have been illustrated in detail elsewhere (Barker & Higham 1982, 41). If this sort of technique was used in the defences it would account for the lack of evidence on the rampart.

The impression within the bailey is that the castle was less crowded domestically in this period. It must be remembered, however, that only half the bailey has been excavated, so that we cannot know what changes were also being made elsewhere. The contrasts between phases X and Y may be more apparent than real if in X the southern half was less crowded than the northern and if

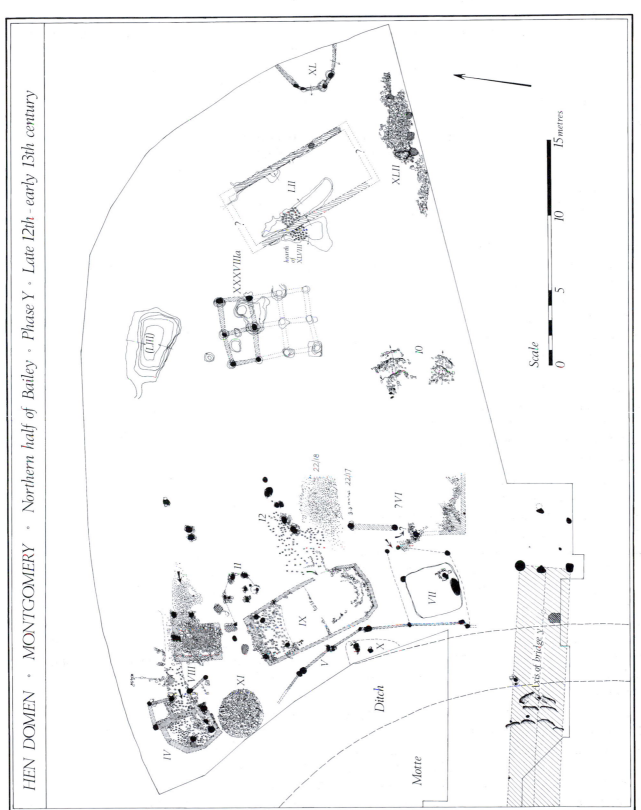

HEN DOMEN · MONTGOMERY · Northern half of Bailey · Phase Y · Late 12th - early 13th century

Fig. 1.5: Plan of northern half of bailey: later period, phase Y (from Barker & Higham 1988)

Fig. 1.6: Artist's reconstruction of excavated areas in later period, phase Y (by Peter Scholefield)

in Y *vice versa*. Nevertheless, in the excavated area, there were certainly reductions in both the number and size of buildings. There were few structures behind the rampart in the north-west corner, Building VIII being the only obvious feature. The granary was reduced in size by half, to become a six-post building (XXXVIIIa). Most notably, the large hall in front of the motte ditch, which had stood in modified form from the castle's foundation, was removed and not replaced by any building of comparable size, at least not in the northern half of the bailey. Other features of this period were the counterparts of buildings in phase X. A second apsidal building (IX) stood on the site of the earlier putative chapel, with the foundation (XI) of a possible bell-tower to its north-west. The cistern continued in use in modified form (LIII) and the massive foundations of a new bridge across the motte ditch lay slightly north of the earlier bridge axis. In the lower part of the bailey a new hall (LII), resting on ground sills in shallow gullies, lay slightly east of its predecessor. At the bailey entrance the cobbled building (XLII) continued in use from phase X. At the point where the bailey slope became more marked, a flight of crude steps (10) was constructed from pebbles and small boulders. This led to the site of a building (VI) of which only the western end was observed. But since this rested on sill beams it may have extended much further east.

Immediately to its west lay a 3.0m square rectangular pit (VII) whose uneroded sides suggest permanent cover in a building formed by post-holes in the palisade along the motte ditch and others to their east. Originally at least 6.0m in depth, its digging destroyed the west wall of the earlier hall standing in front of the motte bridges. For much of its life it was probably a latrine pit, but it was eventually floored with clay 1.5m from its top, perhaps being used as a cellar to a structure above. In its probable latrine use it is not clear whether it served only the adjacent building (VI) or the whole bailey—if the former this building (for which the evidence only partly survives) may have been very important. The proximity of the pit to the chapel is somewhat curious, and it is certainly among the more enigmatic features on the site. A rich sample of material was recovered from this deep pit, whose fill was heavily waterlogged. Analysis by James Grieg (of Birmingham University) revealed a wide range of local flora which had been growing in a variety of habitats: arable land, meadows, marshes, stream sides and woodland. The species included weeds, cereal crops, hedgerow plants, sedges from damp places, and birch, hazel, alder, oak and willow from the woodlands. Peas and beans, known to have been an important element in medieval diet, are probably poorly represented because they preserve badly. Most of the species represented are still found in the modern landscape of the area. In addition, the presence of the dung-feeding beetle and the stable fly suggest that some of the contents of the pit derived from stable sweepings, though interestingly, no building within the excavated area has been identified as a stable. The pit itself, whatever its original intended use, seems to have fulfilled mixed functions as latrine and waste disposal point. Perhaps it was a failed well.

Fig. 1.6 is a hitherto unpublished artist's impression (by Peter Scholefield) of this phase of the castle's development. Although it is more difficult to be precise about constructional details than in the preceding phase, the overall character and position of structures is clear enough. But because some of the evidence in this phase is impossible to interpret fully, the drawing shows two areas as building sites in operation: at the western end of the bailey, where Building ?VI is represented by an incomplete series of ground evidence, and on the motte, where the nature of the tower at this stage is difficult to understand fully (see below, Chapter 4). The defences have been reconstructed as framed and free-standing structures, which is what the excavated evidence suggests, and the outer rampart has been given its own palisade by analogy with the earlier phase. A hall building has been shown at the foot of the motte bridge, though to the south of the equivalent structures in the preceding phases. There is, however, no specific evidence for this.

The Last Castle (figs 1.7 and 1.8)

In the lower parts of the bailey, in the north-east corner, the surfaces of this period (phase Z) lay above a deep layer of silt, whereas further up-slope, to the west, they lay immediately above the surfaces of phase Y. In the subsequent rebuilding there was a major contraction of the built-up area, and most of the structures identified lay in the western half. To the east lay a horizontal building platform (Building XXXVI) with an internal partition, and a probable tower site by the entrance (Building XXXVII). Otherwise the evidence lay west of the north–south division of the bailey which was most obvious in phase X but had its beginnings in the earliest castle and was also apparent in phase Y. As in phase Y, there was evidence of a north-western tower (IV) but no sign of a palisade. This may therefore have been of framed construction, as in phase Y, though in the north-west corner the shallow sockets of the fighting platform supports were also located. The foundations of the motte bridge suggest a much narrower structure than any of its predecessors. Apart from their obvious western concentration, the buildings of this period are difficult to describe. The evidence was wholly of very shallow post-sockets and stone alignments along the edges of buildings. A building of some form stood in front of the motte bridge and incorporated the sunken floor in the top of pit VII described in phase Y. To its north a

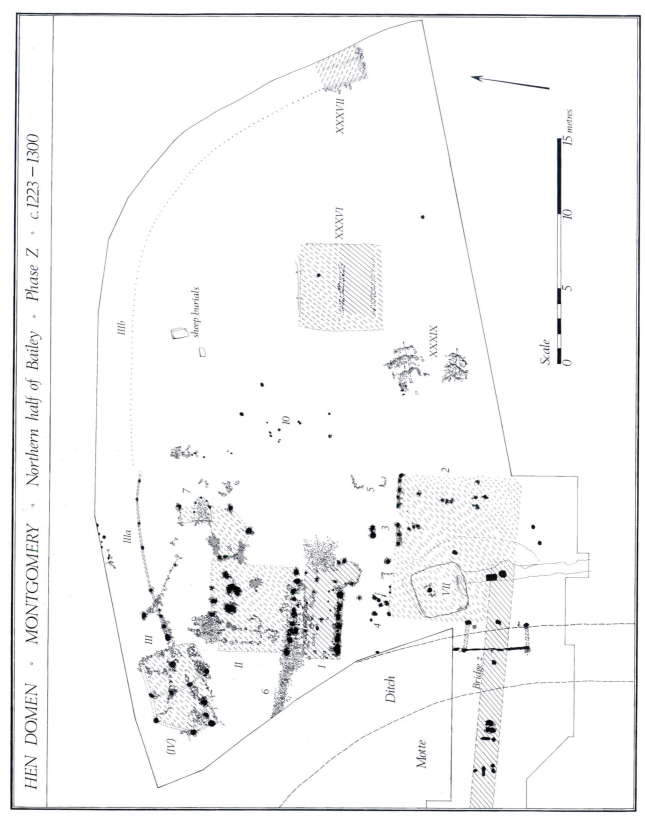

HEN DOMEN · MONTGOMERY · Northern half of Bailey · Phase Z · c.1223 – 1300

Fig. 1.7: Plan of northern half of bailey: last period, phase Z (from Barker & Higham 1988)

Fig. 1.8: Artist's reconstruction of excavated areas in last period, phase Z (by Peter Scholefield)

rectangular structure or structures is indicated as Buildings I and II, with a pebble path (6) between them and a curiously shaped extension (7) at the north-east corner.

The general impression is of a very different sort of bailey from that of the twelfth century, though the slightness of the foundations may disguise a corresponding massiveness in the superstructure of the presumably framed buildings. This phase, we have suggested, represents the ongoing (and final) use of the site as a satellite to the new castle built by Henry III at Montgomery. Fig. 1.8 is a hitherto unpublished artist's impression of what the castle may have looked like at this time. This is, however, a very difficult task owing to the nature of the ground evidence. As in the preceding phase, the defences have been shown as free-standing, framed structures on both the inner and outer ramparts. There was no archaeological evidence to help with this interpretation, though the preserved palisade timbers discussed in the preceding phase may be relevant. But in the works at New Montgomery castle, broadly contemporary with this last phase at Hen Domen, there is good documentary evidence for the use of pre-fabricated and free-standing brattices and other timber defences (Barker & Higham 1982; Knight 1992). A belfry-like tower has been placed on the motte, the evidence for which is discussed below (Chapter 4), reached by a narrower bridge as suggested by the evidence already published (Barker & Higham 1982). The evidence at the foot of the bridge has been turned into a building of similar character to that found much earlier in the castle's life. Since evidence survived only at the northern end of this building site, however, this interpretation is no more than a suggestion and the building may have been smaller than ventured here.

CHAPTER 2

PRE-CASTLE PHASES

Evidence of an earlier date than the castle was located in two areas, in the bailey interior and in a northward extension of the section across the ditch of the outer rampart. The position of the latter is shown on fig. 0.2, and the evidence illustrated in figs 3.24 and 3.25 (see below, Chapter 3). This extension was cut in an attempt to locate the presumed continuation of a linear feature revealed as an anomaly by a magnetometer survey (marked A on fig. 2.1) conducted by the (then) Inspectorate of Ancient Monuments in 1972 in conjunction with a contour survey. The geophysical survey had suggested an otherwise unknown ditch or palisade running parallel to the outer ditch of the motte, as well as other features marked B–E on the plan. The latter have already been discussed in print (Barker 1986, 60–63) and were probably ditches and pits, but of unknown date. The field also contains a group of surface anomalies which did not appear on the contour survey, tentatively identified as building platforms, recorded in a plane-table survey carried out during the training

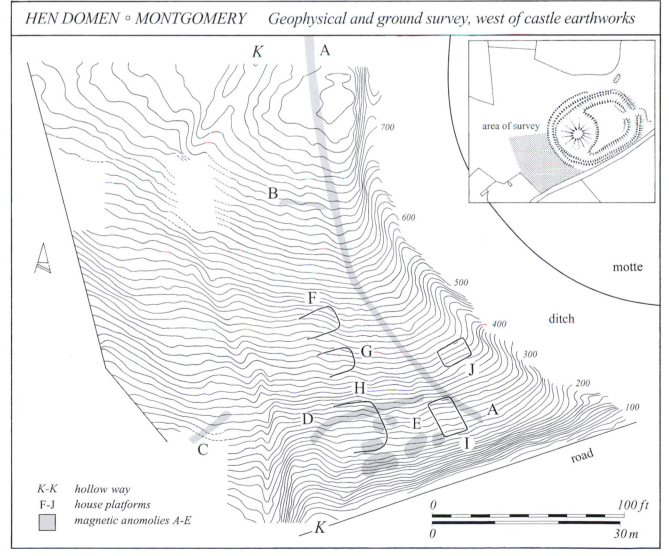

HEN DOMEN ○ MONTGOMERY   *Geophysical and ground survey, west of castle earthworks*

area of survey

motte

ditch

road

K-K   hollow way
F-J   house platforms
▨   magnetic anomolies A-E

700

600

500

400

300

200

100

0   100 ft

0   30 m

Fig. 2.1: Geophysical and ground survey, west of castle earthworks. The contours are at 10cm vertical intervals above the temporary bench mark

Fig. 2.2: Aerial view of castle earthworks, extant ridge and furrow and features to the west, 26th December 1984 (© Clwyd-Powys Archaeological Trust, 84-41-10)

excavation in 1980 and interpolated on the plan at F–J. The field also contains a prominent hollow way (K–K) as well as ridge and furrow belonging to the pre-castle field system. The survey of the ridge and furrow to the west of the site has already been published (Barker & Lawson 1971) and is not reproduced here. Fig. 2.2 is an aerial view showing the surveyed areas covered in fig. 16 of Barker & Lawson 1971 as well as fig. 2.1 in the present publication. Fig. 2.3 is a photograph of ridge and furrow in the field to the east of the bailey entrance (labelled *c* in fig. 1.1 in the present volume). Unfortunately, this was ploughed out as the result of a simple misunderstanding in the late 1960s, the (then) farmer of the land believing it had been surveyed together with the field to the west. The richness of the castle's

surrounds, whose interlocking features reveal several periods of use, is clear evidence of the complexity of the landscape setting of the castle, to which the excavation here described added further.

What the northward extension of the outer ditch section revealed (from south to north on fig. 3.25) was (a) part of a tiny double gulley or slot (19–20), (b) a shallow gulley or part of a shallow pit (14) and (c) part of an apparently linear feature of dry-stone construction (21). The gullies were visible only where cut into the natural subsoil and were not demonstrably related to the castle. All features were sealed by soil continuous with that of the ridged field of pre-castle date so they are also pre-castle in origin. Unfortunately, this excavation threw no light on the ridge and furrow itself in this area because

Fig. 2.3: View of ridge and furrow (now destroyed) east of castle earthworks

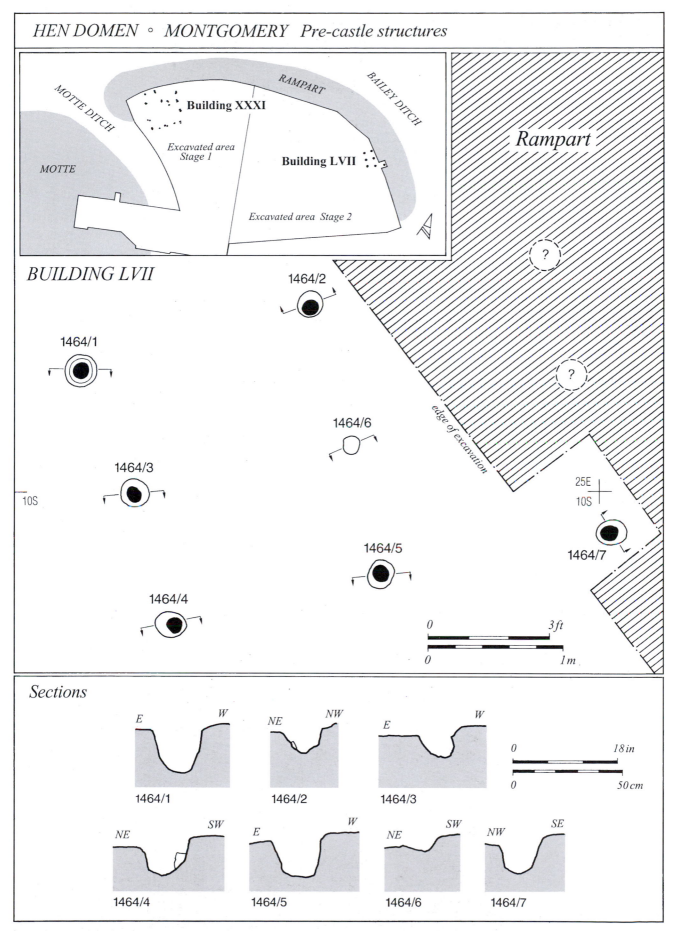

Fig. 2.4: Pre-castle buildings beneath the bailey: LVII and XXXI (latter also shown in detail in fig. 2.5)

it was situated at a point where two areas of ridging (aligned in different directions) converge, leaving an area without distinctive surface features between (Barker & Lawson 1971, 61–62). So little of any of these features was revealed that functions cannot be suggested for them, nor can we know if they are even remotely associated with each other in date. Their relationship with the evidence of the magnetometer survey remains enigmatic. The most to be said is that perhaps the stone feature (21) is part of a field boundary. Unfortunately, part of this was removed in excavation before its potential significance was realised.

Within the north-east sector of the castle bailey, the building of the Norman rampart had sealed earlier phases of evidence as it had in the north-west sector (Barker & Higham 1982, 26–29). In the latter, a pre-castle plough-soil, with evidence of ridging, overlay the site of an earlier building (XXXI) whose northern end had been destroyed by the digging of the bailey ditch. The function and date of this building remain uncertain, though its most likely interpretation was a domestic building of early medieval date. Its plan has been reproduced in figs 2.4 and 2.5, to show its relationship with Building LVII (described below). Similarly, the pre-castle plough-soil survey from the north-west sector of the bailey is also reproduced, in fig. 2.6, in conjunction with the new evidence recovered further east (figs 2.7 and 2.8).

In chronological order, the pre-castle features in the north-east sector of the bailey were as follows:

1. Cut into the underlying natural boulder clay were various small (unillustrated) depressions, some perhaps eroded post-holes, the majority more probably arising

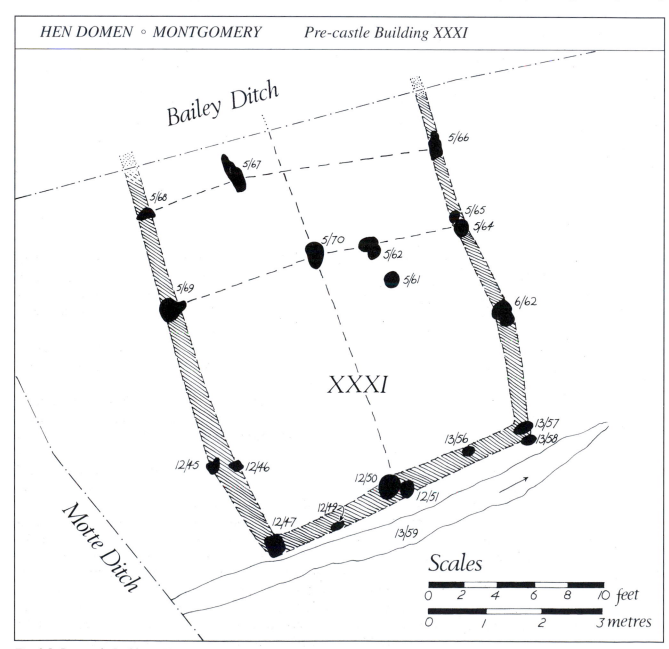

Fig. 2.5: Pre-castle Building XXXI, with wall lines extrapolated (from Barker & Higham 1982)

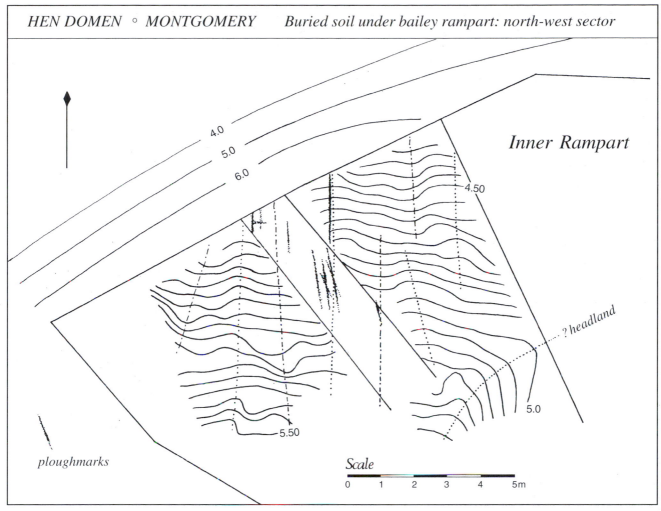

HEN DOMEN ∘ MONTGOMERY   Buried soil under bailey rampart: north-west sector

Inner Rampart

4.0

5.0

6.0

4.50

? headland

5.0

5.50

5.0

ploughmarks

Scale

0   1   2   3   4   5m

Fig. 2.6: Contour survey of pre-castle field surface beneath north-west quadrant of bailey (after Barker & Lawson 1971)

from the removal of stones in the subsequent ploughing. At the east end of the excavated area, however, a group of six features, in two rows of three, clearly represented a small structure (Building LVII, fig. 2.4, features 1464/ 1–6). The full extent of this building is not known: removal of a small portion of the adjacent rampart revealed a seventh post-hole (1464/7) and it seems likely that one end of the structure had been destroyed by the digging of the bailey ditch. Its minimum dimensions were 3.2m × 2.0m. No specific dating evidence for this phase was discovered. Like the building excavated in the north-west sector of the bailey, which had also been truncated by the castle ditch, it could be of any date from prehistoric to early medieval. No internal features were identified and the function of the building is unknown. The two buildings discovered were not necessarily, of course, of the same date, though, for convenience, they are here shown on the same plan. The boulder clay also contained long thin dark marks, visible at the western and eastern ends of the excavated area. Two groups are shown incorporated on the survey of the overlying plough-soil (fig. 2.7) and a third group survived in the surface of the boulder clay immediately south of the eastern end of the illustrated survey area. The north-western group of marks

had definite 'ends', whereas those in the south-eastern group seemed to fade away and may originally have been longer. These marks, like those discovered in the north-west sector of the bailey, presumably resulted from ploughing in the next phase:–

2. Above the boulder clay the plough-soil (context 1083) of the pre-castle field was preserved where it had been buried by the Norman rampart and its southward-extending tail. Further south still, the Norman builders had removed this soil, where it would otherwise have been exposed in the bailey interior providing a very soggy ground surface in wet weather. The soil was progressively exposed as the removal of the rampart and its tail continued over several seasons of excavation. On each occasion, the exposed surface was carefully covered in polythene and a layer of spoil so that eventually it could be cleaned and examined as a whole. As in the north-west sector of the bailey, the surface was carefully cleaned and surveyed, but whereas in the former area this operation had revealed clear evidence of a ridged field, in the area now described no such uniform pattern was apparent, not even ridges on the alignment of the underlying plough-marks. Nor was ridging apparent in the longitudinal section of the rampart (fig. 3.4) in which

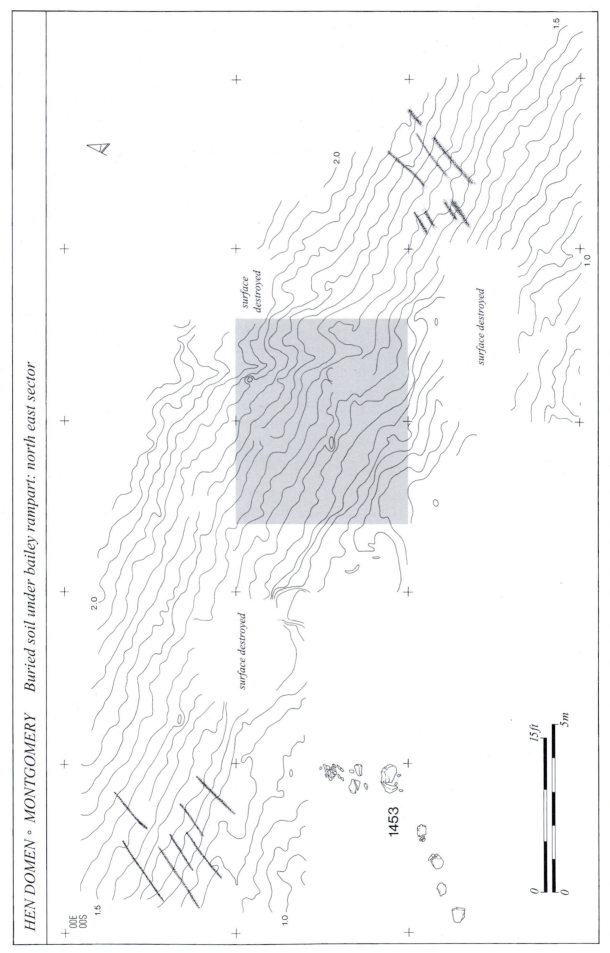

Fig. 2.7: Contour survey of pre-castle field surface (and underlying plough-marks) beneath north-east quadrant of bailey

the buried soil was visible as the lowest layer. This area had either been ploughed in a way which did not produce ridges, or ridges had at some stage been ploughed flat. Much of the soil surface seemed featureless to the naked eye, and one or two areas thought on first exposure (or seen in section in later features cut through it, for example pit 1017—see below, Chapter 3) to contain plough ridges turned out to be isolated anomalies. A survey of the soil (fig. 2.7) was produced, with readings on a grid at 0.2m intervals and contours interpolated by hand at 0.05m intervals. For comparison, the survey of the adjacent area, published in 1971, is also reproduced (fig. 2.6). In addition several computer-manipulated versions of the central portion of the north-eastern area, measuring approx.7.0m × 5.0m, reveal the low banks, perhaps part of a slight enclosure, in more detail. The data and its computer manipulation are discussed fully below (Chapter 5). One of the resulting images is shown in fig. 2.8. A line of boulders (collectively 1453) on the west side of the excavated area were either deliberately laid or left in place when others around were removed (the northernmost may be a piece of shattered bedrock *in situ*). Since ploughing could hardly have taken place immediately above these boulders, they may be part of a boundary. It would appear that the castle was added to the pre-Norman landscape at a point where different parts of a field system converged. It is possible that the feature identified in the earlier stage of excavation as the start of a headland may mark the point at which a change of land-use was beginning. It seems most unlikely that the

Normans somehow managed to leave ridges nicely preserved at one end of their building site while selectively removing them only a few yards away.

Unfortunately, we have no view of the archaeological junction of the two areas of plough-soil examined. In the earlier stage of the excavation, although all the features cut into the top of the rampart were examined, the body of the rampart was not removed along its full length. Immediately to the east of the earlier area removed, under which the plough-soil was exposed, a portion of rampart some 9.0–10.0m long was left intact: the season in question (1969) was very hot, the boulder clay hard as concrete and the labour-force small. Sadly, but perhaps inevitably, the undug rampart conceals the point where the surface configuration of the buried soil changes. The extent of the undug portion is shown on the simplified plan of the early castle (fig. 3.1). This is the only undug part of the northern half of the bailey and it contains potentially crucial evidence. The methodological lesson hardly needs stating.

A strip of the plough-soil some 15m (north–south) by 5m (east–west) was carefully hand-dug at the western end of the excavated area. This revealed further stake-holes of a fence (structure 17) discovered in the north-west sector of the bailey. Gradual removal of the soil, centimetre by centimetre, showed that these stake-holes had been driven through the soil and confirmed the impression gained in the earlier excavation that this fence was part of the castle rather than anything earlier (see

Fig. 2.8: Computer processed data from centre of area shown in fig. 2.7. Vertical scale enhanced: see Chapter 5

below, Chapter 3, fig. 3.1). Despite a combination of meticulous dry- and wet-sorting on site, however, the buried soil proved devoid of all artefactual, floral and faunal evidence. Other parts of this deposit were sampled for pollen and other evidence by Astrid Caseldine (University of Wales, Lampeter and CADW) and also proved barren. The remaining part of the soil was accordingly scraped off by machine. At the end of the exercise, all that had been recovered, either in first exposure of the plough-soil surface, or in its removal, were a few bone fragments and three very small, heavily abraded sherds of Roman pottery. The contrasts between the evidence recovered in the two sectors of the bailey excavation are remarkable. In the north-west sector, not only were there continuous plough-ridges (and a possible headland), but also one or two artefacts and a fruitful pollen sample suggesting abandoned arable (Barker & Lawson 1971). It is a sobering thought that, had the excavation of the site begun in the north-east sector, we would have concluded, quite reasonably, that the pre-castle land-surface was of minimal interest. We may not have bothered to remove any of it, or perhaps removed only a small portion, so that the underlying structure at the extreme east end may not have been discovered. Had the excavation then proceeded to the north-west sector, we would have been in danger of pre-judging the potential interest (or lack thereof) of the pre-castle levels and the evidence they contained may never have been brought to light.

3. The field surface began to slope away at the point where the north-east corner of the bailey interior was eventually to be built. This slope had been levelled up with large stones, a detail of which is shown in fig. 2.9, over an area measuring some 7.0m×3.0m. On first exposure, these were considered as a possible building platform (1396; fig. 2.10). Although there was no specific dating evidence for this infilling operation, it obviously post-dated the creation of the plough-soil over which it lay and pre-dated one of the structures of the castle, Building LIV (see Chapter 3). It seems most likely to have been a preliminary stage in the building of the castle itself, designed simply to level up the sloping ground, rather than a separate building operation: the surface of the boulder spread seemed too uneven to form the footings for a structure, and the clay of the overlying Building LIV was deeply embedded in the spaces between the boulders, suggesting that the latter were newly laid when the clay was deposited. In a few places (1404, 1405, 1406, 1407—all marked on the plan in parentheses) what seemed to be more consistent gaps in the boulders suggested possible post-settings, but excavation produced nothing to confirm this possibility and they are just as likely to have been fortuitous.

4. Further evidence of the pre-castle/castle interface

Fig. 2.9: Detail of stone platform (1396) including 1405

came from the centre of the bailey at a point where the buried soil had been removed by the Norman builders (fig. 2.10). Here, the earliest Norman features, cut into or lying on top of the underlying boulder clay, were not separated stratigraphically from features of potentially pre-castle date in or on the same material. The foundation trench and associated post-pits (features 834, 830, 831, 1056) of the eastern side of the very large (hall) Buildings (LIa and LIb) immediately in front of the motte bridges (see Barker & Higham 1982, 31) had cut through a pebble surface (1111) whose edge followed a line oblique to that of the subsequent building. This pebble surface comprised a major continuous area with, at its southern end, a smaller and almost separate portion. It is not clear whether the two were originally parts of the same feature or not. The pebble surface in turn sealed a shallow gulley some 6.0m long (1132), perhaps an eroded beam slot, and a series of small post-holes (collectively 1138) on a parallel alignment. Eastwards and southwards lay an area of other minor features (collectively 1131). These varied in size, from tiny depressions whose man-made origin was not even certain, through small but distinct stake-holes, to small post-holes the most substantial of which were 0.2–0.25m deep. The pebble surface (1111) seems, in retrospect, to be a continuation of pebble surface 14 published in 1982 as part of phases U/V/W in the north-west sector (Barker & Higham 1982, 32). They were very similar in character and immediately adjacent. Surface 14 has been added to the present plan on this assumption. The pebbles are here shown (fig. 2.10) as a simplified toned area. The actual character of the recorded surface can be seen on fig. 18 of Barker & Higham 1982. On the basis of the stratigraphy it is impossible to be certain whether these features (whatever they represent structurally) pre-date the castle or represent its earliest building operations. In the 1982 report it was suggested that the western end of the pebble surface (14) was more likely to be part of the castle, since the removal of the plough-soil by the Norman builders is not likely to have left such a delicate surface, lying immediately beneath, intact. This interpretation is

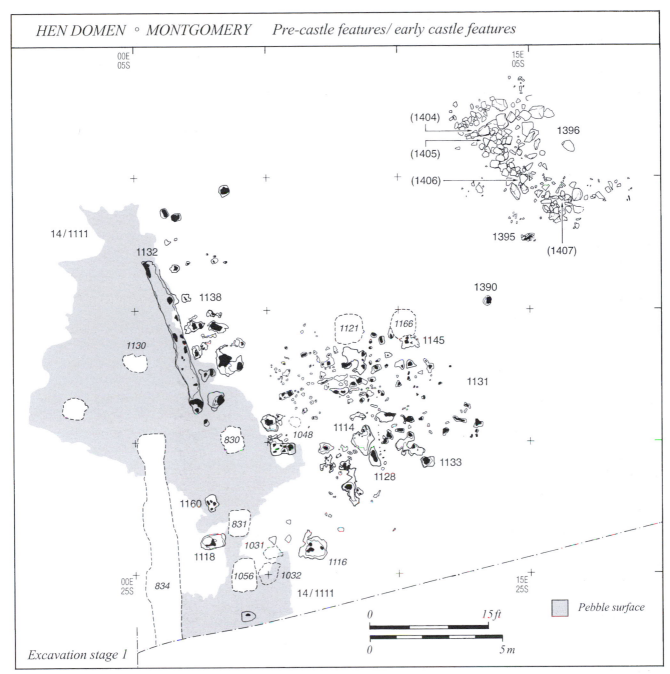

HEN DOMEN ∘ MONTGOMERY   *Pre-castle features/early castle features*

Excavation stage 1

Pebble surface

Fig. 2.10: Pre-castle features/early castle features

likely for the whole surface (1111). But features found beneath this pebble surface could be of any date. A similar problem arises with the interpretation of the scatter of little post-holes and stake-holes (the smaller ones collectively feature 1131, with larger ones individually numbered 1114, 1116, 1118, 1128, 1133, 1145, 1160, and two outliers to the east numbered 1390 and 1395) lying to the south and east, into the northern edge of which had intruded two of the post-pits (1121 and 1166) belonging to the early castle's (?) granary (below, Chapter 3). This scatter of features could either be pre-castle or early castle in date. If any of this evidence represents structures of pre-castle date, it should be seen in the context of the buildings excavated beneath the

plough-soil in the north-west and north-east sectors (above and fig. 2.4). If it belongs to the early castle, it should be seen in the context of the primary palisade and perhaps other structures such as the fence which ran behind and parallel to it (below and fig. 3.1), in which case it may represent temporary buildings in use before the more massive early structures were put up. One possibility is that the pebble surface (1111) represents the interior of a building whose walls have left no trace and which was presumably, therefore, of framed construction. If so, it was an extremely large building, since even the continuous part of the surviving pebbled area was some 12m in length. This hypothesis, though unsupported by other evidence, might explain the survival of a fairly delicate and vulnerable layer. Another feature which may also be associated in date (though this is not provable) is the pebble surface published as structure XXX at the extreme western end of the earlier stage of the excavation (Barker and Higham 1982, 27 and fig. 14). This was, however, demonstrably pre-castle in date, since a thin layer of soil lay between it and the overlying rampart.

CHAPTER 3

THE BAILEY

The Early Castle (figs 3.1–3.16)

The evidence of the early castle recovered in the north-west sector was published in 1982 (Barker & Higham, 29–31), when the north-east sector had been excavated only to the phase published as 'X' (*ibid.* 32–40). Further excavation in the latter revealed the earliest domestic structures and defences encountered. The evidence for the more substantial structures is illustrated individually and the overall pattern is given in slightly simplified form in fig. 3.1. The very earliest features recovered in the centre of the bailey may belong to the castle or alternatively may pre-date it. They have been discussed and illustrated with other pre-castle evidence (above, Chapter 2) and are not repeated here. It should be noted that the feature numbers given in what follows take different forms because the evidence described comes from both the pre- and post-1970 stages of excavation: 1970 saw not only the move from the north-west quadrant of the bailey to the north-east quadrant but also revision of our recording system. The move from the north-west to north-east sectors also involved a change from an imperial to a metric recording grid. The ten-year-old (1960–70) eastern edge of the north-west sector excavation was by now very badly and unevenly eroded and we sometimes experienced difficulties in matching up the evidence on either side of this 'line' in our drawn plans. Most difficulties proved resolvable but others occasionally had simply to be left as they were and these are indicated.

In the following discussion, the evidence of the early castle in the north-west sector (published in the 1982 report) is also summarised and illustrated on the simplified plan and two secondary structures in the north-west sector are illustrated separately. The structures of the early castle are called phase T but because there were additions among them the overall plan is called T/U. This creates deliberate overlap with the plan of the alterations to the palisade (fig. 3.15), which is labelled U/V/W because we simply do not know how many stages there were in the process of change reflected in the accumulation of these structures.

The earliest structure of the castle (fig. 3.1) was a low bank of clay and turf (numbered 5/48–5/49 in the already published north-west sector) piled up along the course of the rampart which was soon to be built over it. This bank levelled up the downward slope at the point where the front timbers of the palisade were to be erected. In the north-east sector of the excavation, this feature was not continuous and it is curious that it did not appear at precisely the points where some of the palisade timber positions were also elusive. Perhaps there were details in the design of the defences which were impossible to detect in excavation. At the extreme north-west corner of the bailey the bank formed a higher and broader mound (5/50), although it was badly mutilated here by rabbit burrows. Perhaps this was the site of a tower. A comparable mound (1416), here of hard clay and stones, lay some 20.0m further east, at the junction of the north-west and north-east sector excavations. Perhaps this carried an interval tower? These putative towers, if they existed, must have been heavily framed structures, since they left no other ground evidence. At the bailey entrance (the evidence of which has undergone some re-interpretation since the publication of our 1988 preliminary report) a curving row of posts was set in shallow holes (1383, 1429, 1428, 1450) up to 0.25m deep (see fig. 3.2). It is not clear whether these represent a tower (tentatively called Building LVI) or simply a revetment holding back the rampart material in a vertical wall flanking the entrance passage. Interpretation is also made difficult by the limits of excavation at this point. First, the entrance was presumably conceived by its creators as a structure or structures occupying both sides of the entrance passage, whereas only its northern side was examined. Second, there is no way of knowing (on present evidence) how far in front of the rampart structures relating to the entrance may have extended. This makes the significance of the forward-most post-position identified (1383) difficult to understand. If it forms part of a tower, this had a curiously 'pointed' front and it may be that this post was either a secondary support, added within the life of the structure to shore it up, or part of something running down the rampart face into the ditch. Our hypothetical outline of the structure (in fig. 3.1) makes this assumption. This post also seems to have had a longer life since this feature was first noted higher up in the rampart clay. A larger post(?)-pit (1411),

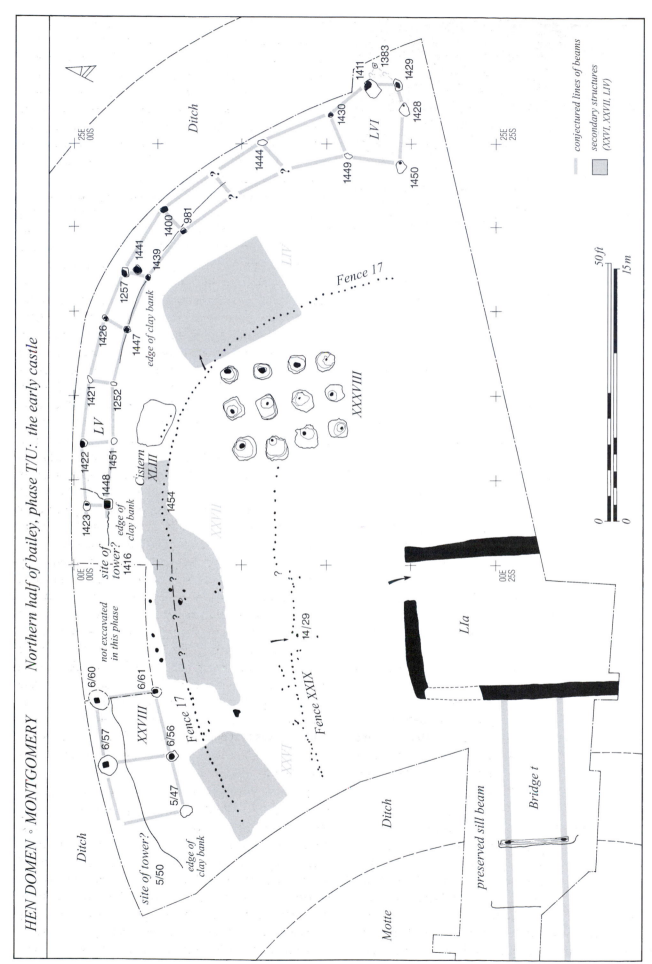

HEN DOMEN ∘ MONTGOMERY   Northern half of bailey, phase T/U: the early castle

Ditch

25E
00S

Ditch

1411
1383
1429
1430
1428
LVI
1449
1450

1444

981
1400
1441
1439
1257
1426
1447
edge of clay bank

Fence 17

LIV

XXXVIII

LV
1421
1252
1422
1448   1451
1423
site of
tower?
1416

Cistern
XLIII
1454
XXVII

25E
25S

edge of
clay bank
edge of
clay bank

not excavated
in this phase

6/60
6/61
XXVIII
6/56
6/57
5/47
5/50
site of tower?

Fence 17

XXVI
Fence XXIX
14/29

00E
00S

00E
25S

LIa

Motte

Ditch

preserved sill beam

Bridge t

            conjectured lines of beams

            secondary structures
            (XXVI, XXVII, LIV)

50 ft

15 m

0

0

Fig. 3.1: Northern half of the bailey, phase T/U: the early castle (secondary features shown as tint)

Fig. 3.2: Building? LVI at bailey entrance

whose maximum depth was 0.6m may represent a support for a fighting platform which bridged the entrance, but its interpretation was made difficult by considerable damage from a rabbit burrow which had partly created its eventual shape (approx. 0.8m × 1.1m).

The palisade defending the northern half of the bailey was not uniform throughout its length. In the north-west corner the posts stood on pads of clay and the rear row was some 3.5–4.0m behind the front row (Building XXVIII, 5/47 and 6/56–6/61) and presumably enclosed occupiable space where they rose out of the rampart itself. It is also possible that these posts represent a building raised above the rampart, rather in the manner of a first-floor hall, whose roof or parapet acted as a fighting platform. Further east, the rear posts lay only 1.5–2.0m behind (collectively called Building LV, 1423 & 1448 in pairs eastward to 1449 & 1430) and presumably supported only a fighting platform. It is unfortunate that some 9.0–10.0m of rampart remains unexcavated in its lower levels at the junction of the two stages of the excavation–when it was left intact at the end of the 1960s the interest of this area had not, obviously, been foreseen (see also above, Chapter 2). This distinction between the upper and lower halves of the bailey became more marked in later phases of the castle's domestic development, for which an 'upper and lower bailey' division, reflecting status and defensibility, has been suggested (Barker & Higham 1982, 40 and 1988, 10). Subsequent palisades, however, were of the narrower design throughout the whole length of the rampart in both halves of the bailey.

Despite the variation in width of the earliest defences, the evidence for all the posts was similar in that, with the exception of the post which presumably occupied pit 1411, none stood in deep post-holes when originally laid. The evidence for the posts varied in visibility: some in the front row (for example 1421 and 1422) were seen only partially at the limit of excavation, some were less convincing than others and some proved totally elusive. (Note that the limit of excavation shown on the plan is

the upper limit, whereas the lower limit was further in on account of the need to batter the slope of the exposed face of the rampart as it was progressively excavated). The presumed approximate positions of the 'missing' examples are indicated, with queries, on the overall plan. The features fell, broadly, into one of three groups. Some stood on pads of clay or stones directly on the laying-out bank (or the pre-castle field surface immediately behind), or in shallow depressions or holes not more than 0.25m deep and sometimes very much less. A few stood in deeper holes, 0.3–0.4m deep. But simply recounting approximate depths is potentially misleading because where a primary post had a longer life, or was replaced exactly *in situ*, the evidence for it was discovered at an earlier stage in the excavation, higher up in the rampart clay, and its measured 'depth' was greater. Nor can we be confident that we actually observed the uppermost evidence for every post where it survived within the rampart. Thus, though originally laid beneath the rampart, either in very shallow holes or simply on stone/clay pads, the positions of the various posts emerged at different stages of the removal of the rampart clay. The majority of these features, with context numbers in the 1400s, were discovered in 1986 and one in 1984. But two of these deeper examples, 1252 and 1257, were found in 1981. The final example (981) was discovered as early as 1976, when a post-position was detected and excavated to a depth (at that time unbottomed) of 0.8m in a location which years later proved to have been continuously used from the building of the earliest defences onwards. The problem of re-use and replacement of the positions occupied by these early timbers is discussed further in the context of the next phase of the defences. The illustration (fig. 3.3) of the early defences in the northern part of the rampart also indicates the nature of this problem. Although the palisade structure described above was put in place before the rampart was piled round it, the photograph shows some of the post-positions (indicated by scale rods) with portions of rampart clay still *in situ*. This is because the photograph was taken when the structural evidence was first encountered, which in some cases was when the position of the post emerged in the lowest part of the rampart.

The raising of the initial bank created a more or less horizontal base for the front and rear posts, possibly indicating that the timbers were cut to pre-set lengths. Although the horizontal dimensions of the features varied, many were similar in size to the pads of clay and stones encountered in the north-west sector, up to 0.5m across in some cases but often about 0.3–0.4m in diameter. It is tempting, but not provable, to see a fairly consistent use of timbers approximately 12in square throughout the early bailey defences, as suggested also

Fig. 3.3: Primary palisade posts of northern rampart

by the evidence on the motte (below, Chapter 4). Perhaps the entire palisade structure was pre-fabricated, but, since the nature of the posts' foundations varied somewhat, this cannot be proved. There was no evidence on the ground of horizontal beams linking the front and rear posts; if they existed they were jointed in slightly higher up, though neither was any evidence for them found in the rampart itself. They have been illustrated, very hypothetically, on the overall plan (fig. 3.1) as 'conjectured lines of beams'. If there were no such beams the uprights must have been supported in position while the rampart was piled around them. From the rampart the palisade timbers must have risen at least 4.0m (14ft), to provide a breastwork tall enough to protect a man on the fighting platform and to allow access beneath.

A cross-section of the rampart in the north-west sector, showing its east–west tip lines, laying-out bank and some intrusive features, has already been published (Barker & Higham 1982, 29–30 and fig. 15) and should be referred to for a detailed view. In the north-east sector (fig. 3.4) the rampart was a largely undifferentiated dump of boulder clay and stones (labelled 904). A few tip lines were again visible, but no major periods of construction were apparent. Several running sections were maintained across the rampart during excavation, in the hope that

details of the rampart's construction would be revealed. These were useful in providing a control mechanism for the excavation, which removed the rampart in careful spits, but proved otherwise unrewarding, showing us more about the annual progress of digging than about the rampart itself. Their positions are indicated on the plan. The longitudinal rampart section, provided by the northern and eastern limit of the excavation, shown in photograph, was drawn in simplified form as a 40.0m long face of boulder clay at the very end of the excavation. It reveals the pre-castle buried soil, the discontinuous laying-out bank (here shown in generalised form—in reality it contained some variation, including the stony mound 1416), and some of the rampart dumping processes, but no stratigraphic history of the rampart. This, defended by successive palisades throughout the castle's life, was more or less the same height throughout its use: some 2.0m at its crest above the buried soil. Except in its surface layers (capped by a few centimetres of turf and soil omitted from the drawing), in features cut into its top from successive palisade rebuildings, and in its thin, southern tail (where it was contaminated by material deposited after its construction), it was sterile: the body contained only a handful of animal bones and a prehistoric flint. In order to make this section safe, it was progressively battered inwards during removal of the rampart. For this reason, the areas truncated by features cut from the top of the rampart occurred at various heights on the standing (and drawn) wall of boulder clay at which we were eventually looking. That the sections published in 1982 (originally drawn in 1969) contain more detail than that shown here arises largely from differences of procedure in the field. The earlier section drawings were of a trench, cut and recorded in one digging season, whose walls contained freshly revealed evidence. The later, longitudinal section arose from a quite different process. Although we cleaned it thoroughly before drawing it, this wall of boulder clay had suffered up to twenty years of weathering and aeration as it was progressively revealed during the excavation of the rampart in 1970–90. It is likely that further detail, of the tip lines and occasional soil lenses which were observed in 1969 in the north-west sector, would have been visible in this area had the section been excavated and recorded in one operation. There is also a wider methodological point here: although the 1969 section produced more vertical detail, the trench itself completely failed to reveal the primary palisade post-positions, which only came to light when the rampart was removed over a bigger area.

Fence 17 comprised nearly sixty stake-holes (collectively context 1454 in fig. 3.1) whose stakes had been driven through the buried soil into the natural boulder clay (above, Chapter 2). It may have been a

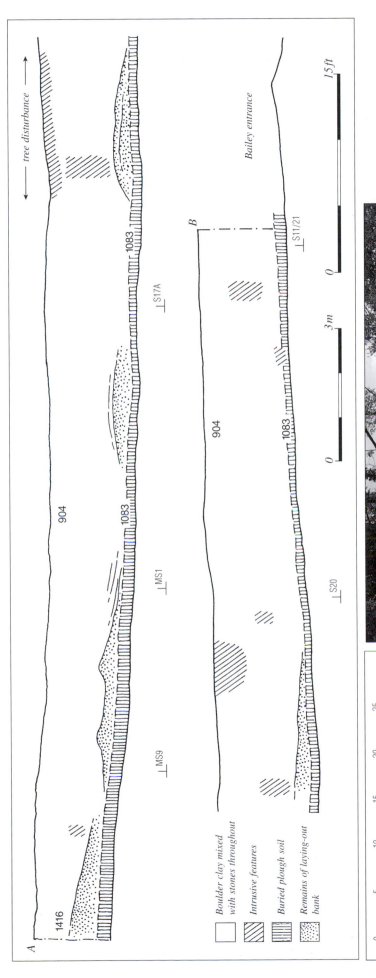

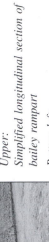

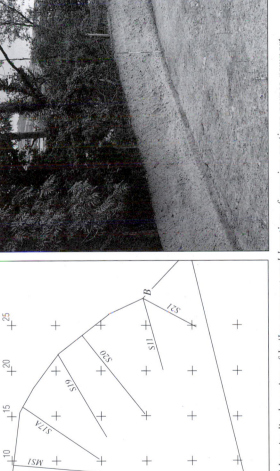

Upper:
Simplified longitudinal section of bailey rampart

Bottom left:
Location of running sections as laid out at various times during excavation of the rampart

Bottom right:
View of section at end of excavation

Fig. 3.4: Simplified longitudinal section of bailey rampart and location of running sections across rampart

Fig. 3.5: View of fence 17 at tail of rampart looking east

revetment to control the tail of the rampart as it was dumped, or perhaps a corral for the protection of the horses and supplies of the men at work building the first castle. Throughout its life, the tail of the rampart tended to collect loose stones and eroded clay, which accumulated downwards both from the rampart slope itself and from the slopes of the bailey interior. This dual process of erosion and deposition created great

stratigraphic complexity in the immediate lee of the rampart, which was often the most difficult part of the site to dissect in a rational manner. Part of this fence is shown in the accompanying photo (fig. 3.5).

The tail of the rampart did not long remain in this form. In the north-west corner of the bailey, two buildings (XXVI and XXVII) were inserted after the rampart was constructed, superseding fence 17 (see Barker & Higham 1982, fig. 16). Building XXVI (the evidence for which is reproduced here as fig. 3.6) had a deliberately laid, stone-free, clay floor (13/54) with hearth (13/55), and the floor presumably indicates its overall plan. Building XXVII, whose remains extended across the junction of the two areas excavated, was probably not as large as the area covered by the burnt clay, charred timbers and charcoal spreads which represented its debris, and no clear outline of its plan can be suggested. A generalized shape, representing this debris, is shown on the overall plan (fig. 3.1). The lack of obvious wall foundations, in both structures, suggests they were built of framed timbers. At the eastern end of XXVII, fragments of

Fig. 3.6: Building XXVI (from Barker & Higham 1982)

apparently unworked carbonised timbers had been dumped in rows, immediately behind the rampart (fig. 3.7). Building XXVI and the eastern part of XXVII were removed, but the western part of XXVII, immediately behind the portion of undug rampart, was not: here the continuation of the stake-holes of fence 17 is presumed rather than known.

Probably also belonging to this phase of additions was the first digging of the water cistern (828) at the tail of the rampart, within the area contained by fence 17. This was to remain, with alterations, throughout much of the

Fig. 3.7: Carbonized timbers at east end of Building XXVII

castle's life (published as Building XLIII in this phase and phase X and as Building LIII in phase Y). Interpretation as a cistern to collect water is suggested by its position in one of the lowest parts of the bailey and, in a later phase, by the gullies which led into it (see Barker & Higham 1982, 36 and figs 21, 23, and 55). To be waterproof, this cistern would (at any stage of its life) have needed a lining of puddled clay or hides. If it was a cistern it can only have been part of the site's system of water containment because it was not very deep, especially in its first phase: we have always imagined that the castle's occupants stored water in butts

filled from the gutters of buildings, though this is, of course, not demonstrable archaeologically. Various plans and sections were recorded at different stages of excavation, but are not published here. Its character is shown on fig. 3.8, which is a composite section/profile running north–south through the bailey (see also section J–J in Barker & Higham 1982, fig. 55, where the (then) unexcavated lower parts of the cistern were shown in hypothetical outline). It was impossible to detect whether this feature was first constructed as a cut through the tail of the rampart, which seems probable, or whether it was somehow constructed as the rampart was being built. But it was certainly cut through the pre-castle plough-soil and into the natural boulder clay beneath. Its outline at this stage is shown on the overall plan of the early castle (fig. 3.1). On its southern side, four stake-holes were identified within its perimeter, perhaps a timber revetment supporting clay which subsequently slumped inwards. The stake-holes are shown on the overall plan and that nearest the section line illustrated has been projected on to it. Unfortunately, an error in excavation destroyed some of the evidence for the original shape of the cistern on its southern side. This loss of evidence has been indicated on the section. The stratigraphy within the cistern (which has not, on this illustration, been labelled and characterised fully) suggests that its early use ended with the accumulation (slump from around its edges?) of deposits in its bottom and that it was subsequently recut to a shape which was larger at the top but narrower at the bottom. Layers higher up seem to derive from slumped rampart material, followed by layers representing deliberate infill. The site of this feature was then covered by a general layer (2) but later disturbed by the cutting of a pit, in post-medieval times, for the burial of a sheep. Fig. 3.9 shows excavation of the cistern in progress and its lowest levels.

Many of the deposits removed during excavation were very thin (as the section J–J published in 1982 illustrates) and for illustration here the data has been simplified in order to reveal the essential character of the site's stratigraphic development. At the southern end of the profile, in the centre of the bailey, even the earliest archaeology was literally under our feet. At its northern end lay the massive rampart described above. In between lay an area of stratigraphy deepening progressively northwards, whose greatest depth and complexity was in the immediate lee of the rampart. Fig. 3.8 illustrates the northern part of a line running through the bailey (shown on fig. 3.4 as MS1). In the southern (unillustrated) part of this line the stratigraphy became progressively thinner towards the centre of the bailey. This illustration is a composite depiction of data drawn *in situ* during excavation of the cistern together with data based on survey records in the immediately adjacent

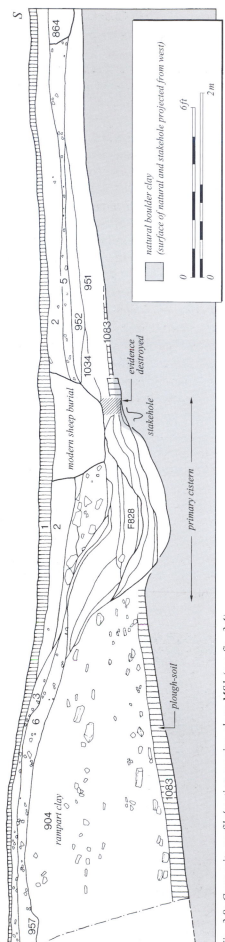

Fig. 3.8: Composite profile/section running along MS1 (see fig. 3.4)

Fig. 3.9: Cistern XLIII during excavation. Left: general view from the south west. Right: bottom of feature during excavation (from east) showing four stakeholes on left hand edge

areas. It shows clearly the relationship between the natural boulder clay, that part of the pre-castle plough-soil which survived *in situ*, the clay of the bailey rampart, the deeper stratigraphy immediately behind it and the shallower stratigraphy extending (upslope) southwards. It contains, of course, a historical paradox: the massive bulk of the rampart clay was the product of a single archaeological event (with relatively little build-up on top, the result of successive reconstructions/demolitions of the defences), whereas the numerous thinner deposits to the south were the accumulation of at least two hundred years. The recorded line runs between (and therefore does not illustrate) pairs of major posts in the rampart (1422/1451 and 1421/1252 in the early defences and their equivalents in phases U/V/W/X) and also misses the surviving portion of primary marking-out bank immediately to its south. But shallow gulley 957, in the top of the rampart, is the connecting feature between structural timbers in the phase X defences (see Barker & Higham 1982, fig. 21). Layers in this area with general stratigraphic importance were: layer 951, which (to the west of the line illustrated) preceded the construction of Building XXII (phase X) and therefore accumulated during the early castle's life; and layer 2, which represents the accumulation of silt over much of the north-eastern part of the bailey sealing the structures of phase Y (including the last use of the cistern) and preceding those of phase Z (notably Building XXXVI which was laid in this deposit—see Barker & Higham 1982).

Further east lay an interesting but somewhat enigmatic structure, also built after the rampart had been constructed. It was erected on a platform of clay and this foundation overlay a deposit of large stones laid on the buried soil. This stone spread, which has been illustrated above (fig. 2.10 in Chapter 2) together with other features at the interface of the pre-castle and early castle phases, added further to the levelling up of this naturally sloping part of the site. The evidence depicted was recovered over three seasons of excavation, during which time we wondered whether it represented two successive buildings on exactly the same site, because features at its northern end emerged before those at its southern end. Fig. 3.10 shows excavation of the structure in progress. In earlier interim reports the evidence was tentatively interpreted in this way. On reflection, however, it seems more likely that there was one building only and that the apparent stratigraphic separation of its structural features was simply a product of the excavation process, the southern end having been covered more deeply by subsequent deposits. We have shown all the evidence together on one plan and called it Building LIV (fig. 3.11). This seems a better option than suggesting the existence of a second, possibly imaginary building. This site was occupied in the next major phase of the castle (phase X) by the northern extension (Buildings XLIX and L) of the large hall (Building XLVIII) which occupied the lower half of the bailey.

Although its general configuration was clear enough, the evidence representing the edges of Building LIV varied from wall to wall. The clay platform conformed more or less to the plan of the building. A series of small post-holes and stake-holes (1266–1277, up to 0.20m deep) formed its northern limit. On the south, an isolated (and presumably internal) shallow post-position (1224) lay near the edge of the platform but the main wall line was represented by a short line of small post-holes (collectively 1368, varying between 0.15m and 0.30m in depth) in the south-west and a line of carbonised

Fig. 3.10: Building LIV partly excavated; see also fig. 3.11. The clay fill of hollow 1261 has been removed

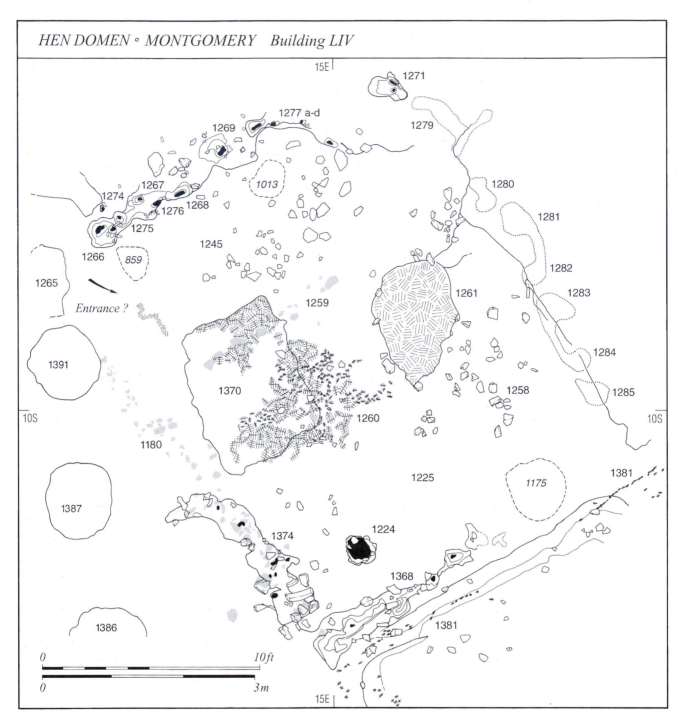

HEN DOMEN ∘ MONTGOMERY Building LIV

Fig. 3.11: Building LIV

timber fragments (collectively 1381) along its whole length. On the west, the wall line was represented by a group of small post-holes (collectively 1374, up to 0.25m deep) at the southern end. On the east, another line of stones (1258) ran at the southern end. Otherwise, structural evidence on the east side proved elusive. A series of dark, damp marks (shown in discontinuous outline as 1279–1285) coincided with the edge of the building platform and were investigated on the assumption that they would prove to be further small post-holes. But excavation failed to 'prove' them. The building seems to have had two floor areas of clay and soil (1225 to the south, 1245 to the north), in which the

more northerly had a more consistently clay composition and more stones, often flat and worn. An area of burnt clay and charcoal (1260) near the centre of the structure presumably represents the site of a hearth. It partly occupied a sub-rectangular shallow hollow (1370). A clay-filled hollow (1261) inside the east wall had no obvious function and may have resulted from the digging out of timbers, or was alternatively perhaps an abortive post-pit for the east wall of the next structure on this site, Building XLVIII. A possible entrance of Building LIV was situated at the north end of its west side, immediately next to the posts of the adjacent structure, Building XXXVIII. At this point was discovered a shallow feature (1265) of which only the eastern side was clear and whose function remains unidentified. Two other features are shown as tinted areas, both distinctive lines of stones. One (1180) ran the length of the western wall and partly overlay 1374. Another (1259) ran across the building and partly overlay hearth 1260 (which must therefore have gone out of use, or at least been reduced in area at some stage). These features may well represent part of the western wall line and an internal cross-partition, but if so may represent developments within the life of the building rather than primary features. Reconstruction of this building is difficult: the total evidence along its wall lines seems to suggest a mixture of slender ground-fast timbers, framing and perhaps clay construction. It was perhaps repaired *in situ*, using different building methods, during its life.

Building LIV was stratigraphically early in the sequence of events excavated in the bailey. It overlay only the levelling-up operation at the tail of the rampart represented by the boulder spread (1396, above, Chapter 2) but was in turn sealed by Buildings XLIX and L (the northern part of hall XLVIII) of phase X, partly sealed by Building LII of phase Y, and finally overlaid by the deep silting of the lower parts of the site which preceded phase Z in the thirteenth century (for all of which see Barker & Higham 1982 and 1988). On the basis of this stratigraphic sequence we had always assumed the structure to be an early feature of the castle, hence its discussion at this point of the report. But in 1995, a calibrated date for a charcoal sample from its hearth area was provided by the Ancient Monuments Laboratory of English Heritage (from an earlier C[14] assessment, Birm-1182, by the University of Birmingham Department of Geological Sciences). This lay, within a 95% confidence range, between AD 1170 and 1290, which seems far later than the stratigraphic sequence would suggest if the castle's 'historical' origin in the 1070s is assumed. Even if the charcoal sample represents activity at the very end of Building LIV's use, or even if it reflects a second building on the site, it puts the subsequent sequence of phases X, Y and Z very much later than previously argued. The matter remains a conundrum. It is, of course, possible that the true date lies outside the 95% probability range, or that the sample was contaminated in the field or with intrusive material from the subsequent buildings (XLIX and LII) of phases X or Y, or even by unobserved root activity. The issue is discussed in the wider context of the site's dating (Chapter 7) but one further aspect is relevant in the structural discussion at this point. If Building LIV is later than we have suggested, the nature of the site it eventually occupied is problematic. As described above (Chapter 2), the building occupied a clay platform laid on top of a boulder spread which had levelled up the steep downward slope of the bailey at this point. The clay of the platform for LIV was embedded within the boulders, the spaces between which otherwise lacked accumulated deposits, suggesting the boulders had been freshly laid when the clay platform was put down. If the clay platform (and presumably therefore the boulders) were not put down until a much later stage in the castle's occupation, it implies that for a very long time its occupants had tolerated a steeply sloping area of exposed pre-castle plough-soil, which must have been regularly very muddy and always inconvenient. This seems most unlikely. Elsewhere in the bailey, the builders always removed the plough-soil except where it would be covered by the construction of the rampart and its tail. A related issue is the longevity of fence 17, which ran through this area. We have assumed, above, that this stood until it was uniformly dismantled when the various structures behind the rampart were added (at whatever date). But this cannot be proved and it is also possible that the fence was removed earlier, or selectively if the three buildings in question (LIV, XXVI and XXVII) were not all built at exactly the same time.

Building XXXVIII, immediately adjacent to LIV, was massively constructed with twelve deeply founded posts in four rows of three set at close intervals. It will be observed (see figs 3.11 and 3.12) that the north-eastern corner of this structure (post-pit 1391) is contiguous with the west wall of Building LIV and is situated exactly where the evidence for that wall (feature 1180) comes to an end, giving perhaps the impression on the plan that the post-pit truncates the wall line. This is an illusion: post-pit 1391, excavated in 1984, was cut only through the eroded southern edge of the buried soil, exposed at the very tail of the rampart, and through the underlying boulder clay. Building LIV, however, was excavated between 1981 and 1983: the illustrated length of the line of stones (1180) which marks the course of its western wall was its real extent. The evidence suggests that both buildings were part of the early castle. Building XXXVIII may have been under construction while the defences were being erected, with Building LIV added after the rampart had been thrown up.

The twelve post-pits of Building XXXVIII, none of which cut through anything other than eroded buried soil and/or natural boulder clay, were dug so that their bottoms were level to within 0.1m, again suggesting some prefabrication of the timbers (note that the published profiles of their post-holes, in Barker & Higham 1982, fig. 32, are slightly misleading, since subsequent excavation showed that some had not been fully emptied on first examination owing to their depth and narrowness). The full evidence of this structure, as revealed in this part of the excavation, suggests that all twelve features were originally contemporary, rather than

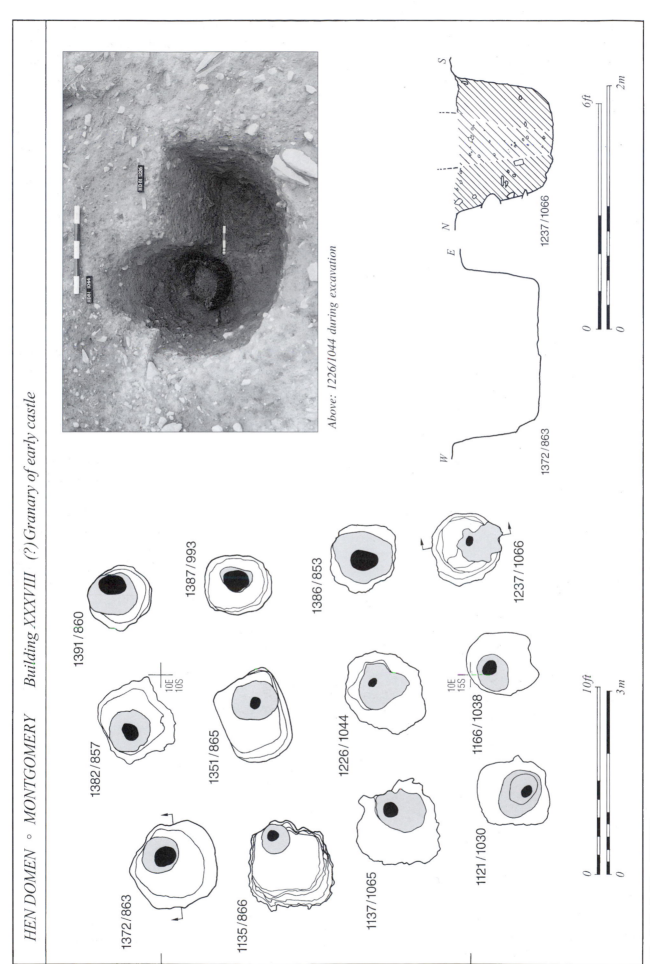

Above: 1226/1044 during excavation

HEN DOMEN ◦ MONTGOMERY   Building XXXVIII   (?)Granary of early castle

Fig. 3.12: Building XXXVIII

representing two groups of six, accumulative or successive in date (though the northernmost six posts remained in use longer and were covered by fewer subsequent deposits—see Barker & Higham 1982, 37, 47). The fills of the pits themselves were sterile, apart from a few animal bone fragments, though one (1237) had a sherd of the earliest type of coarse pottery occurring on the site in general (Clarke 1982; type 11 fabric). But most of the post-holes contained nails, animal bone debris and coarse pot sherds, and several contained glazed sherds (including three instances of developed Stamford ware) which can only have been deposited on the withdrawal of the timbers when the building went out of use (on the pot evidence, probably in the later twelfth century or later still; see Clarke 1982, for Stamford and other wares in the bailey). This process of withdrawal, however, left *in situ* the broken but waterlogged bases of two oak posts (1030 and 1044) which were subjected to C[14] assessment in the 1980s at Birmingham University's Department of Geological Sciences (Birm-1120 and Birm-1121 respectively). This produced results of 1054 ± 70 and 971 ± 70 and this information was subsequently published (Barker & Higham 1988, 7). More recently, these dates have been calibrated at the Ancient Monuments Laboratory of English Heritage and are now, within a 95% confidence date-range, respectively AD 1010–1270 and AD 970–1230. Although this information does not tell us very much, given the good documentary dating for the foundation of the castle in the 1070s, it allows at least the possibility of the re-use of timbers from an earlier structure elsewhere. In the circumstances of its foundation, the bringing in of at least some pre-prepared timbers seems quite likely. The close spacing of these

timbers suggests this building was not a domestic dwelling but a structure designed to resist the thrust of stored material, and a granary is the most likely interpretation. This putative granary had a long life, continuing in use through major reconstructions of the castle, which is why its post-holes (as opposed to its post-pits) were discovered so much earlier in the process of excavation (Barker & Higham 1982, 37–38). In the lowest area of the bailey, the site of this building received washed-down material from all directions which further added to the sealing of its pits while its posts still stood. On the accompanying plan (fig. 3.12) the outlines of the post-pits are shown with the post-holes already published on the phase X plan (Barker & Higham 1982, figs 21 and 23) inserted into them. The top and bottom shapes of the post-holes are distinguished on the plan. Variety in their top shapes may reflect distortions created when some of the posts were pulled out. Some posts were more pointed, others straighter in shape. The features are numbered (with the pit first in each case) 1372/863, 1382/857, 1391/860, 1135/866, 1351/865, 1387/993, 1137/1065, 1226/1044, 1386/853, 1121/1030, 1166/1038, 1237/1066. Fig. 3.12 also illustrates two of the twelve foundations, one as a profile of the original pit (1372), the other as a composite section of pit and post-position (1237/1066). One photograph (within fig. 3.12) is a detail of 1226/1044, partly excavated in quadrants, with the preserved post-base *in situ*. The second photograph shows a general view of the structure (fig. 3.13) from the south-west, taken when only the post-holes had been excavated. The post-pits seem to have been dug wide not only to allow deep digging for the required foundations but also to permit easy adjustment of the post-positions into straight lines.

Fig. 3.13: General view of granary (Building XXXVIII) from the south-west (post-holes only excavated at this stage)

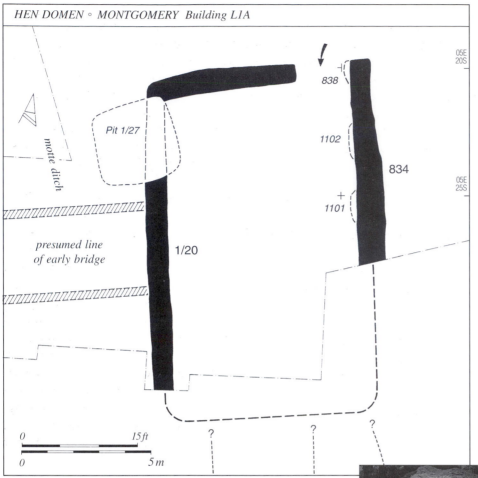

HEN DOMEN ○ MONTGOMERY Building L1A

motte ditch

Pit 1/27

*presumed line
of early bridge*

1/20

838

1102

834

1101

05E
20S

05E
25S

0   15 ft

0   5 m

?   ?   ?

Fig. 3.14: Building LIa

*Above: plan (metric grid only shown in eastern part of
illustrated area)*
Below: western wall during excavation
Right: eastern wall during excavation

Also of massive character was Building LIa, which occupied a central position in front of the motte ditch. The original outline of its foundation trench is shown in fig. 3.14, where features relating to its re-use are not shown except where they extend its shape. The two photographs indicate the character of the building's western and eastern wall lines during excavation (in the 1960s and 1970s respectively). Otherwise omitted are the intrusions created by re-use of its wall lines in the next major phase (X) when it became the site of a post-built structure (first labelled XVII in the 1982 report, but LIb in the 1988 report and thereafter) of similar dimensions except extended eastwards, (Barker & Higham 1982, 38–40 and fig. 23). The original foundation trench (834) was up to 1.0m wide in places and cut deeper on the western, up-slope side so that its bottom (up to 1.0m deep on this side) was more or less level all round the building (this was tested during the excavation of 834 by briefly re-opening a portion of 1/20, excavated in the earlier stage of the excavation). This trench would have comfortably held horizontal timbers similar to the preserved example which lay in a trench cut into the natural boulder clay at the bottom of the adjacent motte ditch and which represented the foundation of the early motte bridge (Barker & Higham 1982, 56–57). A socket in the underside of this preserved bridge timber (and therefore redundant) indicates the re-use of the timber and possibly part-pre-fabrication of one of the early castle's structures. If this was the case, the structure from which the bridge timber was re-used may not have been very old: a recently calibrated date from the bridge timber, produced by the Ancient Monuments Laboratory of English Heritage from an earlier C[14] assessment (Birm-1184), is, within a 95% confidence range, AD 1040–1290. The true date, of course, could still be earlier than 1040. It should also be noted that one small timber slot and one post-hole, also cut into the natural boulder clay at the bottom of the ditch, may be either contemporary with or earlier than the preserved timber (Barker & Higham 1982, 56–57). If these features represent an earlier bridge, then that represented by the timber, though still very early in the castle's life, was not the very earliest. The issue is discussed in the wider context of the site's dating, below (Chapter 7).

Although it is impossible to prove contemporaneity of the bridge foundation and Building LIa, this is suggested by their proximity and parallel alignment (see fig. 3.1). It is quite possible that access to the bridge may have been via the building, there being little space between the motte ditch and its western wall. The size of the foundation trenches also suggests that this building was of two storeys, perhaps a first-floor hall, a major residence (probably *the* major residence) within the bailey of the early castle. Access to the bridge may even have been from its first floor, though this is speculative. Overall interpretation of this building is impossible because its southern end remains unexcavated, but the only ground-floor entrance observed is in its northern wall: thus assailants approaching directly up the bailey would not have an unbroken run at a doorway immediately in front of them. The building was some 8.0m wide and its longest excavated portion (on the west) was nearly 12.0m in length. Its probable southward extent, giving a total length of over 13.0m, has been traced by a radar probing survey carried out by Peter Barker (see below, Chapter 5). The single broken lines shown on the plan represent the likely extent of the building (and perhaps an extension of it further to the south?) and have been interpolated from the results of the geophysical survey. This line supersedes that appearing on earlier published plans, which was a guess based on the assumption that the bridge was situated more or less centrally to the long axis of the building. This guess turned out, in fact, to be basically correct. Building LIa itself became the site of a further structure in the next phase, when it was extended eastward by a row of posts outside its original wall. It was of long-lasting influence in the site's development and its possible reconstruction is discussed further below (Chapter 7).

Fence XXIX, between this building and those behind the rampart, may represent an internal division of the bailey separating this main residence from lesser structures nearer the defences. It comprised a series of stake-holes with a cobbled entrance (14/29) about half way along. The plan (fig. 3.1) shows a hiatus in the evidence for this fence at the junction of the north-west and north-east sectors of the excavation, at which point the stake-holes do not quite match up. This may be illusory, arising from a survey-recording problem where there was a genuine loss of data at the eroded edge of the first excavation. Alternatively, it may be that, coincidentally, another narrow entrance through the fence was situated at this point. The western part of fence XXIX is shown in detail in Barker & Higham 1982 fig. 16.

In the 1982 report, a series of features was illustrated cut into the top of the rampart some time after the completion of the early defences but before the development of the phase published there as phase X. These features were compositely labelled U/V/W because it was not clear whether they represented a distinct phase in the castle's development or simply a piecemeal process of repair and re-building of the first castle prior to a general rebuilding which we called X. It is notable, for example, that the lines of small post-holes separating the postulated structures XX, XXa, XXI and XXII (Barker & Higham 1982, figs 18 and 19) lie more

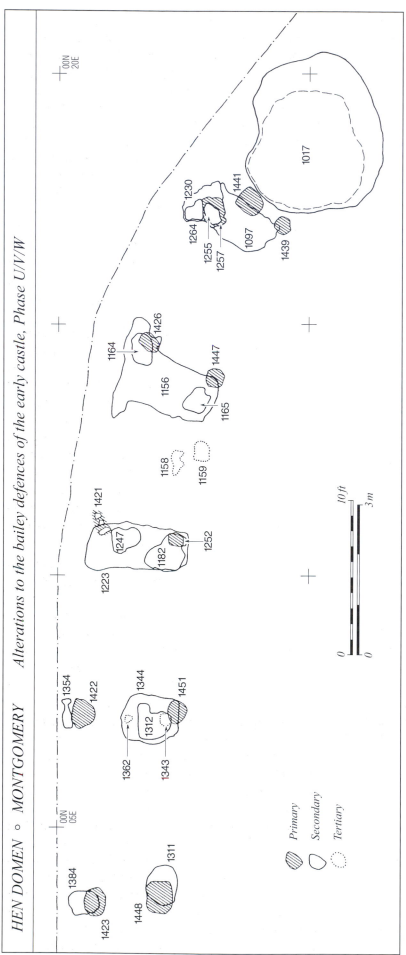

HEN DOMEN ○ MONTGOMERY   Alterations to the bailey defences of the early castle, Phase U/V/W

Fig. 3.15: Alterations to the bailey defences of the early castle: phase U/V/W

Above: primary, secondary and tertiary post postions

Right: pit 1017: excavation of upper levels

Far right: pit 1017: excavation complete

or less above the pairs of major posts belonging to the earliest castle (*ibid.* fig.16). In the north-east sector of the bailey, we also found features which had been cut into the rampart but which preceded the features already published collectively as phase X (*ibid.* figs 20, 21, 22, and 23). Whereas in the relatively small north-west sector such features made a reasonably coherent pattern (*ibid.* fig. 19), in the much larger area of the north-east sector they were not as continuous and we have illustrated here the developments encountered in the northern part of the rampart only (fig. 3.15). From this point down to the bailey entrance, the evidence was less consistently distributed, or at least less successfully identified in excavation.

Fig. 3.15 illustrates various developments, from west to east, in simplified form. Fig. 3.15 can be correlated with fig. 3.1 since both contain the primary palisade features. Features 1423 and 1448 represent a pair of post positions in the primary defences, eventually discovered when the rampart was removed. Features 1384 and 1311 were identified at a higher level during the removal of the rampart but overlay the earlier features and must surely be their replacement. Features 1422 and 1451 represent a further pair of primary post positions beneath the rampart. Above, and again presumably representing replacements, lie 1354 and a complex of features numbered 1312, 1343, 1344 and 1362. The sequence here was that pit 1344 contained a post-hole 1312, which was in turn succeeded by two smaller posts, 1343 and 1362. Further to the east, identifying the primary post positions beneath the rampart proved very difficult. A small group of stones (1421) may represent the remains of a post-pad. Feature 1252 was discovered within, rather than under, the rampart, but its shape, depth and position suggests it is a primary post position. Above, post-pit 1223 contained posts 1182 and 1247, whose positions also reflect those of features beneath. Excavation of pit 1156 suggested that it was dug for the erection of posts 1164 and 1165. The latter lay more or less over primary palisade posts 1426 and 1447, for which they had perhaps been replacements. Two shallow post-holes, 1158 and 1159, may represent additional repairs in this area. They have been tentatively labelled as later in date, though this cannot be demonstrated. Finally, post-pit 1230, containing post-holes 1255 and 1264, and pit 1097 (which cut through 1230 but in which no obvious post-position was detected) succeeded two primary post positions (1439 and 1441) discovered beneath the rampart and a third (1257) which was also early but detected within the rampart. If all three were at some stage contemporary, the pattern is different from elsewhere, where the primary posts were in pairs. Alternatively, one of the three may have been an early addition.

The evidence observed in this stretch of rampart suggests a process of evolution between the earliest erection of the defences and the building of the phase X defences already published (Barker & Higham 1982, figs 21 and 22). This evolution may not have consisted of discrete phases but rather of a more continuous process of repair, replacement and addition. There is no dating evidence to suggest its time-span and no way of knowing how long the primary timbers in the palisade lasted in comparison to those in the granary or the earliest motte tower identified. Excavating this sequence of events in the north-east sector of the bailey rampart was a considerable challenge during which some mistakes were definitely made. Dissection of the rampart was made difficult by the fact that in several locations (both those illustrated and those, further south-east along the rampart, which are not) posts had been placed more or less exactly in the positions of their immediate predecessors. Where this occurred on top of one of the primary posts, originally laid before the rampart was built, the sequence might intrude on a primary post position where it was detectable within the rampart itself (*cf.* post position 6/56 shown in the section of the rampart published in fig. 15 of the 1982 report: the bottom of a post from a higher level intrudes into it). For this reason, we sometimes experienced difficulty establishing the lower edges of what we began excavating, at a higher level, as a post-pit or post-hole: we dropped into features which, while detectable within the rampart, had no pits at all. Deciding exactly how many structural events there were was not always possible, let alone easy.

A further feature of the rampart's early development also deserves discussion here. In the published phase X plan, a large pit (feature 1017 or structure 15) is shown in the north-east corner of the defences (Barker & Higham 1982, 36 and figs 22 and 23). It was there noted that during this phase what had originally been a simple but deep pit had been largely filled and then lined with small timbers whose positions were observed on its west and south sides. Perhaps by this stage in its life (see first photograph in fig. 3.15) it had become a storage space of some sort or the shallow basement of a tower or other building located within the defences. The original digging of this pit belonged, however, to the earlier alterations made to the rampart described here. It had been dug right through the rampart itself, through the buried soil beneath and into the underlying boulder clay, a total depth of some 2.5m. Its upper surface diameter was some 3.0m at the widest point, but this shape (as illustrated) was perhaps the result of collapse or erosion and lower down the shape was sub-rectangular and the diameter 2.0m at most. The digging of this pit was a substantial undertaking (see second photograph in fig. 3.15) if it was created after the rampart was

Fig. 3.16: The early castle: an artist's reconstruction of the excavated areas (by Peter scholefield)

complete, which the available evidence suggests. But it could, alternatively, have been planned before the rampart was built, with the rampart thrown up around a strong timber lining but the bottom already dug through the pre-castle ground surface, perhaps to aid drainage. There was, however, no direct evidence for such a timber inner structure. The most obvious interpretation is that it was a very deep basement in a tower or other structure, supported by the flanking groups of palisade timbers (1257, 1441 and 1439 to its west; 1400 and 981 to its east). It would certainly have been a very secure place, though a storage place for valuables would surely have been provided on the motte rather than on the site's perimeter? If it had been completely lined, perhaps with hides, it would have held a large volume of water: perhaps it was filled from gutters draining from the roofs of the defensive structures around it. It remains, however, like other features on the site, something of an enigma.

Fig. 3.16 is an artist's impression (by Peter Scholefield) of what the early castle may have looked like. The evidence for the tower on the motte is discussed below (Chapter 4) and the evidence for the wide motte bridge has already been published (Barker & Higham 1982). The drawing illustrates the main features of the bailey as described above. The hall (LIa) below the motte bridge has been shown with two storeys and with entrances (ground- and first-floor) to the north. The wide defences in the north-west corner have been built up to include a structure (XXVIII) at first-floor level and the assumed corner tower even higher. The interval tower on the bailey rampart has been shown open, simply for visual contrast. As with all our reconstruction drawings, depiction of the entrance is limited by its incomplete excavation and we do not know how the passage-way was bridged nor whether other structural evidence lay forward of the inner rampart crest. Since it has been argued, above, that the 'early' castle underwent considerable development, a decision has been necessary about what to depict among the secondary additions. To create visual interest, two secondary structures (XXVI and LIV) are shown, but between them XXVII has been omitted and fence 17 has been left *in situ*. The outer rampart has been shown with palisade because practical defence of the site seems to demand one; the excavated evidence here, however, probably belonged to the middle of the castle's life-span (see below, fig. 3.24).

The Bailey Ditch (figs 3.17–3.23)

Several sections across the extant bailey ditch were dug as specifically targeted exercises. Their locations are shown on fig. 3.17, which should be compared with fig. 0.2, the overall site plan. The latter also shows the positions of two earlier ditch sections, whose evidence has already been published (Barker & Higham 1982,

71–72, and fig. 10). Of the two earlier sections, dug in 1966, the westernmost had been dry whereas the easternmost had been waterlogged and produced preserved portions of a timber palisade base (*ibid.* fig. 40).

In the early 1980s, four sections were dug: two at the north-east corner of the site, where the ground is still heavily waterlogged; one immediately next to the bailey entrance, to examine the causeway across which entry is now gained; and one on the northern side of the site, between the two sections dug in 1966. The general character of the unexcavated ditch, looking southwards from the position of section A towards that of section D, is shown in fig. 3.18. The corresponding northwards view, showing the waterlogged area, is shown in figure 3.19.

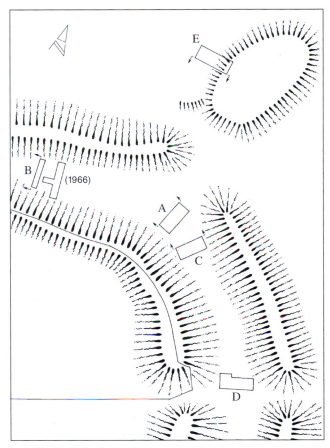

Fig. 3.17: Location of excavations: inner ditch of bailey and outer earthwork

The wet section (fig. 3.20, A) illustrated how strong the bailey defences had originally been since the ditch itself was nearly 2.0m deep. It was clear from the countless number of very thin layers which had accumulated (collectively layer 7), almost like sedimentary geology in miniature, that the ditch had been a muddy-bottomed feature for a very long time. This is clearly a product of the site's natural drainage, since one of the sections cut in the 1960s only a few metres further west, as well as that described below (B), was totally

Fig. 3.18: Bailey ditch looking southwards from section A

Fig. 3.19: Bailey ditch looking northwards from section C

dry. (A similarly wet environment is to be found at the corresponding corner of the ditch on the south-east side of the bailey). The surface volume of water had, however, been increased in the area where the section was dug by the laying of a deposit of cobbles (2 and 4), perhaps by a farmer in relatively recent times, probably to prevent grazing cattle from sinking too far into the mud. Earlier, a sump or drainage channel (5) seems to have been dug in the ditch top, by now filled with clay (6), and had subsequently filled with organic debris. The section also reveals that clay (8) had slumped into the ditch from both sides during its filling up. A view of the excavated ditch is shown in fig. 3.21.

A complete wooden stave-built tub was found at the bottom of the ditch. Apart from its intrinsic interest as a utensil, it tells us something unexpected about the history of the defences at this point. Dendrochronological study shows that, although the evidence will bear alternative interpretations (below, Chapter 5), the oak tree from which it was made may well have been felled in the late eleventh century. It is possible that the tub had a very long life and was discarded late in the occupation of the site. But if it was discarded, say, after one generation of use, it suggests that the ditch at this point was not re-cut, or even cleaned after the second quarter of the twelfth century. This evidence contrasts sharply with the periodic re-cutting of the motte ditch and the assumed re-cutting of the bailey ditch which was originally argued (Barker & Higham 1982, 51–59 and 71–72). The difference may have been mundane—mud in the outer ditch may have added to its defensive character—or it may have been social, the ditch beneath the high status residence on the motte being kept cleaner. The motte side, being taller, would also have produced more natural silting into the ditch, and rebuilding operations on the motte top would also have added to the accumulation below, in each case adding to the need for cleaning out some of the ditch silt as the sequence of bridges succeeded the primary one.

Two further bailey ditch sections were also dug (fig.

3.20), one (B) in a dry deposit on the north side, the other (C) in the wet deposit immediately south of section A, described above. Section C produced further items of waterlogged wood including a wooden shingle and a shovel blade. Such finds provide direct evidence of a form of roof-cladding otherwise not seen in the excavated evidence as well as of what must have been an array of everyday wooden artefacts (below, Chapter 5). Section B had evidence of a re-cut (through 10 and 7) on its north side as well as slumping (5 and 6) from both sides. Section C also had rampart material slumped in at different times (9/10 and 2/7). Above its waterlogged levels (11, 12 and 13) a layer of cobbles (3) had been deliberately laid (as in section A). A shallow clearance operation may be represented by the profile of 8 (cutting 9, 10 and 11). It is notable that several of these sections show horizontal shelves where the ditch profiles meet the natural ground surface at the base of the inner and outer ramparts. Perhaps these narrow berms reflect the construction methods employed in the digging of the ditches and the piling up of the ramparts, when platforms for the management of spoil would have been very helpful?

The varied patterns of evidence (in profiles and wet/dry character) recovered from the bailey ditch sections confirm not only the varied history of the site but also an important methodological lesson: the story provided from any one of them could not be safely extrapolated to other parts of the site, even a few metres away.

Section D (here illustrated in plan, fig. 3.22) was designed to test whether the present entrance causeway is an ancient or modern feature. Because of the restricted size of this cutting, approximately 5.0m×2.0m, and its location in the bailey entrance upon which the excavation itself depended daily, investigation did not proceed beyond the latest surface of the underlying ditch. One short but deep timber slot (5, measuring some 1.7m×0.75m and up to 0.5m deep), containing many iron nails, was discovered at the foot of the inner rampart.

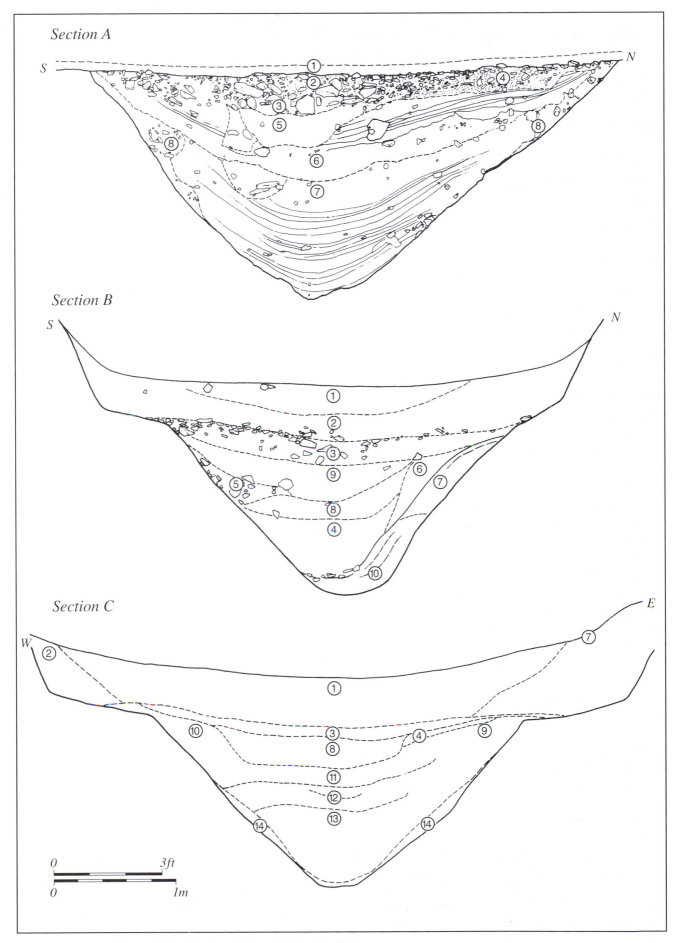

Fig. 3.20: Sections of inner ditch of bailey: A, B, and C (see fig. 3.17)

Fig. 3.21: The recording of section A

The tentative conclusion to be drawn from this limited excavation is that in the earlier periods the ditch had run continuously around the entrance and had been spanned by a timber bridge. Part way through the life of the castle, the ditch had been allowed to silt up, or had perhaps been partly filled deliberately, and the infill shaped to make a causeway. Later silting, particularly with wash-down from the bailey, had also been sculpted, perhaps by a farmer, into the existing causeway.

A Second Enclosure?

A short stretch of separate earthwork lies to the north-east of the outer rampart (fig. 3.17). This we had supposed to be the result of modern farming activity, or perhaps the spoil from the adjacent break in the rampart. It was cleared of vegetation during the seasons when the bailey ditch sections, described above, were excavated. It proved to be a substantial earthwork and in order to

Plan of cutting D

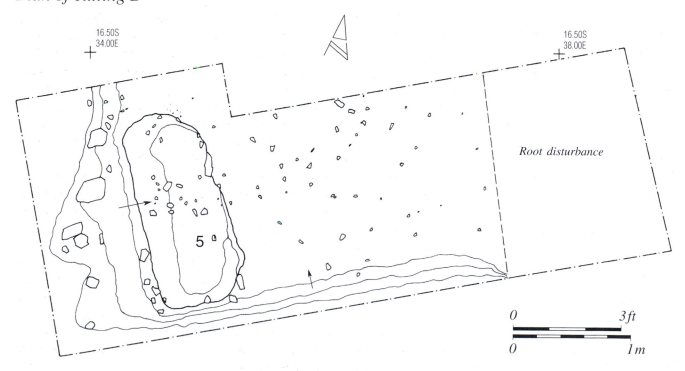

Fig. 3.22: Plan of cutting D, by bailey entrance (see fig. 3.17)

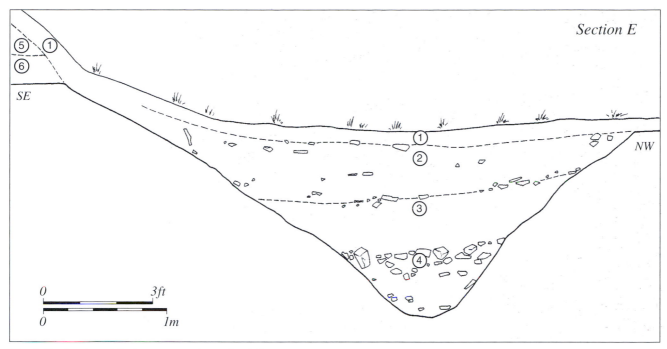

Section E

SE

NW

0   3ft

0   1m

Fig. 3.23: Section of ditch in cutting E (see fig. 3.17)

gain some indication of its origin a section was dug across what appeared to be a silted ditch on its north-west side (fig. 3.23, E). This small excavation produced a quantity of medieval pottery and evidence of nearby iron smithing in the form of a good sample of waste products (see below, Chapter 5). A buried soil (6) was also observed in the section, sealed by the earthwork (5). Since the survival of ridge and furrow outside the castle shows that the field has not been ploughed in modern times (in which case medieval material might have got into a feature dug at a later date), it appears that this ditch is medieval. It was filled with a succession of three layers of clay/silt (2, 3, 4) with stones and charcoal near the bottom and capped by the modern turf (1).

Two interpretations of this earthwork are possible. It may represent the start of an abortive attempt to build an outer bailey for the castle or an enclosure for an attached settlement. The documentary evidence for a nascent borough encouraged by the later twelfth-century lords of Montgomery may be relevant here (Barker & Higham 1982, Chapter 3). Alternatively, it may represent simply protection, from the prevailing westerly wind and rain, for some activity such as smithing. The present character of the earthwork makes this seem less likely, since it is a very substantial feature to build for such a purpose, for which a solid fence would presumably have sufficed. But it is also possible that in its present form, the earthwork also carries an overburden resulting from the demolition of the adjacent stretch of the outer defences. This demolition, indicated by a gap on the site survey (fig. 3.17), was perhaps a post-medieval attempt by a farmer to drain the wet part of the ditch. If it resulted in dumping on the outer earthwork, then a medieval predecessor, of smaller dimensions (better matched to the size of the ditch?), may lie beneath. Further excavation of the crest and interior of the earthwork might elucidate the problem.

The Outer Defences

In order to gain some impression of the outer defences a small excavation was conducted on the crest of, and below, the outer rampart on the north-west corner of the site (fig. 3.24). Dense tree cover limited the extent of excavation on the crest, which covered an area only 8.0m × 2.0m. Stripped of its turf and a thin layer of clay and pebbles, it revealed a pattern of post-holes, stake-holes and wattle slots which prove beyond doubt that, at least in its later life, the outer rampart was defended with a palisade and fighting platform. The evidence comprised: at the front, a more or less continuous slot with some individual post-holes; at the rear, a series of discrete post-holes; between, two short slots linking front and rear. It seems probable that the palisade was a clay wall strengthened with slender posts and wattles (a technique for which there is good evidence elsewhere in the bailey) and that the clay soil and pebbles which had to be removed in order to expose the excavated features represent the debris from the collapsed wall. The fighting platform seems to have stood on the rampart crest, rather than being raised above it as on the inner rampart. The whole construction would form a mantlet lying behind the outer ditch, providing a formidable obstacle in front of the inner defences. Its height cannot be known, but it seems reasonable to assume that it would be lower than the inner defences so that it did not obstruct the view from the latter. Given the closeness of the two lines of

The crest of the outer rampart looking west (1985)

The outer defences 1966, 1985 and 1986

Below: plan of crest of outer rampart excavation (1985)

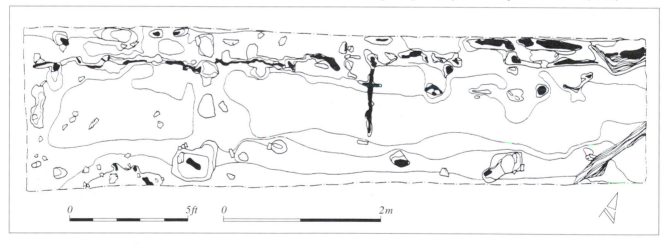

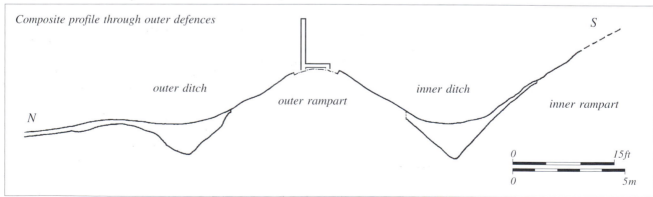

Fig. 3.24: The outer defences: the rampart and overall profile (and suggested palisade)

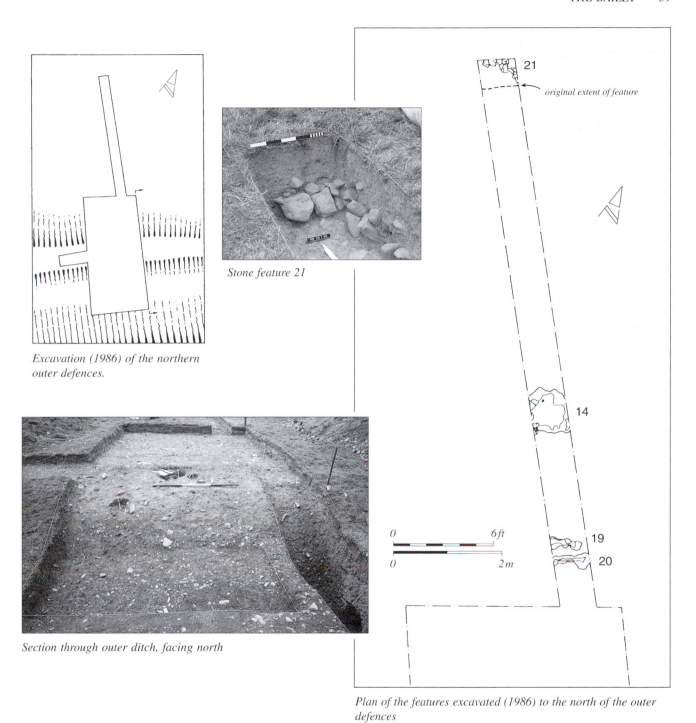

Excavation (1986) of the northern outer defences.

Stone feature 21

Section through outer ditch, facing north

0   6 ft

0   2 m

21

original extent of feature

14

19

20

Plan of the features excavated (1986) to the north of the outer defences

Section through outer ditch and counterscarp

←— counterscarp —→   ←— ditch —→

N

S

0   10 ft

0   3 m

Fig. 3.25: The outer defences: the outer ditch and features to its north

defence, there is some parallel with the later design of 'concentric defences' in which an inner line overlooked an outer one.

Although only a small stretch of the outer rampart was explored, and one of the lessons of the whole excavation has been how the character of the site could change over short distances, it seems reasonable to suppose that a palisade of some sort ran round the whole circuit of the outer rampart. It must, however, be stressed that only the uppermost evidence was examined and that nothing is known of the outer rampart's earlier history: if it had an earlier palisade, perhaps it had risen up from the underlying ground surface, like that of the inner rampart of the bailey? No dating evidence for the construction of the excavated palisade was recovered, but since it was dug into the top of the rampart and made use of clay/timber construction, the closest parallel is with the middle periods of the bailey, collectively called X, in the twelfth century. We have assumed throughout that the outer rampart was of one build with the inner defences. Only extensive excavation, at various points on the site's perimeter, could demonstrate whether this was the case or whether the outer defences had at some stage been added to the inner. The surviving earthworks, however, give the impression that the site was designed with double defences from the start.

A profile from the crest of the inner rampart to the outer ditch is shown in fig. 3.24. It conveys a good general impression of the nature of the defences, to which, of course, the heights of the inner and outer palisades must also be added. The investigation of the outer defences continued with the cutting of a section (fig. 3.25) across the outer ditch immediately below the rampart excavation. The area also included the top of what appeared to be, before excavation, a counterscarp bank. A strip some 4.0m wide was examined in its upper levels and the ditch bottomed in a cutting 1.0m wide on its eastern side. The illustrated section is compiled from two contiguous field records in which, unfortunately, a hiatus of information prevents a continuous presentation of evidence. Nevertheless, the sequence of events observed during excavation was clear enough. The outer rampart itself had been dug from a V-shaped ditch, some 1.5m deep, and in its first phase no counterscarp had existed. A few shallow and irregular depressions (not illustrated on the plan, but visible in the photograph) forming no coherent pattern, including two possible, and very small, post-holes, lay immediately outside the ditch. But there was no evidence of a palisade here. After a period (for which there was no dating evidence) of silting and perhaps some collapse of the front face of the rampart, the ditch was re-cut to a slightly shallower profile, the debris from the re-cut being thrown outward to form a low counterscarp of clay and small stones. This low bank, no more than 0.2m high, sealed the shallow features referred to above. The ditch subsequently filled up with clay, soil and small stones, though it survived clearly as a surface feature prior to excavation.

A narrow, northward extension of this excavation revealed the pre-castle features discussed above (Chapter 2), including parts of two gullies and a dry-stone construction, perhaps part of a field boundary.

CHAPTER 4

THE MOTTE

The excavation of the motte top began in 1988 in an area whose shape was laid out partly so that it joined up with the excavation carried out in the 1960s on the east face of the motte (see Barker & Higham 1982, 51–59) and partly so that it covered what appeared to be the summit of the surviving earthwork. During excavation and in the light of the features discovered, the area was extended to the north and west, but the temptation to extend down the slopes was resisted since there would be no obvious point at which to stop. The mound as surveyed in 1987 had many surface features—curves, slopes, straights and irregularities, presumably the cumulative effect of constructional events, demolitions, erosion and even possibly unrecorded archaeological explorations. There was no way of knowing in advance whether the centre of the motte top in the twentieth century coincided with its medieval counterpart. In the event, the main building platform, described below, turned out to be on the western side of the apparent centre. Fig. 4.1 illustrates the pre-excavation contour survey of the motte and the various areas excavated from the 1960s onwards. A north–south profile of the motte has been extrapolated from the contours and the overall extent and depth of the area excavated in 1988–92 indicated (but omitting depths of individually deeper features). Although some individual features were set much more deeply within the motte, the sequence of structural events described below was exposed by the removal of only about 0.5m of stratigraphy in the area as a whole.

There are respects in which the information recovered from the motte is obviously, or potentially, deficient. First, features run from the building platform to the edge of, and beyond, the excavated area, so that their interpretation is problematic. In an ideal situation, excavation of a motte would involve total examination of its whole surface area, but with the resources available this was not a practical proposition. Second, and related, is the question of depth of excavation. Through lack of time, it was not possible, in the final season of work (1992), to explore fully every part of every wall foundation of the building excavated. This limitation did not, however, prevent an overall interpretation being achieved. More general, however, is the problem of the total vertical history of the motte. Only complete removal of the mound down to the pre-castle ground surface would reveal any structural evidence which may lie buried far below the levels excavated: it was only with the removal of the bailey rampart that its earliest palisade was discovered. Finally, and conversely, it is not certain that the archaeological deposits excavated in the early seasons on the motte top represent the latest occupation. During evacuation/demolition/abandonment, but before a turf-line consolidated the motte top and sides, some material would have been lost through erosion: it is possible that a complete phase of occupation has disappeared. The material excavated in the motte ditches on the bailey side (Barker & Higham 1982, 51–59) and cut through on the opposite (western) side for the excavation's annual latrine pits must have come largely from the top and sides of the motte. For these reasons, equating the phases of the motte's use with those of the bailey is a hazardous process. Approximations are suggested below, but there is no reason why the motte should necessarily have been developed in parallel with the bailey. They may have had somewhat different histories, as often with the nave and chancel of a church. Moreover, the caveat made in the discussion of the bailey also applies here: the major phases suggested are simplifications which no doubt disguise many minor stages of alteration.

Fig. 4.2 shows the excavated features as recorded at the end of the excavation in 1992. They represent the earliest building identified on the motte top, in the form which it took when first constructed, but modified in use over a long period. This illustration, therefore, is not a 'phase plan'. Fig. 4.12 shows evidence of substantial burning which at some stage affected the modified structure, and a later phase of development, in which the evidence took a quite different form, is shown in fig. 4.13. A simplified sequence of development is shown in fig. 4.21. The challenge of analysing the structural sequence here is analogous to that described (above, Chapter 3) on the bailey rampart, where there was also a complex accumulation of features overlying the earliest ones. In the bailey, however, we had the advantage that the eventual removal of the rampart revealed most of the earliest palisade positions

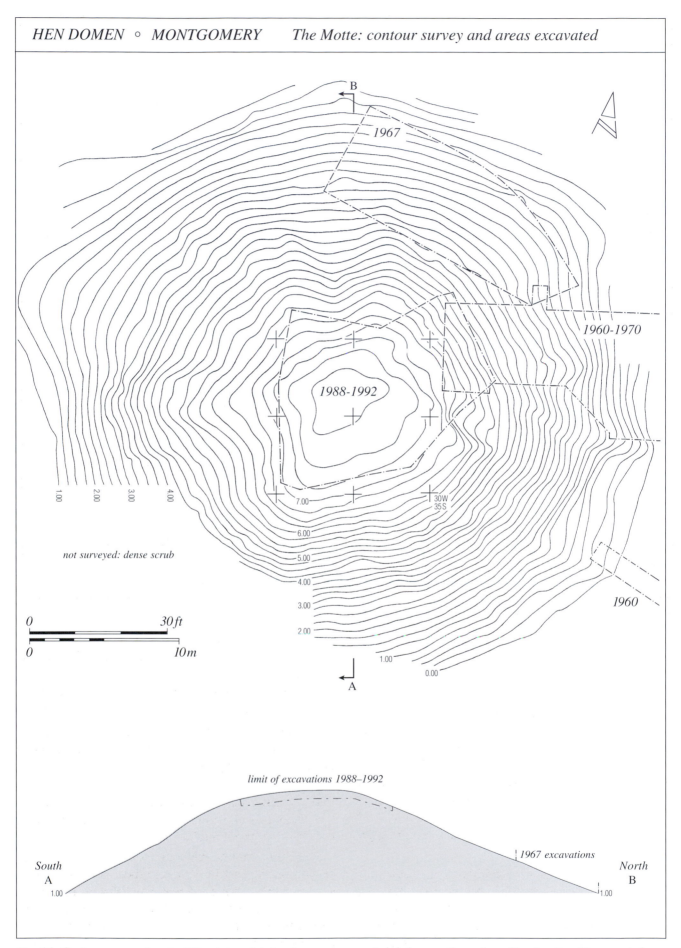

HEN DOMEN ○ MONTGOMERY   *The Motte: contour survey and areas excavated*

B

1967

1960-1970

1988-1992

1.00   2.00   3.00   4.00

30W
35S

7.00

6.00

5.00

4.00

3.00

2.00

not surveyed: dense scrub

1.00

0.00

A

1960

0   30 ft

0   10 m

limit of excavations 1988–1992

1967 excavations

South
A
1.00

North
B
1.00

Fig. 4.1: *Contour survey of motte (25cm intervals) showing areas excavated; below, north–south profile of motte with excavated areas*

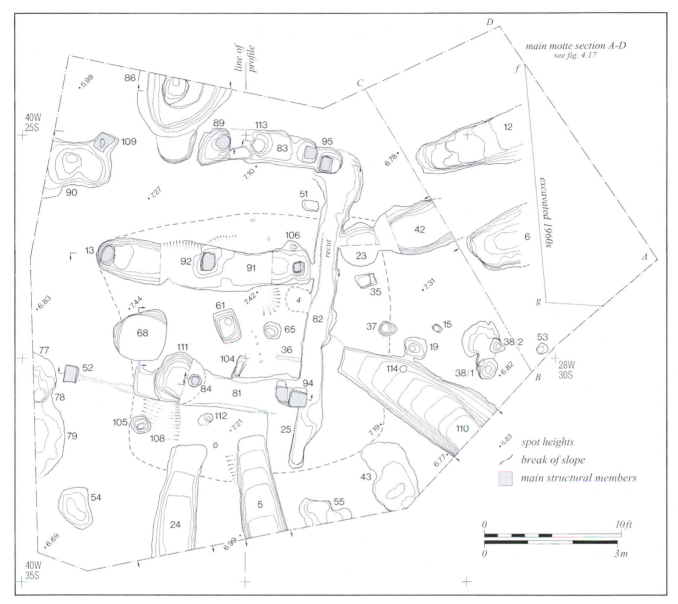

Fig. 4.2: The motte: the structural evidence, phases T – X

unencumbered by later developments. On the motte, in contrast, we were tackling the whole task of dissection from above without eventually being able to see all of the earliest features in isolation.

It was originally our intention to maintain cumulative sections across the motte, north–south and east–west, as the excavation proceeded, so that at the end there would be an overall vertical record of developments to complement the plans. Inevitably, the lines chosen for these cumulative vertical records created difficulties in the rational excavation of several features encountered during successive seasons. They were accordingly abandoned at an early stage.

There is no specific archaeological dating evidence for the start of the events described below. Two sherds of the earliest type of pottery found in the bailey were present in early features encountered on the motte, notably the (?)cistern 68 and post-position 89 in the north wall of the building. But, as in the bailey, pottery was

not common in the earliest levels explored and became more plentiful only in the middle period. The pottery from the motte had much the same character as that from the bailey, the latest types in each area suggesting occupation until *circa* 1300 (see below, Chapter 5).

In what follows, however, we have assumed (as in the bailey) that the motte sequence starts in the late eleventh-century context suggested by the documentary evidence because:–

a) the major posts of the primary building seem to have been laid in the motte as it was completed rather than laid in pits cut into its top;

b) the upper motte material, examined in the major section on the east face, was sterile apart from a few scraps of animal bone and charcoal; had it resulted from a heightening of the motte well into the castle's life, earlier building horizons and incorporation of earlier occupational debris would presumably have been visible in this section;

c) there is a structural analogy between the squared timbers used in the primary building and that preserved *in situ* in the motte ditch (see Barker & Higham 1982, 56–57 and above, Chapter 3) from the early motte bridge (and possibly elsewhere in the bailey's early buildings, for example the primary palisade and Building LIa, at the foot of the motte, whose foundation trench would have comfortably accommodated such timbers).

Nevertheless, absolute certainty about the initial date is impossible because the excavation examined only the upper portion of the motte. It will be seen from what follows that it is not possible to demonstrate uniformly that all the major posts of the earliest building encountered were laid as the motte was built. The example of the central post-position in its south wall shows how a post-pit (argued below to be secondary) was discovered at a late stage in the excavation. However, the squared timber post-positions encountered

undoubtedly represent the earliest building actually discovered in the excavation. Whether this was actually the first building ever constructed in association with the motte is a wider question which is addressed in general discussion of the site's dating evidence (below, Chapter 7).

In illustrating the evidence which represents the structural sequence on the motte, we have adopted the same approach as in illustrating the bailey. Excavation of the motte involved the removal of many successive deposits of boulder clay (and derivatives of it) which were frequently very localized and often not easy to distinguish from each other. We have not illustrated the results of this process of dissection but rather illustrated the structural features which this process revealed. Description of the deposits is therefore confined to contexts whose relevance to the structural sequence is crucial and numerous deposits noted in excavation are

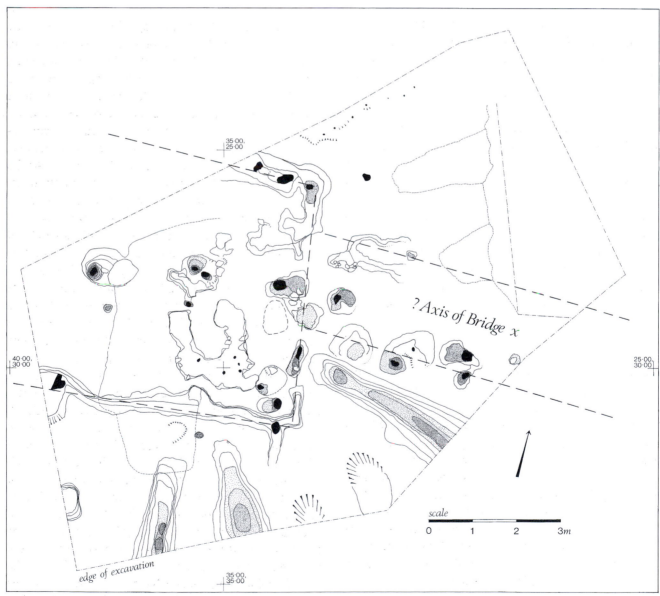

Fig. 4.3: The motte: plan of '?phase X' during excavation (after Higham & Barker 1992)

not individually enumerated or illustrated here. The earliest building encountered seems to have been occupied and modified over a long period. We did not, as we had expected, reveal a succession of buildings, of distinct sizes and forms, to be conveniently labelled as a series of 'phases'. This only occurred at the end of the sequence recovered (phase IV, below), but what we have labelled as phase II (and, less confidently, as phase III) represents the ongoing occupation and development of the building laid out in phase I. Once excavation of the uppermost building had been completed (in 1989), the ensuing process involved peeling off numerous deposits, frequently thin and localized, to expose features inside, outside and along the wall lines of a building whose shape gradually emerged and whose earliest structural evidence was eventually revealed and recorded in 1992. This process, which produced the pottery and other artefactual material, was challenging not only because making stratigraphic distinctions was often extremely difficult, but also because variations in dryness or wetness of weather sometimes gave us 'false' results. Despite efforts to create controlled dampness in the ground by regular spraying with water, we frequently found ourselves returning to re-excavate features and deposits, previously thought to have been fully examined, when ground conditions were better. Every year we recorded what we had revealed but the evidence thus recorded did not permit simple separation into a series of separate plans. When, in 1990, our general discussion of timber castles was being prepared for publication (emerging as Higham & Barker 1992), we were part way through this process and a plan was published (here reproduced, in modified form, as fig. 4.3) which we tentatively labelled 'phase X', by analogy with the bailey, because the building's walls seemed to consist of irregularly sized timbers. We could also see that this evidence was earlier than the latest phase of the motte, already removed, but later than deposits which still lay beneath. It must be emphasised that this was simply a snapshot of one point in the development of the excavation. It does, however, illustrate how lesser post-positions were added to the original plan, or replaced its original timbers, as well as a methodological lesson. At this stage, the shape of the excavated area did not encompass what we later knew to be the full extent of the building site. The excavation had been laid out using the summit of the motte as a guide. The total building site, however, turned out also to occupy the sloping shoulders of the motte. As first laid out, the excavation revealed little of the northern part of the building. It would have taken only a modest retraction of the northern limit of excavation, as originally planned, to have deceived us into thinking the building was only half its actual size.

Note: the issues of reconstruction which are discussed

in what follows are reflected in the depiction of the motte top in the overall reconstruction drawings of the site (see Chapters 1, 3 and 7). The reader should refer to those drawings in conjunction with this discussion.

Phase I, possibly equivalent of bailey phase T, the earliest castle (figs 4.2, 4.4–4.11)

A building (LVII) approximately 5.5m/18ft square was laid out towards the western end of the motte. An overall photograph of the structural evidence, taken at the conclusion to the excavation, is shown in fig. 4.4, in which major structural posts are indicated by ranging rods. It was apparently designed before the motte itself was completed, since its corner posts stood within the motte material, not in pits dug into its top surface. There was no sign of pits for these posts in the surfaces excavated, no visible stratigraphy in the walls of the post-voids (or those of other features cut into the motte clay), and no earlier horizons were visible in the main motte section (fig. 4.17) which lay only 1.5m from the north-east corner post of the building. The character of the south-western post (52) is particularly revealing: its void was deep and squared, isolated in the motte clay in an area where the motte was trowelled repeatedly in the search for a post-pit or related features, but where none came to light. Several of the post-voids were c.0.3m/12in square and at the north-east and south-east corners were up to 1.1m/3ft 6in deep (95 and 94). Photographs of these features are shown in figs 4.5 and 4.6. At the south-west corner, the (eroded?) slope of the motte meant the post (52) was buried less deeply (0.6m) and at the north-west corner, where the slope is very steep (perhaps enhanced by erosion—it faces the prevailing wind and rain), only a few inches of the bottom of the post-position (109) were recovered. It seems highly likely that midway along the northern and southern walls there were other major posts and that three posts also stood along a spine wall which divided the building into two halves at ground-floor level. The positions of these intermediate and internal posts, however, are suggested by features which in their excavated form may represent replacements of the original timbers (89 on the north, 84 on the south, and, west to east in the centre, 13, 92, 106). This replacement of timbers is suggested by the more irregular shape of some, and the fact that another (84), though squared in shape, was set in a feature which was cut into the motte top: during the final stages of excavation of the south wall it became clear that its central post was not buried within the motte but had been placed in a large post-pit (111). Since it seems pointless to finish building a motte and part of a building and immediately dig a new post pit for a timber (the need for which must already have been known), it seems likely that the post had been placed in a pit dug after

Fig. 4.4: Structural evidence for the early/middle period building viewed from above (west) at end of excavation

extraction of an earlier post laid within the motte itself. Unfortunately lack of time prevented us from establishing whether this was also the case elsewhere, particularly in the lowest levels of the dividing wall around posts 92 and 13.

Fig. 4.7 illustrates the profiles of the foundations, along the building's three wall lines, as they were recorded towards the end of the excavation. The lines of these profiles, and the related limits of excavation, are shown on the main plan (fig. 4.2). These profiles reveal that the depths of the original posts in the centre and south walls were comparable and that the four corner posts in particular were very substantial settings. It is also notable that the pit/post (84/111) in the centre of the south wall, argued above to be a secondary feature, was shallower than the wall's corner posts (94b/52). Either the (presumed) original mid-post was also shallower or it was as deep as the corner posts and its remains still lie in the motte beneath 84/111. If the secondary interpretation of 84/111 is correct, it is perhaps no surprise that it was shallower, as it had to be cut into the motte from above.

It seems probable that in its earliest phase the whole building made consistent use of squared timbers, built within the motte as its upper deposits were laid, but that some of these timbers were later replaced by others, inserted from above. Excavation of the fills of 94b and 106, in the southern and central walls respectively,

suggested that successive posts of similar shape may have occupied exactly the same positions.

The analogy with the earliest bailey palisade, and with the sole-plate of the early motte bridge, is strong: both used timbers of similar dimensions (often about 12in square) and both were later replaced by structures using posts, often of more miscellaneous dimensions, dug in from above. The foundation trench of the early hall (LIa) would easily have accommodated timbers of these dimensions and it, too, was rebuilt as a structure (LIb) using more irregularly sized posts. It may be that the early castle made use of pre-prepared timbers and/or timbers re-used from a dismantled building or buildings of high quality somewhere in the vicinity. The bridge sole-plate was certainly re-used, since it had a redundant socket on its underside (Barker & Higham 1982, 57).

No specific evidence for the nature of the walls connecting the major posts of this first building was recovered. But on the south, east and centre there were trenches (81, 82, 91) of varying dimensions, suggesting either that sill beams were laid in the upper levels of the motte as the latter was finished off, just like the main posts themselves, or that lesser vertical timbers stood side by side between the more deeply laid ones. However, no demonstrably primary post-positions were detectable in these features, whose shapes seem to have been affected by their subsequent re-use during the evolution of the building. That on the east (82), which was shallow,

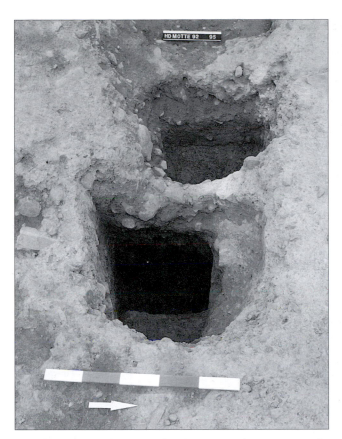

Fig. 4.5: Evidence for squared timbers at north-east corner of Building LVII. (95a & b) looking west

Fig. 4.6: Evidence for squared timbers at south-east corner of Building LVII. (94a & b) looking east

was fully excavated. On the south and in the central wall, the overall extent of these features (81 and 91) was observed, though they were deeper and their earliest profiles were not completely excavated in the time available during the last season of excavation. On the western slope all trace of a foundation gulley, if there ever was one, had disappeared and the evidence on the north and south did not extend as far as the western wall line. Perhaps there had been extensive erosion on this side (which faces west, from which the prevailing wind and rain comes). Or perhaps the motte top already sloped here and the foundations on this side partly over-sailed its surface. On the north, where the wall lay not only along a slope but also down one, the foundation consisted of a shallow trough (83) containing an extra post (113) with the result that individual posts (westwards from the north-east corner to the mid-point, 95, 95a, 113, 89) stood more closely to each other in steps down the slope. Since there is no equivalent of post 113 in the central or southern walls, it may have been a secondary post inserted in the subsequent development of the building.

It is assumed that the principal chamber of this structure was at first-floor level. Whether there was a third storey above that we cannot know, nor can we be certain whether the building was uniform in width throughout its height or whether some or all of its superstructure was jettied out . The northern half of the basement was virtually featureless, apart from one

shallow feature (51) and a few stake-holes. The dividing wall may have been wider than the outer walls: its trench was up to 1.0m wide whereas the latter's trenches varied between 0.5m and 0.8m wide. Perhaps this reflects flooring above in two lengths of timber rather than a single span, so that the dividing wall had to carry the butted ends of two sets of timbers? Although the foundation suggests this was a solid wall, it is possible that at some stage it comprised an open arcade of three major posts supporting the floor above, thus allowing easy access from one half of the basement to the other. Another feature of the dividing wall is that its end timbers did not line up with those in the corners of the building, suggesting that they stood against the internal faces of the east and west walls. Whether the dividing wall was a feature of the basement only, or whether, in the manner of a spine-wall in a stone keep, it continued up through the structure, creating sub-division of the rooms and providing support for the roof, we do not know.

The southern half of the basement had some minor features cut into its floor, including a short row of stake-holes and two shallow depressions (36 and 104). Two post-holes (61 and 65, 0.4m and 0.25m deep respectively) may have been primary features of the building (perhaps representing a ladder to the floor above?) or perhaps insertions to support the floor at some time during the building's life. The most substantial internal feature was a roughly circular pit (68), some

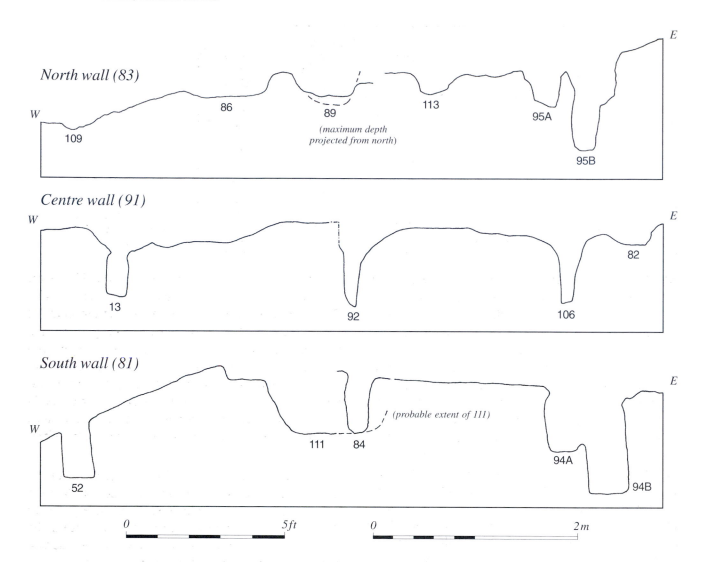

North wall (83)

W

109   86   89   113   95A

(maximum depth
projected from north)

95B

E

Centre wall (91)

W

13   92   106   82

E

South wall (81)

W

52   111   84   (probable extent of 111)   94A   94B

E

0   5ft   0   2m

Fig. 4.7: The motte: profiles of building foundations (see fig. 4.2 for profile lines)

0.6m deep and 1.0m in diameter, at the western end of the basement. This pit is shown in its final excavated profile (north–south) in figs 4.8 and 4.9, which shows it was flat-bottomed and vertical-sided for the most part. When the shape of this pit was first observed, substantial charcoal flecks were seen distributed around its uppermost perimeter. These were sufficiently uniform to suggest that the pit's walls may have been lined with wattling at some stage. The bottom of the pit bore a thin, dark layer, though it is impossible to say whether this was the remains of a lining, of silting during use, or indeed of some residue from the pit's contents. It was also impossible, in excavation, to dissect and illustrate these tenuous deposits separately from the clay infill

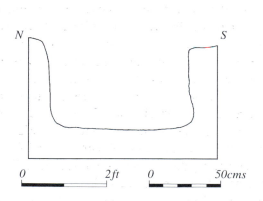

N   S

0   2ft   0   50cms

Fig. 4.8: Profile through ?cistern (68)

Fig. 4.9: View of ?cistern (68) looking east

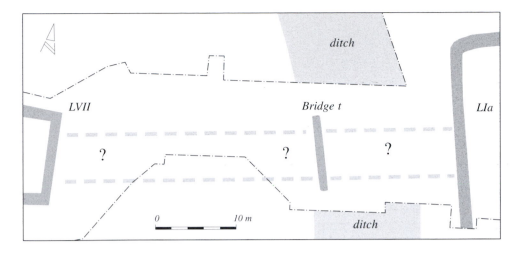

Fig. 4.10: Early motte tower and bridge in relation to Building LIa

which otherwise filled the pit. The drawn profile accordingly only shows the pit's overall form, without these details. The first stage in the excavation of this pit was investigation of a small feature (69) thought initially to be a post-position in the centre of the fill of the underlying pit. It remained, however, an unconvincing feature and has not been illustrated. The pit itself is tentatively interpreted as the seating for a large timber water cistern. If built to waist height, this would have contained many gallons of water, perhaps collected from the roof and directed in a clean down-pipe. This would be a useful facility, without which frequent carrying of water from the bailey would be necessary. But there is no specific evidence for this interpretation, and other functions, for example a storage or garderobe pit, are also possible. At the western end of the building, a planked floor may have provided a level interior above the sloping shoulder of the motte, though no direct evidence of this was discovered. Erosion of this (western) end of the motte may have destroyed considerable evidence.

No entrance into this building at ground-floor level was revealed in its foundations, though the latter would not necessarily have shown this. On the other hand, access to the basement may simply have been down a ladder from the presumed principal room above. In the period in question first-floor entry is to be expected in a high-status/defensible building in a castle. Though impossible to prove, it is possible that access to its upper floor was direct from the bailey bridge on the east side. This idea finds some support in two observations:–

(a) first, the alignments of the eastern wall of the motte building (LVII), of the sole-plate of the early motte bridge, and of the western wall of the hall (Building LIa) adjacent to this bridge on its bailey side were more or less parallel, particularly the bailey building and the sole-plate (positions shown in simplified form in fig. 4.10). Despite the distance separating these three lines, it is tempting to see them joined together by a bridge which entered the upper storeys of both the bailey hall and the

motte building. We cannot know that all evidence for support of this bridge was discovered in excavation. Preservation of the timber sole plate arose from localised waterlogging in the ditch bottom, and it is possible that related evidence further up slope had disappeared without trace. The bridge may have followed an irregular course, but without complete knowledge of the points at which it may have been supported, certainty is impossible. This bridge, whatever its alignment(s), must have been built with many lengths of the longest timbers available.

(b) second, the character of the eastern wall of the motte building described above may indicate that the bridge entered at first-floor level. Immediately next to the deeply set square corner posts, and within the northern and southern wall lines, were two other squared posts (94a and 95a) buried less deeply in the motte. Two interpretations seem possible. They may simply have been extra posts later inserted to support the corners of the building during one of its phases of repair. But, if so, no trace of pits in which to set these timbers were discovered. Alternatively, if they were primary posts designed to give extra support at the building's corners, they could have supported the ends of a horizontal timber (whose mid-point was perhaps supported by the eastern post of the dividing wall, with which they form a straight line) on which the end of the bridge rested. If this were the case, there is a sense in which the motte building, as well as being defensively located, may have been the detached chamber block of a high-status residence whose hall lay immediately below in the bailey. The bridge, too, as well as having the simple function of access, would have been part of this prestigious complex. However, this hypothesis cannot be proved and in reality the situation may have been much simpler. In the reconstruction drawing (see Chapters 3 and 7) various choices among the options of interpretation discussed above have been made, and the bridge has been shown narrower at the top and entering at first floor level. The basement has been made low and without windows, with

Fig. 4.11: Artist's reconstruction of the early motte tower (by Peter Scholefield)

two storeys above partly jettied-out. A detail is reproduced here as fig. 4.11. In the interpretative plans (4.10 and 4.21) both the alignment and width of the early bridge at its motte top end remain hypothetical. In the reconstructed model (7.10) the bridge has been given a slight change in alignment.

Phase II, possibly equivalent of bailey phases U/V/W and X (figs 4.2, 4.3, 4.4 and 4.7)

It seems clear that the primary building underwent several stages of modification, which are (very tentatively) equated with the processes which, in the bailey, gradually transformed the early castle. The evidence for this period of evolution emerged from the laborious identification and removal of many deposits of clay and clay-derivatives. Some parts of this transformation were described above: post-pit (111) and its post-hole (84) in its south wall, post-holes (61 and 65) in the southern part of the interior, the possibly secondary nature of post 113 in the north wall and the suggestions of replacement timbers on the sites of posts 94b and 106. Further evidence includes the disuse of the putative water-tank (68), which was backfilled at some stage. On the east, there was evidence for a re-cut of the wall foundation gulley (82) and irregularities in the gulley's shape may here (and elsewhere) represent alterations to accommodate secondary posts not otherwise identified. Whereas the first building seems

to have made extensive use of massive timbers, the impression now is of a building (notionally labelled LVIII) whose walls, approximately 0.75m/2ft 6in thick, had a skeleton of old and new timbers, the latter more irregular in size, and perhaps with a correspondingly higher proportion of clay-cladding, a fragment of which, burned *in situ*, survived in the south wall. The overall plan of the building, an incomplete 'snapshot' of which is represented by fig. 4.3, however, remained as first laid out, though it is not clear whether the southward extension (25) of the eastern wall line occurred only at this point or whether it had been a feature of the original building. There is no specific evidence for the dates of the changes described, though three glazed sherds of twelfth-century date were found in the position occupied by the south-east corner post (94b), presumably embedded there when a post was pulled out, or rotted *in situ*, either at the building's abandonment or during its repair. Although this pottery is analogous with material from Haughmond Abbey in a later twelfth-century context (see below, Chapter 5), the latter is simply a dated context for its occurrence and its actual production/circulation may have started much earlier in the century. No specific dating conclusion can therefore be drawn from it at Hen Domen. Perhaps the de Boulers, who received the castle soon after 1101 (Barker & Higham 1982, 16–19), maintained the original castle and re-developed it as parts fell into decay. This process has already been described (Barker & Higham 1982, 31–40) in the bailey where some analogies with the evidence on the motte are apparent, particularly (a) the replacement of the first palisade (within the rampart) with one dug into the rampart top and (b) the re-use of the wall trench of the bailey hall (Building LIa) for a second hall built with ground-fast posts in the same wall lines (Building LIb).

Outside the building, other developments occurred whose significance is unclear. One post-hole (78) was found just outside the south-west corner and another shallow, eroded depression (90) outside the north-west corner may also have been the site of a post, or perhaps the eroded top of one of the large gullies around the motte perimeter (see below). Some of these external features may represent timbers added to give extra support to the building. In addition, 105 and 112 were a pair of posts, on the south side, perhaps supporting a subsidiary structure such as a garderobe chute, staircase, or some other narrow extension, perhaps even a jettied upper storey. These two post-holes were discovered during removal of an area of burnt clay and charcoal (unillustrated), immediately outside the south wall of the building, which also exposed a shallow depression (108). This could have been the burnt debris of whatever structure they had supported.

We have assumed that the early bridge had been a wide one, represented by the sole-plate found surviving at the bottom of the motte ditch. How long this bridge may have remained in use is not known, though if it was linked directly to the building on the motte it may not have survived the alterations to the east wall of the latter mentioned above. In the excavation of the motte side in the 1960s evidence of numerous successive bridges was discovered (Barker & Higham 1982, 51–59) but correlation of their foundations with some very large features excavated at the eastern end of the motte (see below) is difficult. But from at least one period within this stage of the motte's occupation there seems to have been a bridge of very different style—resting at its top end on small posts, sometimes in pairs, set in the platform in front of the building and supporting a walkway perhaps as little as 3ft wide. Features 53, 38/1, 38/2, 15, 19, 37 and 35 follow a line leading more or less to the centre of the building's east wall. Perhaps this is the top end of one of the bridges excavated in the 1960s, but this cannot be proved.

The reconstruction drawing of the middle period (see Chapters 1 and 7) does not show the motte top because it was made before the motte top was excavated. The main building itself, however, as it evolved through this period, retained the overall shape of its predecessor. The date to which this building survived is not known. Given the massiveness of the primary timbers and the gradual process of re-building described above, there is nothing inherently unlikely in an overall life-span of a hundred years or more from the 1070s onwards. Its wall timbers may also have been protected from the weather by clay-cladding for much of the structure's life. Whether its use was continuous into the period (after 1223) when New Montgomery was established, or whether it was abandoned at the end of the de Boulers' occupation in the early thirteenth century and dismantled at some later date, we cannot determine. These and related issues of dating are discussed below (Chapter 7). But before it was finally swept away, the building may have undergone a major reduction in its extent, as described next.

Phase III, possibly equivalent of bailey phase Y (fig. 4.12)

The evidence for this change comes, however, not from its construction but from its destruction, which seems to have been the result of a major fire (see fig. 4.12). This rendered both timbers and their clay cladding into a mass of burned debris, much of which must have been cleared away but some of which was levelled out before the erection of the next building to occupy the site (below). The extent of this burning and the effect it had on the underlying boulder clay were not, however, uniform. It is interesting, however, that the condition of the pottery

assemblage did not reveal independent evidence of a major episode of burning (below, Chapter 7). The indications of burning extended hardly at all north of the dividing wall of the building described above but were uniformly intense across the southern half of the building and extended in places slightly outside its south wall. It is possible that the extent of this burning arose from a strong wind which fanned the flames southwards, or that the fire was quickly put out on the north whereas on the south the building was left to burn. But in either event one might expect some evidence of burning throughout the building. But the evidence might be explicable if, before the fire occurred, the northern half of the building had already been demolished and the former dividing wall rebuilt as an external wall, so that the structure (putatively Building LIX) was now a little over half its original size but with the narrow extension southwards postulated in the previous phase (105 & 112). It may also be relevant that the fill of the north wall foundations was of clay and large stones, perhaps deliberately replacing extracted timbers, whereas on the south and in the dividing wall there was a greater proportion of dark soil—perhaps representing the bases of timbers which had been cut off and rotted *in situ*. This alteration, if correctly interpreted, produced a smaller building which occupied the flat top of the motte and avoided its sloping shoulders. But the picture may be distorted by the contours of the motte top itself, since the surviving extent of burning is very much coincident with the flatter area of the summit and it is possible that other evidence, on the sloping shoulders of the motte, had eroded before the next structural phase. The plan shows the surviving extent of the burnt deposits, in relation to the break of slope. The burning was more intense in some areas than in others, though this distinction seemed to have no pattern.

The smaller building suggested here cannot be dated independently. But it may be relevant that in phase Y in the bailey the tower at the north-west corner of the rampart also burned down and there was a general contraction of the built-up area (Barker & Higham 1982, 41–48). It is clear, however, that this postulated smaller building is the most difficult part of the motte's building sequence to demonstrate. For this reason, it has been shown as a building site in operation, rather than a complete structure, on the reconstruction drawing of this phase (see Chapters 1 and 7). An alternative and simpler interpretation of the evidence is that the burnt deposits represent a fire within, or at the end of, the life of the whole building, but for some reason affecting only its southern half. The removal of the latest evidence encountered on the motte (see below) revealed, gradually but simultaneously, the burnt deposits and the structural features. The argument for a smaller building rests upon

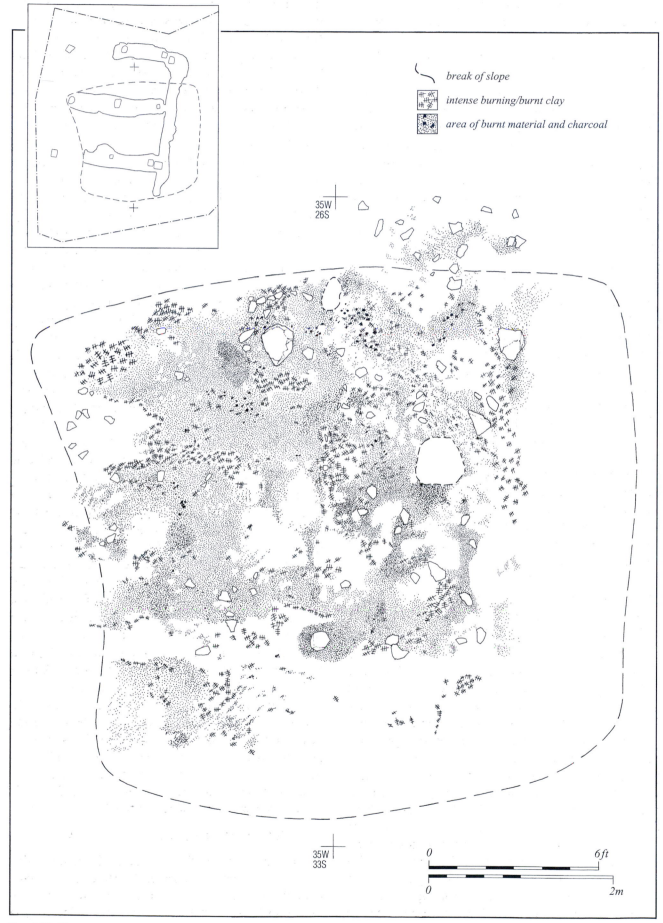

break of slope

intense burning/burnt clay

area of burnt material and charcoal

35W
26S

35W
33S

0   6ft

0   2m

Fig. 4.12: The motte: burned deposits (destruction of phase Y?)

the southward distribution of the burning rather than upon a stratigraphic separation of structural events.

Phase IV, possibly equivalent of bailey phase Z (figs 4.13 and 4.14)

Removal of the turf and topsoil on top of the motte revealed a layer of clay and small stones. This, obviously, cannot have been deposited after the site was abandoned. It presumably represents degraded fabric, presumably clay wall-cladding, of a building. But at this level there were also apparent the surfaces of some features which subsequent excavation showed to belong to the underlying building. Their visibility at this stage arose from a number of circumstances. Sometimes, what we observed was a deeper level of topsoil in their slumped tops. In other cases, their tops may have been exposed by erosion before the turf consolidated, particularly where, nearer the edges of the motte, they had been covered less in the subsequent structural phase. For these reasons, we had a first sight of a few features now whose significance did not become clear until a later stage in the excavation, when the underlying building was exposed. These are identified in fig. 4.13 by the feature numbers originally allocated to them. In parenthesis are given the numbers of the underlying features subsequently excavated: in the north wall, 16 (95); in the central wall, 13 (number retained) and 14 (92). Nearer the perimeter of the excavated area we also had a first sight of other features which only later made sense: 15 (which subsequently included bridge post-holes 15 and 19); 5 and 11 (110), two of the large gullies which are discussed below; and 6, which proved to be the continuation of a feature related to the bridges excavated in the 1960s (see Barker & Higham 1982, fig. 60, feature 51). The distribution of darker soil (for example, context 9) in the uppermost plan also gives hints of the main wall-line gullies (83 and 91) lying beneath.

The evidence which suggested the structure occupying the motte top in this phase, however, took quite a different form from that so far discussed. The burned debris of postulated Building LIX had been levelled out and covered in a layer of boulder clay (context 7). Upon this a building (LX) seems to have stood, occupying the flat crown of the motte. The evidence for it comprised banks (collectively labelled deposit 3) of relatively clean whitish/yellow clay, perhaps the footings of a timber-framed tower or the eroded remains of clay wall-cladding from such a building. The total absence of post-holes along any possible wall lines demonstrates its free-standing nature. How exactly the distribution of this material reflects the shape of the building is not clear. Its extent is indicated on the accompanying plan and on the simplified version (fig. 4.21) we have suggested an outline similar to that of Building LVIII but extending

further south. In retrospect, we may wonder whether these deposits simply represent the collapsed walling of Building LVIII itself. But had this been the case, more of the timber positions of the latter would surely have been visible at this stage of the excavation? And if these deposits were simply the collapsed walling of Building LVIII then the evidence of the fire and the contrasting fate of the foundations in that building's walls remains unexplained.

On the whole, the evidence points rather to a succession of structural events. The fact that some of the underlying structural features (especially on the north side of the building) had been deliberately backfilled with large rocks also suggests that a further structural event followed—otherwise there would have been no need for the backfilling. The date of this last building is uncertain, but on the evidence discussed below (Chapter 7) it may be from the mid or later thirteenth century. By this date it is assumed that Hen Domen had only a minor military role (subsidiary to that of New Montgomery) and had lost its former social importance. Although certainty is impossible, our reconstruction drawing (see Chapters 1 and 7) offers a free-standing, belfry-like tower as a possible interpretation of the evidence. Its principal timbers have been left exposed and its wall panels rendered. This type of structure is known from both documentary and pictorial sources of medieval date (Higham & Barker 1992, Chapters 4 and 5). A detail is reproduced here as fig. 4.14. It is impossible to say how long this building remained in use, whatever form it took. The layer of clay and small stones immediately below the turf presumably derived from the footings and wall-cladding of this building. Whether or not erosion had already removed the evidence of any subsequent structural phase, before the growth of turf consolidated the motte, we simply cannot know. The first discrete feature to be discovered after the removal of this overburden was a post-hole (2) and its post-pit (4) near the centre of the motte top, sufficiently deep to be still visible when the underlying surfaces were recorded at the end of the excavation (above, figs 4.2 and 4.13). Perhaps this was an internal feature of the postulated last building on the site. Alternatively, and more probably, it may be much later in date, an individual post sunk in the motte by a farmer at some stage for some unknown purpose—perhaps even a flag-pole erected for some event of celebration?

The Motte Section (figs 4.15, 4.16 and 4.17)

A standing section at the east end of the motte, which was already heavily truncated by large features (see below), was dug partly by hand first, to reveal the junction with the 1960s excavation (fig. 4.15; line *f–g* from Barker & Higham 1982, fig. 60). Cutting of the

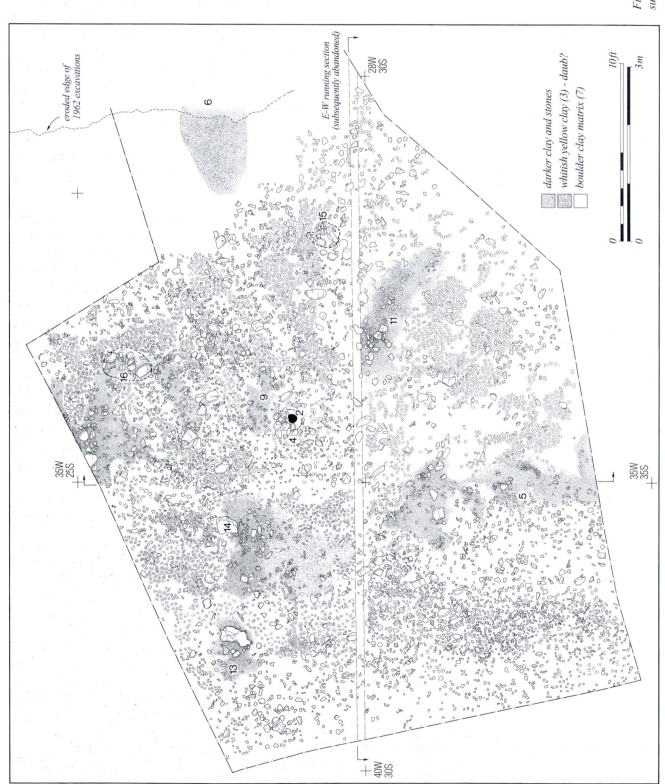

eroded edge of
1962 excavations

6

E-W running section
(subsequently abandoned)

28W
30S

15

11

9

2

4

16

35W
25S

14

5

35W
35S

13

40W
30S

darker clay and stones

whitish yellow clay (3) - daub?

boulder clay matrix (7)

10ft

3m

0

0

Fig. 4.13: The motte: uppermost
surviving evidence (phase Z?)

Fig. 4.14: Artist's reconstruction of the last motte tower (by Peter Scholefield)

section was completed by machine (and cleaned manually) down to a platform level with the top of the 1960s excavation of the eastern side of the motte, giving a vertical face up to 2.0m high (fig. 4.16). This revealed the upper parts of a ring-bank whose construction was presumably the result of tipping material upward and inward from the surrounding ditch (fig. 4.17). This bank consisted of various layers of clay capped by a layer of grey gravelly clay, dipping down into the centre of the motte. The lower bank comprised layers 98 and 99 at the north end and 97, 100, 101 and 102 at the south end. The material (dug presumably from the lowest levels of the ditches) with which the central hollow had been filled

was, in contrast, clean boulder clay with small stones and no apparent tip lines. It is numbered layer 96 on the drawn section. It was within this material that most of the posts of the first building (LVII) discussed above stood, and it would appear that it was spread around and consolidated as the timber foundations were set, presumably because this would create a firmer foundation. It may be that motte builders did not consider steeply tipping deposits as a secure building foundation. At Okehampton (Devon) the late eleventh-century motte was built by tipping except at the end where the first (stone) building was erected. Here, in the uppermost metre of the motte, the layers were built horizontally as the foundations were also laid down (Higham 1977). Features within central infill (96) and visible in the upper part of the section at Hen Domen were: 12 (?) possibly an otherwise unobserved westerly extension of this feature as previously excavated; 42, truncated by this section; 38 (?) possibly an otherwise unobserved easterly extension of the feature. All these features are shown in plan in fig. 4.2.

If we project the possible extent of the ring-bank from the standing section, where it was actually visible, it would appear that the first building (LVII) created was not wholly contained within its perimeter. At the north-west corner (and perhaps also the south-west) the building oversailed, so that here it lost the protection with which its foundations were provided elsewhere. An advantage of ring-bank construction (apart from the fact that it is a logical response to the challenge of building a mound) is that it contains, and perhaps protects from erosion, the material which is subsequently used to fill in the central hollow. The fact that the north-west corner of the building was more difficult to find, and was located only in the form of an eroded post-hole (109), perhaps arises from lack of protection by the ring-bank and consequently greater erosion of the motte. The post-hole at the south-west corner (52) was also shallower in its surviving form than its more easterly counterparts. The

Fig 4.15: Western ends of gullies 6 and 12 (continued from 1960s excavation)

Fig. 4.16: Main motte section A–D looking west (excavation spoil heap on motte face)

need to oversail presumably arose from the desire to build the biggest structure possible as well as maintain a space outside the east end of the building where it overlooked the bailey and was approached by its bridge.

The Motte Perimeter (figs 4.2, 4.18, 4.19 and 4.20)

A series of large gullies or trenches, running away from the building platform beyond the limits of the excavation, was encountered throughout every season of the motte's excavation. These features were frequently difficult to excavate, as changing patterns of weather made their fills either rock-hard or very soft. On several occasions a feature thought to be fully excavated in one season proved, in the next, not to have been. It eventually became clear that, despite our best efforts, we had not always identified their full extent: the east end of 42 was lost in the cutting of the main standing section; the west end of 12 and part of 38 were under-dug (they were subsequently visible in the main standing section—see above).

Three possible interpretations were discussed as excavation proceeded: drainage gullies, garderobe chutes and structural foundations. The size and number of these features eventually made the first two seem less likely. In any case, the steep motte sides would create good natural drainage and run-off for all sorts of detritus. It must be remembered, however, that their apparent contemporaneity may be misleading—erosion of the motte's shoulders may have removed stratigraphy which, if intact, may have separated them from each other in time. Of all the features excavated on the motte, arguably on the whole site, these remain the most enigmatic. They are illustrated together on the accompanying plan (fig. 4.2) for the sake of simple presentation, but this must not be assumed to indicate a single phase for their construction and use. They are numbered, clockwise

starting at the east end: 12, 42, 6, 110, 43?, 55?, 5, 24, 77/79?, 90? and 86. A selection of sections showing their fills is shown in fig. 4.18. Those with queried feature numbers had only a small part visible in the excavated area, making identification as large gullies more problematic, and 90? may just as easily have been an eroded secondary post-position near the north-west corner of the building, as suggested above. Fig. 4.19 is a photograph of 24, 5 and 110 viewed from the west.

There are two possible structural interpretations—as bridge terminals or as foundations for other major timbers. On the side facing the bailey, use as bridge terminals is a strong probability and the lower portions of two of these gullies (6 and 12) were excavated, together with other evidence for bridges, in the 1960s (Barker & Higham 1982, fig. 60, features 51 and 67), confirming this suggestion. Contemporary bridges facing in various directions seem superfluous, even a security risk. But we may here have evidence of more bridges, of various dates, in addition to those encountered in the motte ditch—for all we know, bridges may at some time have risen from the unexcavated (southern) half of the bailey, reaching the motte top where the gullies on its southern shoulder were found.

Other structural possibilities include massive raking timbers to support the first building under construction, internal revetments to prevent slippage of the newly constructed motte top, trenches for a succession of palisades running down the motte sides, and, finally, supports for a horizontal timber apron around the building which would effectively increase the summit area of the motte and perhaps provide an additional fighting platform on the sides not occupied by the bridge. A sketch illustrating this last suggestion, but not representing specific archaeological features, is shown in fig. 4.20.

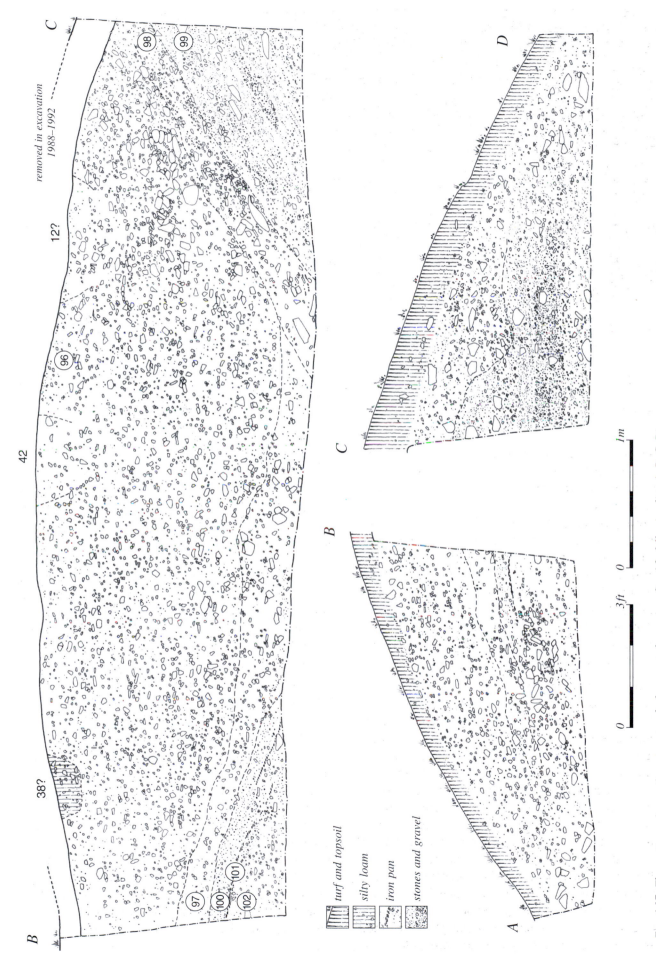

Fig. 4.17: The motte: major section at east end of excavated area (see fig. 4.2, following line A–B–C–D)

turf and topsoil

silty loam

iron pan

stones and gravel

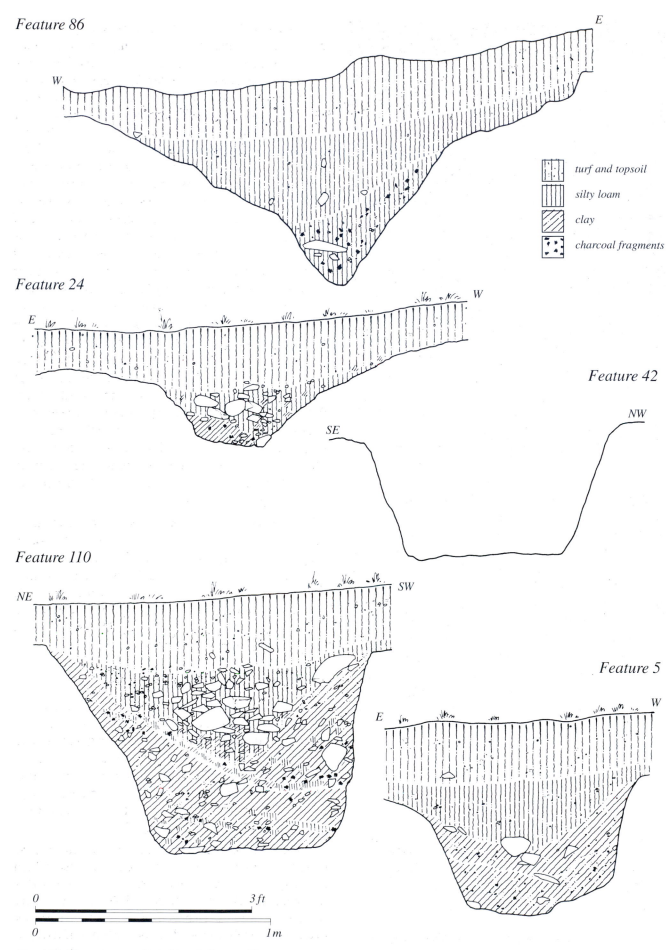

Fig. 4.18: The motte: sections through large gullies

Fig. 4.19: Gullies 24, 5 and 110 from the west

In practice, some of these functions might have coincided where these gullies reached the motte top. At least one of them runs much further down the motte — that on the north was identified in the section of the motte cut on this side in 1967, where it was tentatively interpreted as an old archaeological excavation (Barker & Higham 1982, 72). But further excavation down the motte sides, while possibly revealing more evidence, would not necessarily help our interpretation if the evidence simply consisted of longer gullies and trenches. Two of these features (12 and 6) contained a sherd each of imported French pottery of late twelfth to early thirteenth-century date, suggesting either that they were

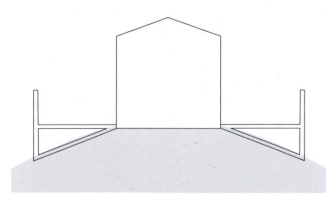

Fig. 4.20: Sketch of one possible structural interpretation of large gullies on motte perimeter

first dug at that date or that old timbers were being dug out when major alterations were being made at that date to the motte top. The local pottery recovered from these features (see below, Chapter 5) suggests a mainly twelfth-century horizon, though some pieces of earlier fabric are also present. But, without knowing whether we are dealing with finds contemporary with their construction or later digging out, or indeed with residual material, this tells us little. Indeed, in their excavated shape, these features may reveal more about their dug-out form than their original constructed form. Like the foundations of the first building on the motte, some of these timbers may have been buried within the motte as it was built rather than dug into it, so that as excavated features the gullies reflect their removal, not their insertion. A further possibility is that of secondary uses for some of these features: sometimes there were hints, during excavation, of a separate post-position at the top end of these features, notably on the north (86), south-east (110) and east (42). These could perhaps have been raking posts supporting the building or perhaps (except on the east) the ends of palisades running down the motte. But these suspected individual post-positions were never satisfactorily 'proved' and the post-hole (23) shown on the plan at the end of large gulley (42) may be completely illusory since examination of this feature remained incomplete at the end of the excavation and it may simply have been part of the gulley.

The excavation and interpretation of these features, despite their massiveness (sometimes up to 0.6–0.7m deep), leaves many problems unsolved. For this reason they have not been included in the reconstruction drawings of the whole site. Although frustrating, it is nevertheless a valuable methodological lesson to note that massiveness of evidence does not always lead to ease of interpretation.

Conclusion

The overall development of the motte top is illustrated in fig. 4.21. The sequence discussed above is depicted in simplified form, but without the large gullies around the motte perimeter. Fig. 4.22 shows a view of the excavation, looking from west to east, with excavation in progress on the south and east walls of the building. Fig. 4.23 finally shows most of the main structural evidence which eventually emerged.

The evidence recovered from the motte can be compared with that from excavations elsewhere which also exposed foundations of timber structures (for references see Higham & Barker 1992, 353–60). There was no suggestion, at Hen Domen, of a functional interior to the motte itself, as found at South Mimms (Herts.) or Goltho (Lincs.). As at Abinger (Surrey) and elsewhere,

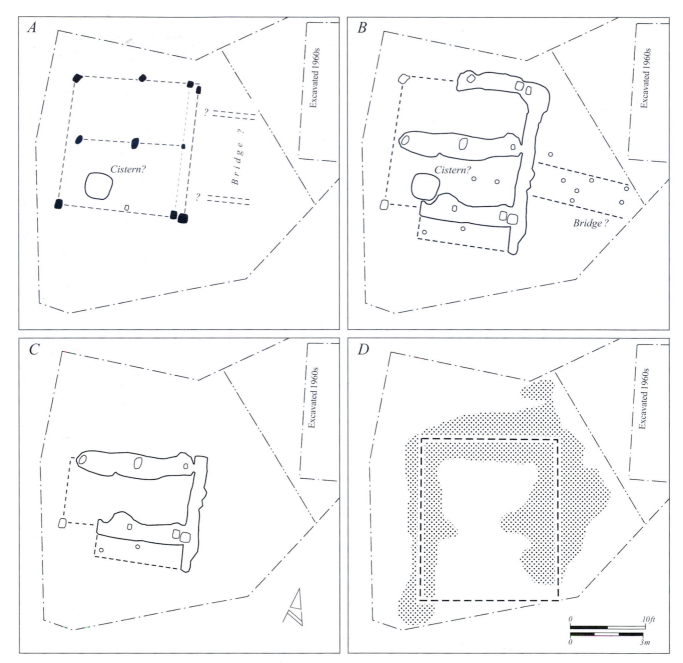

Fig. 4.21: The motte: simplified sequence of building development, tentatively equated with phases T–Z in the bailey. For A and B see fig. 4.2; for B and C see figs 4.2 and 4.12; for D see fig. 4.13

A: early period structure (?T): Building LVII
B: middle period structure (?U/V/W/X): Building LVIII
C: later period structure (?Y): Building LIX
D: last period structure (?Z): Building LX showing spread of probable building material (stippled area) and suggested outline of building

the Hen Domen structures stood on a solid motte (though at Hen Domen the motte top had been built around the footings of the first building). The motte at Hen Domen was a primary feature of the site (see Barker & Higham 1982, 72). This contrasts with the evidence from some other sites where the motte was a secondary feature (for example Neroche, Somerset) or where the motte resulted from the enlargement of a pre-existing site (for example Lismahon, Co. Down). At Hen Domen we have probably the most detailed timber structural sequence so far

known. It is certainly possible to construe the main building on the motte in terms of the few medieval written descriptions available and the final building encountered in terms of the prefabricated structures for which there is also documentary evidence (Higham & Barker 1992, Chapter 4). Whether the main building carried any of the ornate details suggested by the Bayeux Tapestry we cannot know, but the possibility should not be ignored. Timber towers on mottes were part of the wider tradition of castle *donjons*, currently the subject of renewed

Fig. 4.22: Excavation of east and south wall lines in progress, viewed from the west

Fig. 4.23: Structural evidence at end of excavation, viewed from the south-west

debate. The evidence from the motte at Hen Domen and elsewhere has the potential to contribute to the wider issues of defence, status and domestic planning which are more easily studied in stone castles.

CHAPTER 5

THE ARTEFACTUAL, ENVIRONMENTAL AND SURVEY EVIDENCE

POTTERY FROM THE MOTTE AT HEN DOMEN

by Stephanie Ratkai (illustrations by Steve Rigby)

A selection of pottery from the early seasons of excavation at Hen Domen was published by Barker (1970) as part of a study of Shropshire medieval pottery. In this study, the production, uses, dating and distribution of pottery were considered within a framework provided partly by sites chosen because of their good documentary dating (including Hen Domen) and partly by others from which data was available from rescue excavations. It was concluded that, at Hen Domen as at other sites in the area, little pottery was in use until some point, difficult to define exactly, in the twelfth century. The ensuing pottery culture was conservative in approach, although containing diverse forms, and not easy to sort into a typological sequence with strictly chronological significance. After *circa* 1300 forms and fabrics occurred which were not present at an earlier date, which created a useful dating horizon. The Hen Domen pottery contributing to this study came from the north-west quadrant of the bailey, the motte ditch and the deep pit 1/27. Three fabrics were identified (by visual examination) among the coarse cooking pots, varying in fineness of fabric and size of inclusions. Various jug forms with brown or green glazes also occurred, like the coarse wares, in twelfth and thirteenth-century contexts. One strap handle from a Stamford ware jug (closely paralleled by one recovered from Stamford castle itself) also occurred, in the lowest silting of the motte ditch of late eleventh-century date. An overlap of the pottery occurring at Hen Domen and its successor, New Montgomery castle, was observed. Some two hundred vessels or part-vessels were illustrated in Barker's publication.

A further study was published by Clarke (1982), who included most of the pottery from the excavation of the north-west quadrant of the bailey, totalling approximately 1,200 sherds. These were overwhelmingly medieval, though a few Roman sherds (presumably from nearby Forden Gaer) and post-medieval sherds (representing occasional use of the site in its later agricultural setting) were also found. Some basic conclusions from Barker's earlier study were confirmed: virtually none of the pottery on the site was independently datable (though by now sherds of developed Stamford ware, perhaps later twelfth century in date, had been found) and the documentary framework remained crucial to dating the pottery. There was a demonstrable overlap with the early pottery sequence at New Montgomery castle (which had by now been more extensively excavated). On the other hand, it was now shown that a very small amount of local pottery was used on the site in the late eleventh century. Clarke also laid out a more complex collection of fabrics than had been earlier suggested, identifying the various types in the sequence of the site's structural development and cautiously putting forward a basic chronology for the pottery, though this was essentially a relative chronology since only at the start and end of the site's life were real historical dates available. It was stressed that the true ceramic phases (meaning the dates at which pottery production was itself changing) did not necessarily (indeed were unlikely to) coincide with major events in the physical evolution of the site. Complications arising from the problem of identifying residual material were also noted. Petrological analysis of a selection of sherds (by Alan Vince) supported Clarke's (visual) division of the pottery into fabrics containing fragments of sedimentary rocks and others containing predominantly quartz sand. The former may have been manufactured somewhere in the site's vicinity since they bore reasonable (though not exact) similarity to clay samples studied from Hen Domen itself. The latter came from further afield and represented a tradition whose products are found in Shropshire, Herefordshire and Worcestershire. Within these two major classes, Clarke identified a type series of over twenty variations in fabric, further divided by variations in glaze types. Since a very good range of vessels had been illustrated by Barker (1970), Clarke's study included a complementary set of tables showing the incidence of fabrics and glazes in the stratigraphic sequence of the site.

The Motte

In the period since the publication of Clarke's report there has been an increase in knowledge of the pottery of Shropshire and the Welsh Marches, although this area is still under-represented in terms of published assemblages. Publication of the pottery from New Montgomery castle has begun (Knight 1990–91), further documenting the ceramic overlap between the two sites noted above. In addition, information about ceramics and castle sites has increased and there have been improvements in the methodologies of pottery study. With this in mind, this report on the pottery from the motte contains a brief review of Clarke's observations and includes modifications to her published type series. For the purposes of the present publication it was felt that examining the motte material was of a higher priority than dealing with the pottery from the north-east quadrant of the bailey. The latter, comprising a continuation of the data published by Clarke, remains to be studied at some future date, though occasionally pottery finds from this area are referred to in the main text of this volume. The motte, in contrast, is a separate part of the site, of possibly different social status and, given its restricted summit area and steeply sloping sides, with potentially different circumstances of rubbish deposition and survival.

The database created during the preparation of the current report, containing far more information than is presented here, could be used (together with Barker's and Clarke's earlier work) as the foundation for further study of the site's pottery. A separate assessment report has also been written, exploring possible lines of analysis for the (unpublished) pottery from the north-east quadrant of the bailey.

Hen Domen is a difficult site for the study of pottery. The levels of stratigraphy are often shallow. Successive building operations have caused intrusion into and redeposition of earlier deposits. This has resulted in pottery sherds appearing in contexts other than those in which they were originally lost, as intrusive or residual material. It is therefore difficult to gauge at what period pottery was first routinely used on the site and with such small groups in the early phases of occupation it is almost impossible to gauge the amount of residual material. Although meticulous, Clarke's work has tended to underestimate the effect of residuality in her proposed published chronology and the bias which must follow from such small phase groups. Therefore, although the present author accepts the general trends highlighted by Clarke, there is perhaps insufficiently definite dating evidence for some of the closer dating of pottery types suggested. Both the general and the more detailed trends were kept in mind during the analysis of the pottery from the motte, but as work progressed it became apparent

that there had been several episodes of disturbance resulting in both residual and intrusive material. In short, the pottery *sequence* from the motte was unreliable. Further work on pit groups in the bailey might help elucidate matters if only as far as taphonomy was concerned.

A total of 667 sherds weighing 6377g was recovered from the motte. The pottery was divided into fabric groups by eye. Type sherds from Clarke's fabric type series were examined under x20 magnification and brief notes made on the size and range of inclusions. All the pottery was quantified by sherd number, sherd weight, rim percentage and number of rims. Sherd type (i.e. body, base etc.), vessel form and vessel diameter were recorded. A 'comments' column contained details of glaze, decoration, sooting etc. A form book with sketch drawings of vessel forms, handles and decorated sherds was also kept. Illustrations within this report have been chosen to demonstrate the main vessel forms. These have been cross-referenced to Barker's Shropshire survey (Barker 1970) where possible.

Once the pottery had been recorded, the whole assemblage was laid out in a chronological sequence, based on the succession of building operations, to see if there were any obvious trends or developments in vessel form or fabric and to check for sherds from the same vessel occurring in different contexts (cross-joining sherds).

The Pottery Fabrics

A good quantity of sherds forming Clarke's fabric type series is still accessible. Unfortunately, as a result of the passage of time, one or two of the original type sherds are no longer with the rest of the type series. The pottery from Hen Domen can be split into two main groups: siltstone/mudstone (sedimentary) tempered wares and sandy, quartz tempered wares. Clarke's subdivisions according to glaze type have been abandoned here since there is no good evidence from either Hen Domen or from elsewhere in Shropshire that these differences have any chronological significance or indicate the likely source of production.

Siltstone/mudstone tempered wares (SMT)

These comprise Clarke's fabrics 1, 5, 6.1 and 9.3. There is some variation in colour from reduced black to oxidized, sometimes very pale, browns. Red-black speckled surfaces mentioned in Clarke are also present among the motte pottery. A local source is likely for these.

Sandy wares (SAND)

The remaining fabrics from the motte belong to this group with the exception of developed Stamford ware

(DSTAM) and the north French import (FRIMP). The developed Stamford ware was found amongst unstratified material. Stamford ware has such a wide distribution that its occurrence in the Welsh Marches is of no significance other than to reinforce the extent of its distribution. The date of the sherd would fit in with any time during the castle's occupation. Developed Stamford ware appears to have stopped being produced by the first quarter of the thirteenth century (Kilmurry 1980). It may also be relevant that in the later twelfth century the de Boulers, lords of Hen Domen, were linked by marriage to a family with lands in Lincolnshire and Yorkshire, so that the movement of pottery from eastern England may also have occurred in personal baggage, an explanation which was earlier suggested for the appearance of this material in the bailey (Barker & Higham 1982, 94).

There were two main groups of sandy wares: predominantly glazed sandy wares (fabrics SAND1–SAND5) and predominantly unglazed cooking pots (fabrics SANDC and SANDVC).

The first group consists mainly of vessels with oxidized orange or red surfaces with often patchy or poorly glazed surfaces. Glaze has often flaked away from the surface and over half the glazes are dull/opaque. Clarke suggested that this may be due to soil conditions but the same effect is often seen in pottery from Shropshire and suggests a poor knowledge of glazing or insufficiently fluxed glazes. There are also some unglazed cooking pot/jars in these fabrics.

SAND1 and SAND2 are comprised of a re-ordering of Clarke's fabrics 4, 6.1, 6.2, 8, 9.1, 9.2, 13 and 18. Both fabrics contained very occasional pieces of mudstone amongst the predominantly quartz temper. SAND1 contained moderate quartz whereas SAND2 contained fine quartz. The differences between the two fabrics may well be of little significance. Two further variants of SAND1 and SAND2 were noted: a hard fired fine fabric SANDHF and a fine fabric with sparse quartz sand, SANDF (Clarke's fabric 12). SAND3 is the same as Clarke's fabric 19 and was split into two groups SAND3 and SAND3a, although only fabric SAND3a was found on the motte. The latter had white slip beneath the glaze. This is reminiscent of the glazed Worcester ware jugs of the twelfth and thirteenth centuries. Clarke's fabric 14 type sherds were subdivided into SAND4 (moderate–abundant sub-angular quartz) and SAND5 (moderate ill-sorted quartz, <0.25mm–1mm). SAND5 was not found on the motte.

SAND1 and SAND2 can be paralleled by early material from Haughmond Abbey (Ratkai forthcoming), near Shrewsbury, where glazed pitchers were found associated with the construction of the claustral range,

dated architecturally to 1180–1200. Glazing and decorative motifs in this material (and in residual pottery from the same site) are the same as those from Hen Domen and point to a strong regional tradition, if not the movement of potters within the region.

The second group of sandy fabrics consisted of SANDC (coarse sandy cooking pot, Clarke's fabrics 2 and 11.2) and SANDVC (similar to SANDC but with a more 'hackly' fracture, containing abundant sub-angular quartz and ferruginous inclusions). SANDC and SANDVC belong to a regional type of sandy cooking pots/jars which are concentrated in Worcestershire and Staffordshire but which occur also in Herefordshire and Shropshire.

A new buff sandy fabric BUFF was represented by one sherd (see below). This too is likely to be local. Buff wares seem to represent a later pottery tradition in Shropshire (cf. Buteux 1998 and Ratkai forthcoming). This sherd may date to the later thirteenth century and may indicate continuing occupation at Hen Domen after the construction of New Montgomery castle.

Imported Pottery (FRIMP)

Two, fine, red bodied sherds with tan glaze were recovered from the motte perimeter (see below). They were first examined by K. Barton, who thought them to be northern French. The sherds were subsequently studied by J.G. Hurst, who writes: '[The pottery] is very similar to north French wares, the red fabric being typical of the Paris area, but these are rare, only being known in Devon, Southampton and a couple of sites in Ireland. North French jugs have rilled necks but not usually so pronounced [as the Hen Domen example]. They usually do not have lips or if they do, they are bridge spouts not lips .... the simple rounded rim is unlike the usual more squared French rims.' Dating is not secure but given that the pottery is most likely northern French a date of late twelfth to early thirteenth century seems probable (see *Medieval Archaeology* 29, 1985, 47–48, for north French imports of this date range found in London).

Note on the 'phases': the following analysis separates the pottery according to the main structural phases identified during excavation of the motte (see Chapters 1 & 7, for reservations about 'phasing'). Phase I is the earliest building. Phase I/II represents the piecemeal rebuilding of this structure, culminating in the general re-use of the building site (Phase II). Phase III is a possible reduction in the area of this building. Phase IV is the final building observed, of different form from its predecessors. The large gullies found around the perimeter of the motte may be of various dates: it was impossible to relate them stratigraphically to the structural sequence of the building. Unstratified sherds were those found in the topsoil, in circumstances where ascription to a particular context was insecure, or in the first cleaning operation at the start of each season's excavation, when sherds had weathered out of the exposed deposits during the intervening winter. In the following tables and text, individual sherds are referred to by fabric, function and form, thus: SMTcpj7 (Siltstone/mudstone tempered, cooking pot/jar, form no. 7). Numbers in brackets are context/feature numbers from the site record. Reference will be found here to context numbers which do not occur in Chapter 4 because pottery came not only from the structural features enumerated there but also from other, non-structural deposits identified during excavation.

In the following text reference is made (thus: ill. 10) to sherds illustrated and numbered in figs 5.1 and 5.2.

Phase I

Fabric SANDC is probably the earliest fabric from the site (Clarke 1982) and it is therefore to be expected associated with the earliest motte structures. Fabric SMT is likely to begin in the twelfth century. However, there is strong evidence for intrusive material in this phase. For example the glazed wares, three small sherds, all from context (94), are unlikely to belong to the earliest phase of the castle and probably arrived in this phase during the removal/replacement of timbers at the corner of the first motte building. It is also significant that these sherds join with others from later contexts. Fabric SMT sherds (ill. 10) from the fills of depression (36), and ?cistern (68), and post-position (106), which join with sherds from later contexts, obviously mirror this intrusive process also. Without the evidence of the glazed sherds this would be seen as a straightforward case of residuality in later layers. However, the evidence from the glazed sherds demonstrates that intrusion is also possible, so that it is difficult to be certain if the SMT sherds are intrusive in this early phase or residual in later levels. Defining features as 'early' does not tell us directly that their fills were equally early; indeed in the case of ?cistern 68 this is less likely to be so. Unfortunately these problems leave the pottery chronology for the first phase suspect, although it is tempting to see fabrics SMT and SANDC as associated with the use of the building. Average sherd size and weight is small. The one exception is the rim and body sherds from form SMTcpj7 (see phase I/II) which is made up of four sherds weighing 60g (ill. 10). This may strengthen the argument for its contemporaneity with the structure.

Table 1: Phase I

Fabric	Sherd No.	Sherd Wt (g)	Rims	Form
SMT	17	85	0	cpj
SANDC	2	7	0	cpj
SANDHF	1	12	0	jug
SAND1	1	6	0	jug
SAND2	1	4	0	jug
Total	22	114	0	

Form	Sherd No.	Weight	Rim%	Rim No.
cooking pot/jar	19	92	0	0
jug/pitcher	3	22	0	0

Phase I/II

This phase covers structural alterations and subsequent use of the first building, the material coming largely from the re-worked wall lines. The dominant fabric is fabric SMT followed by fabric SANDC. The two glazed sherds (SANDHF and SAND2) may be intrusive since they come from contexts with cross-joining material. However fabrics SMT, SANDC and SAND4 are likely to be contemporary with this phase. Three cpj forms are present, SMTcpj2a, SMTcpj7 and SMTcpj8. The first form is paralleled in Barker 1970 (HD24 and HD70d). The other two types, one with a slightly splayed rim with a thickened squared terminal (cpj7) and the other with a slightly splayed rim with a flattened top and external bead (cpj8), are perhaps also paralleled in Barker 1970 (HD1 and HD58b, respectively).

Table 2: Phase I/II

Fabric	Sherd No.	Sherd Wt (g)	Rims	Form
SMT	45	491	5	cpj
SAND4	2	32	0	cpj
SANDC	4	51	0	cpj
SANDHF	1	8	0	jug
SAND2	1	4	0	jug
Total	53	586	5	

Form	Sherd No.	Weight	Rim%	Rim No.
cooking pot/jar	51	574	28	5
jug/pitcher	2	12	0	0

Phase II

The largest group of pottery comes from this phase and seems to mark the point at which pottery use becomes more common and less restricted in fabric and form. This would compare well with layer IV in Clarke's (1982) report. However, as she pointed out, this sudden upsurge may relate to contemporary use and breakage or it may be mainly residual, reflecting the pottery in use in the preceding phase. The situation on the motte and within the bailey are dissimilar in that the motte represents a much more enclosed space from which rubbish is likely to be ejected over the motte side at the earliest opportunity. Scobie (pers. comm.) has suggested that rubbish is not usually allowed to accumulate within a building whilst that building is in use. It is therefore important to examine the features associated with the pottery in order to try to understand the taphonomy of the area.

The phase II contexts have been divided into four groups: Da, contexts outside the building; Db, post-holes associated with the bridge which may be of this phase; Dc, deposits within and along the wall lines of the building; and Dd, deposits within the building.

The building and features within the building (groups Dc and Dd)

Only a small quantity of pottery was recovered from deposits within the building. As in previous phases the dominant fabric was SMT, with the first occurrence of fabric SANDVC. Fabric SANDC was also present. A small quantity of glazed wares was represented by six sherds. There were seven cooking pot rims, six in fabric SMT and a single rim in fabric SANDC. The fabric SMT vessel forms were SMTcpj7, SMTcpj2, SMTcpj2a (two examples), SMTcpj10 and a small unidentifiable fragment. The fabric SANDC vessel was SANDCcpj3a. The proportion of cooking pot/jars to jugs/pitchers and the forms of the cooking pot/jars were very similar to the preceding phase. This and the comparative paucity of sherds and the large size of some of the sherds suggests that the pottery was associated with the use of the building during this phase.

A much greater proportion of pottery was recovered along the wall lines of the building. It is clear that these sherds have found their way into these features from both the interior and the exterior of the building. This can be demonstrated by evidence from cross-joining sherds, for example parts of the same vessel have come from the wall line (26) (14) and (29) and the perimeter area (3). Likewise another vessel came from both the wall line (8) and internal feature (39).

A greater proportion of fabric SANDC is evidenced along the wall line than is represented in the interior of the building, which demonstrates how inconsistent and misleading small groups of pottery can be. Four rim sherds were represented (SMTcpj5, SMTcpj4, SMTcpj7 and an unidentifiable fragment), and four in fabric SANDC (SANDCcpj4 [2 examples], SANDCcpj5 and an unidentifiable fragment). There also seems to be a higher proportion of glazed pottery from along the wall line.

Caution is needed in the interpretation of these observations, however, since sherds along the wall lines came not only from inside and outside (above) but could also derive from three distinct processes: re-deposition of residual earlier material, deposition of material contemporary with structural events, and intrusion of later material during structural alterations/demolitions.

Table 3: Group Dc

Fabric	Sherd No.	Sherd Wt (g)	Rims	Form
SAND1	17	121	0	cpj+jug
SAND2	7	57	0	cpj+jug
SAND3a	1	13	0	jug
SAND 4	2	11	0	cpj
SANDC	19	280	4	cpj+jug
SANDHF	1	3	0	jug
SANDVC	2	8	0	cpj
SMT	82	714	4	cpj
Total	131	1207	8	

Form	Sherd No.	Weight	Rim%	Rim No.
cooking pot/jar	113	1063	36	8
jug/pitcher	12	125		
?	6	19		

Table 4: Group Dd

Fabric	Sherd No.	Sherd Wt (g)	Rims	Form
SAND1	3	12	0	jug
SAND2	2	29	0	jug
SAND4	1	16	0	cpj
SANDC	4	19	1	cpj
SANDHF	1	10	0	jug
SANDVC	1	12	0	cpj
SMT	60	534	6	cpj
Total	72	632	7	

Form	Sherd No.	Weight	Rim%	Rim No.
cooking pot/jar	66	581	32	7
jug/pitcher	5	46		
?	1	5		

The area outside the building (groups Da and Db)

A very small amount of pottery was recovered from the exterior of the building. This really is very surprising as the motte area outside the keep would presumably be a repository for at least some of the waste and rubbish produced by its occupants. But our understanding of the archaeological data is limited by not knowing how much pottery was used to start with, how much eroded off the motte into the surrounding ditch and how much may have been taken off the motte for deposition elsewhere. In group Db fabric SANDC is well represented. This may suggest that more of the pottery found along the wall line (see above) derived from the exterior of the building than from the interior. One fabric SANDC rim sherd was present: SANDCcpj5. There was also a cooking pot/jar rim sherd in fabric SMT: SMTcpj2a. There was a single glazed sherd, a strap handle, decorated with combing (ill. 24).

Group Da contained only two sherds. The glazed sherd (sf 157, ill. 23) was decorated with a 'flower' stamp. Two further sherds with the same stamp, and almost certainly from the same vessel, were found in contexts (12) and (42). Barker illustrated part of a vessel with this stamp (Barker 1970, HD114) from the latest layers of the motte ditch and adjacent bailey and it is not impossible that the sherds are all from a single vessel. If this is so, in which case the sherd excavated earlier was residual, it illustrates one of the processes which affected the eventual pattern of evidence: pottery discarded on the motte top ending up, in whole or part, in lower areas of the site.

Table 5: Group Db

Fabric	Sherd No.	Sherd Wt (g)	Rims	Form
SMT	16	96	1	cpj
SANDC	14	176	1	cpj
SAND1	1	51	0	jug
Total	*31*	*323*	*2*	

Form	Sherd No.	Weight	Rim%	Rim No.
cooking pot/jar	30	272	8	2
jug/pitcher	1	51		

Phase III

No pottery-bearing features or deposits were demonstrably associated with the construction or use of the smaller building postulated for this structural phase (as opposed to those of the preceding phase which already existed when the burning of the southern parts of the site took place).

Phase IV

This material came mainly from clay material interpreted as the collapsed wall-cladding of a timber-framed tower, and from associated deposits beneath the turf/topsoil covering of the motte.

Table 6: Phase IV

Fabric	Sherd No.	Sherd Wt (g)	Rims	Form
SAND1	1	4	0	jug
SAND2	2	13	1	jug
SANDC	4	28	0	cpj
SMT	21	148	1	cpj+jug
Total	*28*	*195*	*2*	

Form	Sherd No.	Weight	Rim%	Rim No.
cooking pot/jar	20	128	4	1
jug/pitcher	8	67	7	1

The Motte Perimeter (probably multi-phase)

This pottery does not come from a single 'phase' of the site but from a series of deep gullies, of possibly more than one function, around the motte perimeter. The collection contained the largest group of pottery. This was similar in nature to that from phase II, particularly that described above as phase II Dc (i.e. the wall lines of the main structure), which was the second largest stratified group. There was a comparable range of fabrics in more or less the same proportions. There were a number of cross-joins within this area, i.e. between contexts (6), (12) and (42). Other cross-joins relate material from these gullies to material in the wall lines and internal features of the main building (e.g. gulley 43 and internal structural feature 33). A significant cross-join within the gullies was a ?northern French import (FRIMP) dating to the late twelfth/early thirteenth century (see above), sherds of which were found in (12) and (6). However sherds of the more usual glazed type also occur both in this phase and in contexts (12) and (42). The difficulty in dating these gullies lies in the fact that, not only do we not know how many of the gullies were contemporary with each other, but, equally, it is not clear whether the deposited sherds are associated with the first digging of the gullies or with their infill on disuse. The pottery itself is unlikely to be earlier than the mid-twelfth century or later than the early thirteenth century, which (allowing for all the difficulties of chronology discussed here) *may* confirm our general impression (see Chapters 4 & 7) that the main building on the motte top was fully developed (into what is here described as phase II) in the mid-twelfth century (i.e. what for the bailey was published as phase X). The glazed sherds contained the usual run of decorative motifs, e.g. ring and dot, combing, roller stamping and stabbing, which have a wide currency in the region and

Table 7: Motte perimeter

Fabric	Sherd No.	Sherd Wt (g)	Rims	Form
BUFF	1	4	0	?
FRIMP	2	29	1	jug
SAND1	11	74	0	cpj+jug
SAND2	11	139	1	cpj+jug
SAND3a	6	26	0	cpj+jug
SAND4	2	22	0	cpj
SANDC	21	188	1	cpj+jug
SANDHF	1	23	0	jug
SANDVC	14	106	2	cpj
SMT	83	1183	11	cpj+jug
Total	*152*	*1794*	*16*	

Form	Sherd No.	Weight	Rim%	Rim No.
cooking pot/jar	103	1416	85	14
jug/pitcher	34	297	25	2
?	15	81		

are not closely datable. There was one new fabric, a fine buff sandy ware represented by one sherd, which may belong to the second half of the thirteenth century.

Unstratified Pottery

This pottery contained a similar range of fabrics and forms as the stratified material. A very small amount of post-medieval and modern pottery was present. Even in the unstratified pottery, glazed wares are not frequent, which reinforces the general picture produced by the stratified pottery. This would tend to suggest that there was not much occupation on the motte in the thirteenth century and any that there was is almost certainly confined to the first half of the century, although this may be contradicted by the single BUFF sherd from the motte perimeter.

Table 8: Unstratified Pottery

Fabric	Sherd No.	Sherd Wt (g)
DSTAM	1	12
POSTMED	2	13
MGW (*1)	4	5
SAND1	25	222
SAND2	22	125
SAND3a	1	14
SANDC	9	128
SANDHF	8	56
SANDVC	1	8
SMT	101	899
Total	174	1482

(*1) MGW = modern glazed wares of the eighteenth/nineteenth centuries

Form/Function

Form codes consist of the fabric code and vessel type and number. The form in each fabric group are numbered from 1 onwards, i.e. SMTcpj1 is a different form from SANDCcpj1. Ten main forms were observed in fabric SMT (ills 1–4 and 6–11). These forms have been illustrated (fig. 5.1) with the exception of SMTcpj4, which is similar to SANDCcpj2 and also to a form from Dothill (Barker 1970, DO10) and SMTcpj11 which is similar to SANDCcpj5 (ill. 17). There was a smaller number of forms in fabric SANDC. All five forms in SANDC have been illustrated.

Few jug rims were found and most of them were too small for illustration. Several decorated sherds were found which were divided into six decorative schemes: square or rectangular roller stamping (*cf.* Barker 1970, HD204), complex roller stamping (which is not paralleled in Barker 1970), applied decoration (*cf.* Barker 1970, HD141), variations of ring and ring and dot motifs (*cf.* Barker 1970, HD120), a notched circular stamp (ill.

23; *cf.* Barker 1970, HD114), and incised line, usually horizontal, decoration.

The range of forms observed was limited. The predominant form was the cooking pot/jar, usually straight-sided although more rounded forms were also present. Fabrics SMT and SANDC had some forms in common, but generally the rims with an internal projection or infolded rims (e.g. ills 9, 15, 19 and 25) were more common in SANDC. Thumbed rims (e.g. ills 7 and 15) were only found in SANDC.

Glazed wares were greatly outnumbered by unglazed cooking pots/jars. This is the normal pattern in post-Conquest to late twelfth/early thirteenth-century assemblages, where cooking vessels predominate, with some unsooted storage vessels and a few jugs/pitchers for the storage and serving of liquids. The uses of the material excavated in the early parts of the excavation, particularly the sitting of the sizeable cooking pots in the embers of fires, have been discussed elsewhere (Barker 1970, 44–45).

The spatial distribution of the pottery suggests no functional bias. For example, the pottery from the gullies on the perimeter of the motte contained a similar mix of pottery to that from other areas.

Cross-joining Sherds

The identification of sherds from the same vessel, in separate contexts, often of differing date, has been referred to several times in the foregoing discussion. In addition to those already mentioned, sherds from a cooking pot in fabric SMT (ill. 10) were found in a number of contexts (phase I 36, 68; phase I/II 81, 82, 91, 106; phase II 14, 26, 29, 32, 33, 34, 47, 48; phase III 65; and phase IV 3). This was by far the most extensive series of cross-joins. Generally speaking, sherds from the perimeter tended to join with others from the perimeter although exceptions were: phase IV 3 (clay wall-cladding from the last building) and joins between bridge post fill 38, replacement post fill 92, internal building feature 33 and perimeter gulley 43. There were several joins between pottery from the disturbed wall line/post replacements of the building and between the latter and internal features 14+28, 8+39, 94+49, 94+34, 94+23 and 94+81. This clearly indicates a good deal of disturbance, intrusion and re-deposition of material during the successive building operations encountered.

Interestingly, despite the conflagration which, it has been suggested (see Chapter 4), affected part of the motte building, none of the pottery showed any sign of being burnt. If the suggestion of the major fire is correct, this may have bearing upon the matter of rubbish disposal discussed above.

General Conclusions.

The overall impressions from the foregoing analysis are as follows:

1. The quantity of pottery recovered from the motte was small compared with that from the north-west quadrant of the bailey published in 1982. This may tell us something about relative frequency of use, but on the other hand the motte top was a restricted area and one from which some loss of material through erosion may be expected. However, it is notable that the motte pottery contained types including a range of examples from the earliest to the latest identified from the bailey in 1982. In this, general sense, there was similarity.

2. Little pottery was associated with the earliest occupation of the motte but it became more common thereafter, in the middle and later periods of occupation. Evidence for occupation of the motte after the middle of the thirteenth century is limited to one sherd, which may be late thirteenth century or later. This framework is broadly coincident with that identified in the bailey by Barker and Clarke, though here a few more sherds may have been later thirteenth century in date. However, in all parts of the site, the possibility of early pottery being found as residual material in later contexts must be borne in mind.

3. The assemblage contained an overwhelming preponderance of cooking pots and jars, with relatively few glazed wares and jugs. In this respect, too, the evidence from the motte compares with that from the bailey. Despite, in contemporary terms, the high-status character of the site, the range of pottery used seems no different from that encountered on rural and urban sites of the period. Nor, within the site, would the motte have been identified as a place of higher-status occupation on the basis of the pottery. Allowing for other uses of pottery vessels (storage, medicinal, heating of water etc.), it would appear that cooking took place on the motte (perhaps in the basement of its main building?). Sizeable pots, not only heavy when full of food/liquid, but also hot, would not be easy to carry up from the bailey.

4. The occurrence of joining sherds from different contexts (sometimes of different dates) is notable. This confirms the impression, gained in the excavation, that successive structural developments involved disturbance of earlier deposits and re-deposition of existing material. Sherds were consequently discovered in contexts of different character and date from those in which they had been originally lost. This observation is helpful to our understanding of the site formation processes, but obviously limits the value of the pottery as a means of dating the structural sequence. Equally, spatial distribution of the material tells us little under these circumstances. This aspect of the pottery evidence, though acknowledged in the earlier published studies, may have been underestimated for the bailey. Study of the slag deposits (by Juleff, see below) in the bailey also revealed wear patterns consistent with much movement and re-deposition of material.

5. Occurrence of independently datable sherds is very limited: two sherds of French import and one of developed Stamford ware (the latter also occurring in the bailey). On the whole, the site (through its historical record) dates the pottery rather than vice versa. But the general twelfth to thirteenth-century range of the material is also provided by the wider regional framework (Barker 1970) and the parallels discussed above.

6. The basic two-fold classification of fabrics established in Clarke's report, through visual observation and some petrological analysis, remains valid. Most of the fabric varieties within Clarke's classification occurred on the motte, though some revisions of the detailed type series have emerged from the study of the motte material.

7. The economic connections of the occupants of Hen Domen, revealed by the pottery evidence both from the bailey and the motte, were various. On the basis of both visual comparisons/distributional studies and the earlier petrological analysis by Alan Vince (Clarke 1982), it appears that most of the pottery used came from a source not far from Hen Domen (but not immediately adjacent), whereas the rest, particularly the sandy wares, came from further afield, in Shropshire, Herefordshire, Worcestershire and Staffordshire, but from sources which at the moment are not specifically known.

Table 9: Illustrated vessels

No.	Vessel type	Context (Group)	Comments
1	SMTcpj 9	24(G)	
2	SMTcpj 2a	47(Dd), 33(Dd)	
3	SMTcpj 10	38(Db), 8(Dc)	
4	SMTcpj 2a	81(C)	cf. Barker 1970, HD24, HD70d
5	SMTcpj 2	43(G), 33(Dd)	
6	SMTcpj 3	46(G), 6(G)	
7	SMTcpj 2	46(G)	
8	SMTcpj 3a	12(G)	cf. Barker 1970, HD172
9	SMTcpj 8	82(C)	cf. Barker 1970, HD1?
10	SMTcpj 7	106(C) etc.	cf. Barker 1970, HD58b
11	SMTcpj 1	1(u/s)	cf. Barker (1970) HD69c
12	SMTcpj 3b	1a(u/s)	
13	SMTcpj 6a	3(F)	
14	SANDCcpj 2a	22(u/s)	
15	SANDCcpj 3	5(G)	
16	SANDCcpj 4	8(Dc)	
17	SANDCcpj 5	37(Db)	
18	SANDCcpj 5a	46(G)	
19	SANDCcpj 1	1(u/s)	
20	SANDCcpj 2	1a(u/s)	
21	SANDCcpj 3a	39(Dd)	
22	SAND1jug2	46(G), s3(F)	
23	SAND1dec8	12(G), 42(G)	
24	SAND1handle4	37(Db)	
25	FRIMPjug	12(G), 6(G)	

Table 10: Total of fabrics occurring in all phases (and unstratified)

Fabric group	Fabric codes	Sherd no.	Weight (g)	Min vess	Rim%
Siltstone tempered	SMT	425	4164	40	193
Sandy cooking pot	SANDC, SANDVC	96	1038	12	48
Sandy glazed wares	SAND1-SAND4, SANDHF	137	1132	3	40
Developed Stamford	DSTAM	1	12	0	0
Buff sandy ware	BUFF	1	4	0	0
Continental import	FRIMP	2	29	1	1
Post med	MANG	2	13	0	0
Modern	MGW	4	5	0	0
Total		668	6397	56	282

Table 11: Total percentage of fabrics occurring in all phases (and unstratified)

Fabric group	Fabric codes	Sherd no.	Weight (g)	Min vess	Rim%
Siltstone tempered	SMT	63.62	65.09	71.43	68.43
Sandy cooking pot	SANDC, SANDVC	14.37	16.22	21.37	17.33
Sandy glazed wares	SAND1-SAND4, SANDHF	20.51	17.71	5.41	13.88
Developed Stamford	DSTAM	0.15	0.19	0.00	0.00
Buff sandy ware	BUFF	0.15	0.06	0.00	0.00
Continental import	FRIMP	0.30	0.45	1.79	0.36
Post med	MANG	0.30	0.20	0.00	0.00
Modern	MGW	0.60	0.08	0.00	0.00
Total		100.00	100.00	100.00	100.00

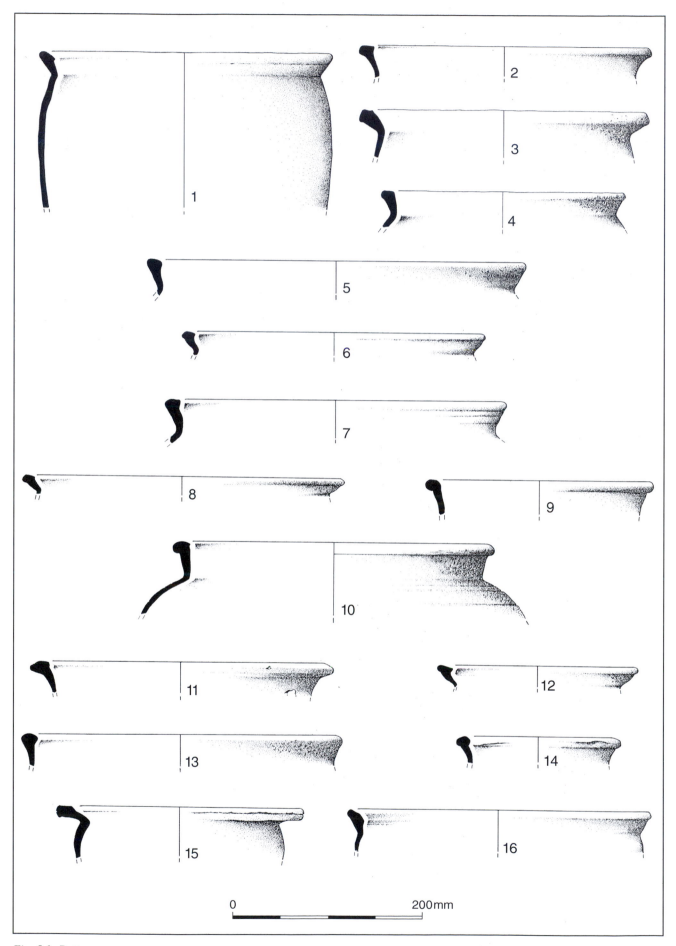

Fig. 5.1: Pottery

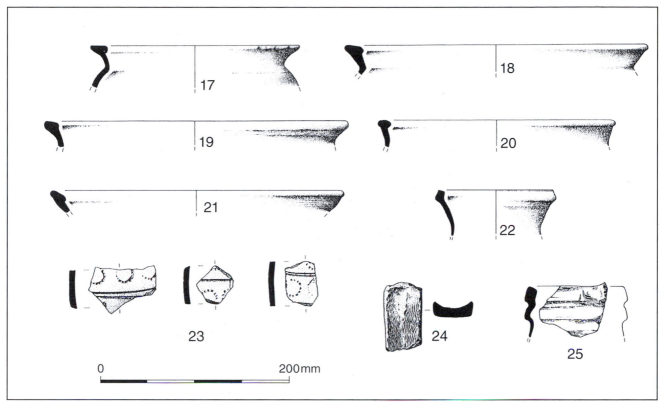

Fig. 5.2: Pottery

METALWORK FROM THE MOTTE EXCAVATIONS AT HEN DOMEN 1988–1992

by Dr Ian Goodall (ferrous items) and Alison Goodall (non-ferrous items)

The following items came from deposits along the wall lines of the building, the major gullies around the motte perimeter and one or two clay deposits inside and outside the building. A few unstratified items came from the topsoil or insecurely identified contexts. No chronological deductions can be made from the contexts in which the finds were discovered. Some may be residual from the early period of the motte's occupation, but most probably relate to the middle to later periods of its development, when the wall lines were re-worked and when the main building was removed, its features deliberately backfilled or gradually filled up. Finds from the perimeter gullies are as likely to have been deposited when the timbers were dug out as when they were laid. The collection is best regarded simply as an assemblage whose date range is between the later eleventh and later thirteenth centuries. Although not a large collection, both categories, ferrous (fig.5.3) and non-ferrous objects (fig.5.4), include high quality items.

Fig. 5.3: **Ferrous Items**

1. Auger bit, irregularly shaped, with flattened terminal and circular-sectioned stem lacking any blade. Length 130mm. Such bits were used to bore holes in wood, and the lost blade would probably have been spoon-shaped, by far the commonest type among such medieval bits.

2. Surgeon's fleam with slender blades for cutting flesh, the shape similar to those of knives depicted in post-medieval medical treatises. Length 44mm.

3. Knife blade, tang lost. The tang, at this date would have been a whittle tang inserted into a handle. Length 90mm.

4. Shears with plain bow and blades. The size and plain form of the blades suggest that these shears were used for cutting cloth and the like (Cowgill et al. 1987, 58–61, 106–7). Length 166mm.

5. U-shaped staple, both arms broken. Not illustrated.

6. Timber nails. Three types were recognised:

   6a. Type A, flat round head: three examples, two with complete shanks 38mm and 43mm long.

   6b. Type B, flat rounded square head, one example, shank 25mm long, broken (Example illustrated is from bailey).

   6c. Type C, figure eight-shaped head, five examples, two with complete shanks 40mm and 45mm long.

7. Spring arm from padlock bolt, one leaf-spring broken. The arm comes from padlock bolts some of whose range is indicated by examples from Castle Acre Castle, Norfolk (Goodall in Coad and Streeten 1982, 228, fig. 39, nos 72–80). Not illustrated.

8. Key with ring bow and bit rolled in one with hollow stem. This type of key was the most common type in use during the thirteenth century, but the plain bit suggest that it is an incomplete forging. Length 113mm.

9. Strip fragment, 49mm long, 7mm deep, 1mm thick. Not illustrated.

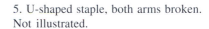

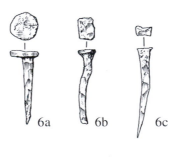

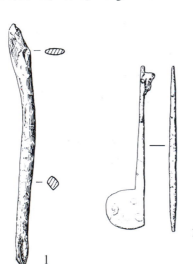

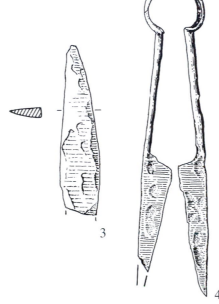

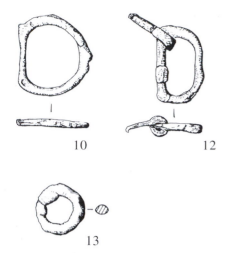

10   12

13

10. Buckle with D-shaped frame and incomplete pin rest. Non-ferrous plating: XRF detected tin and lead. Pin axis 44mm.

11. Buckle with D-shaped frame and fragment of moulded pin. Non-ferrous plating: XRF detected tin. Not illustrated.

12. Buckle with elongated D-shaped frame and plain pin. Non-ferrous plating: XRF detected tin. Pin axis 25mm.

13. Circular buckle frame with butt ends. Diameter 12.5mm.

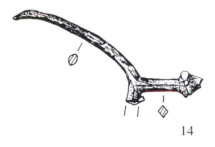

14

14. Prick spur with quadrangular lozenge-shaped goad on a short, gently-curved neck. Length 100mm. The D-sectioned sides, both broken, curve gently under the wearer's ankles. This type of spur was introduced during the twelfth century and became common during the thirteenth century (Ellis in Clark 1995, 55, 62, fig 17, no 3).

15. Horseshoe arm fragment with countersunk nailholes and calkin at tip. This type of horseshoe, with a marked wavy edge around countersunk nailholes, was introduced during the eleventh century and continued in use through the twelfth and thirteenth centuries (Goodall in Biddle 1990, 1054–55). Not illustrated.

16. Horseshoe nails. Two types were identified and may be compared with examples from Winchester, London and elsewhere (Goodall in Biddle 1990, 1055–56; Clark 1995, 86).

Type A is of so-called fiddle-key form with a semi-circular head, sometimes worn down, no thicker in side view than the shank, and in use from the tenth to the thirteenth century. Fourteen examples were found, complete examples being between 28mm and 42mm in length, two of which are illustrated (16a, 16b).

Type B is the succeeding type, used in the thirteenth and fourteenth centuries, which has an eared head which broadens out in side view. Two examples were found, both broken. Not illustrated.

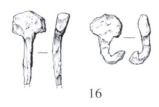

16

17–22. Arrowheads, all socketed: 17 (length 41mm) and 18 have lozenge-shaped heads; 19 and 20 (85mm) triangular heads with slight barbs, the latter with a pinned socket; 21 (length 65mm) a triangular head with a central rib; 22 retains only the stub of the blade. (18, 19, 22 not illustrated).

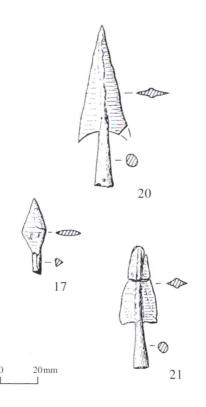

20

17

21

0   20mm

Fig. 5.4: **Non-Ferrous Items**

23. Stirrup-shaped finger ring of copper alloy with undecorated shoulders and raised bezel containing a purplish coloured stone. The material of the stone has not been identified. The ring is much worn. Maximum diameter 25mm.

A very similar ring, set with a glass cabochon, was found unstratified in excavations in London (Egan & Pritchard 1991, 326–27, fig. 215.1609) and two further examples, made from gold and set respectively with a sapphire and an emerald, are illustrated in the Salisbury Museum Medieval Catalogue (Cherry in Saunders & Saunders 1991, 41, fig. 10. 1 & 2). The Salisbury rings are dated to the twelfth and thirteenth centuries, but this type of ring had a long life.

23

24. Incomplete decorative fitting of gilded copper alloy. The flat top is embellished with traced linear ornament. There is a thick shank at the back for attachment, possibly to wood. Max. width 46mm.

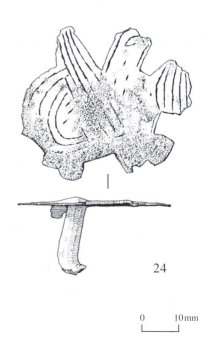

24

0   10mm

25

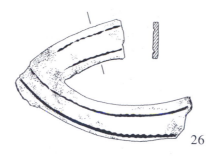

26

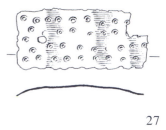

27

25. Incomplete decorative fitting of gilded copper alloy with linear traced ornament. Length 39mm.

26. Fragment of gilded fitting, possibly part of no. 25, above. Length 45mm.

The form that these fragments took when complete cannot be established. It is possible that they are related to the strips, such as nos 28–30, below. Goltho manor in Lincolnshire, where a large number of gilded strip fragments were found, also produced gilded decorative fittings, one of them depicting a lion with its tail curling between its hind legs (Goodall 1987, 173, fig. 153. 11 & 12).

27. Rectangular copper alloy plate decorated all over with rows of rings-and-dots. There is a rivet hole at one end and there may originally have been another at the other end. The long edges are slightly scalloped. Length 34mm.

28. Fragment of gilded copper alloy binding strip. It is a shallow U-shape in section, expanded to form an oval boss; there is a pin or rivet-hole at one of the broken ends. Length 70mm.

29. Fragment of U-sectioned binding strip with one pin-hole. Length 51mm, width 6.5mm.

30. Fragment of D-sectioned copper alloy binding strip with a spoon-like expansion at one end. There is a faint diagonal gadrooning. No gilding survives, although the strip was probably originally gilded, and there are no surviving pin-holes. Length 76mm.

Binding strips of gilded copper alloy of the types represented by nos 28–30 have been found at many castle and manorial sites with occupation in the twelfth and thirteenth centuries. In a number of cases, as at Castle Acre castle, Norfolk (Goodall 1982), Loughor castle, West Glamorgan (Lewis 1993, 142–46, figs 20–21) and Goltho manor, Lincolnshire (Goodall 1987, 173–76, figs 154–55), the strips comprise the majority of the copper alloy finds. The large numbers of examples from these sites demonstrate the wide range of forms that the strips can take and the complexity of the openwork bosses that they are often associated with. Their function has not yet been established, but it is clear that they were attached to a base, perhaps of wood and possibly covered with leather or fabric, to make up designs of considerable size and complexity.

0   10mm

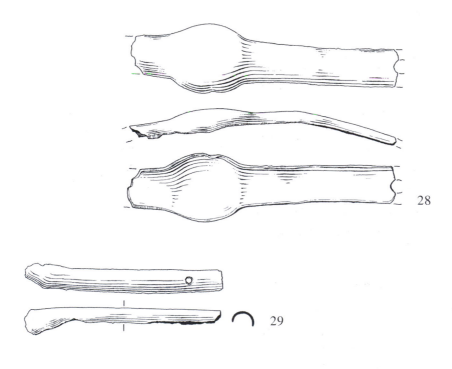

28

29

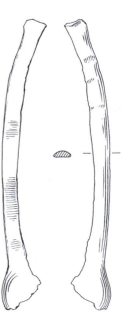

30

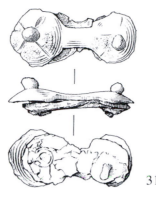

31. Dumb-bell-shaped fitting of gilded copper alloy mounted on leather. One end, which is slightly larger than the other, is ornamented with incised radial lines; it is not clear if these are present at the other end. Both ends are pierced with large-headed rivets. Possibly a belt-mount. Length 32.5mm.

32. Fragment of copper alloy strip with a rivet at one end. Two diagonal lines of uncorroded metal run across the upper surface and may indicate where the strip has been in contact with another material.

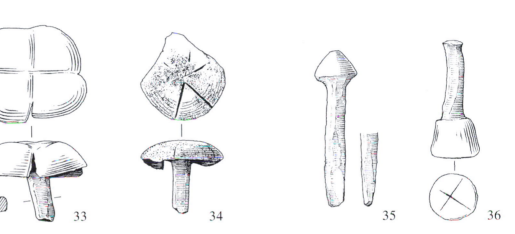

33. Large quatrefoil-headed stud of gilded copper alloy. It has a short rectangular-sectioned shank. Head 24mm x 28mm. Length of shank 22mm.

 Quatrefoil-headed studs were also found at Goltho manor and Loughor castle (see above) and the similarity of the assemblages of copper alloy finds from these sites and a number of others is worthy of note.

34. Large convex-headed stud of copper alloy with a thick rectangular-sectioned shank. The head is decorated with six incised radial lines and there are traces of gilding. Length 19mm, head diameter approx. 20mm.

35. Large 'pin' of copper alloy. It has a heavy conical head and the shank is flattened at the tip. Length 41mm.

36. Copper alloy object with heavy, almost cylindrical head. It is covered with a soot-like patina. Length 31mm.

37. Copper alloy object resembling a double-looped buckle frame or strap distributor. It is crudely made and appears to have been cut from a thick sheet. Length 36mm.

38. Irregular runnel of fused lead. Not illustrated.

39. Lump or runnel of fused lead. Not illustrated.

40. Fragment of lead. Not illustrated.

41. Perforated lead disc. Max. diameter 22mm.

41

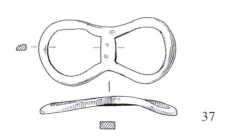

37

0   10mm

METALWORK AND OTHER MATERIAL FROM THE BAILEY EXCAVATIONS AT HEN DOMEN, 1960–1990

by Robert Higham and Mike Rouillard

The following items are the better preserved from a collection including other fragmentary and unidentifiable pieces. Some well-preserved items are not illustrated here because there were several similar or identical examples, only one of which has been included (whether here, from the bailey, or, above, from the motte). These included buckles, hooks, staples, horse-shoe fragments, padlock and key fragments and miscellaneous fittings and bindings. The descriptive phrases given are simply a means of identification and do not arise from specialist examination (as is the case with items from the motte, described above). Many of these objects are deserving of fuller study than has been possible here. The remarks about dating made above in relation to material from the motte apply here also. The objects came from a wide array of contexts and many were probably subject to re-deposition during the site's occupation and development. They are best regarded simply as an assemblage of late eleventh to late thirteenth-century date. Since few objects came, however, from early contexts, it may be that little of the late eleventh century is represented, though some of the objects could easily be residual finds of early date. There is a notable general similarity between the Hen Domen material, especially the metalwork, and that from Castle Acre (Coad & Streeten 1982) and Goltho (Beresford 1987), where occupation of the excavated areas extended to the late twelfth century.

Fig. 5.5: **Ferrous Objects**

42. Incomplete spearhead. Fragment of wood in situ in socket.

43–49. Arrowheads, conforming to socketed types found on the motte, with lozenge or triangular heads, some with slight barbs and central ribs. Generally representing multi-purpose warfare/hunting types (as defined by Jessop 1996). (48 not illustrated).

50. Arrowhead of different type, with long narrow barbs and broad triangular head. Designed to inflict maximum damage in hunting use.

51. Sword hilt with bone panels on both sides riveted to iron base.

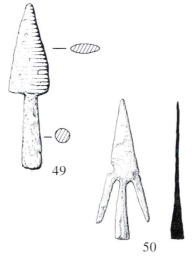

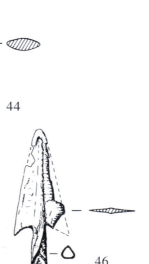

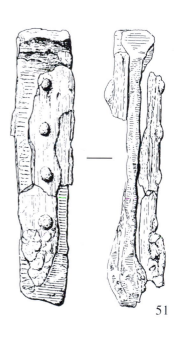

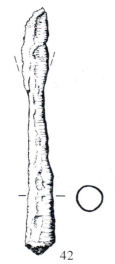

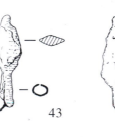

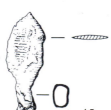

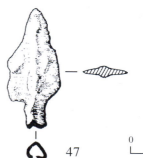

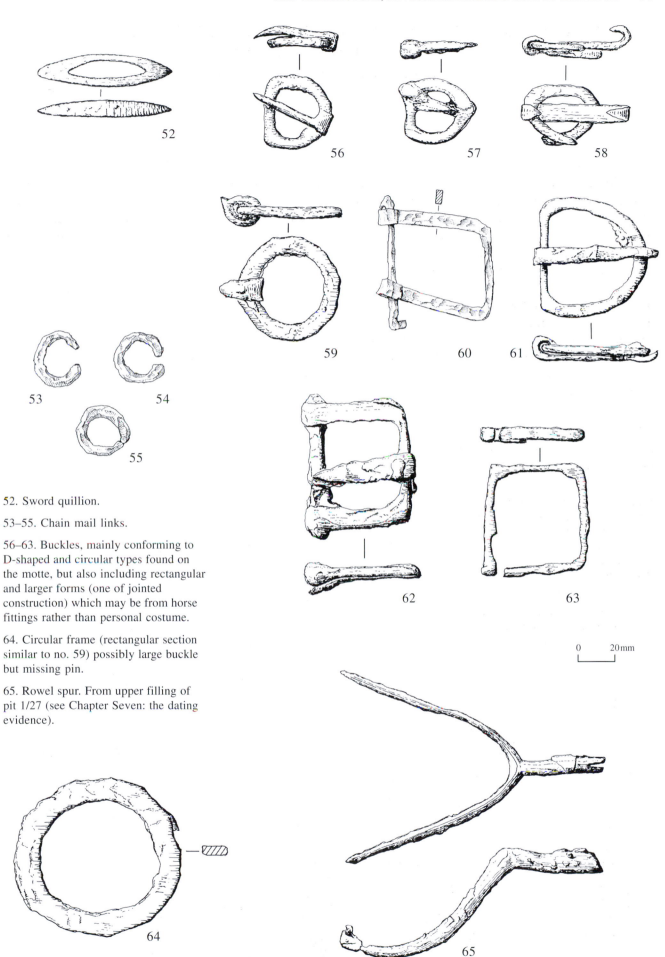

52. Sword quillion.

53–55. Chain mail links.

56–63. Buckles, mainly conforming to D-shaped and circular types found on the motte, but also including rectangular and larger forms (one of jointed construction) which may be from horse fittings rather than personal costume.

64. Circular frame (rectangular section similar to no. 59) possibly large buckle but missing pin.

65. Rowel spur. From upper filling of pit 1/27 (see Chapter Seven: the dating evidence).

0   20mm

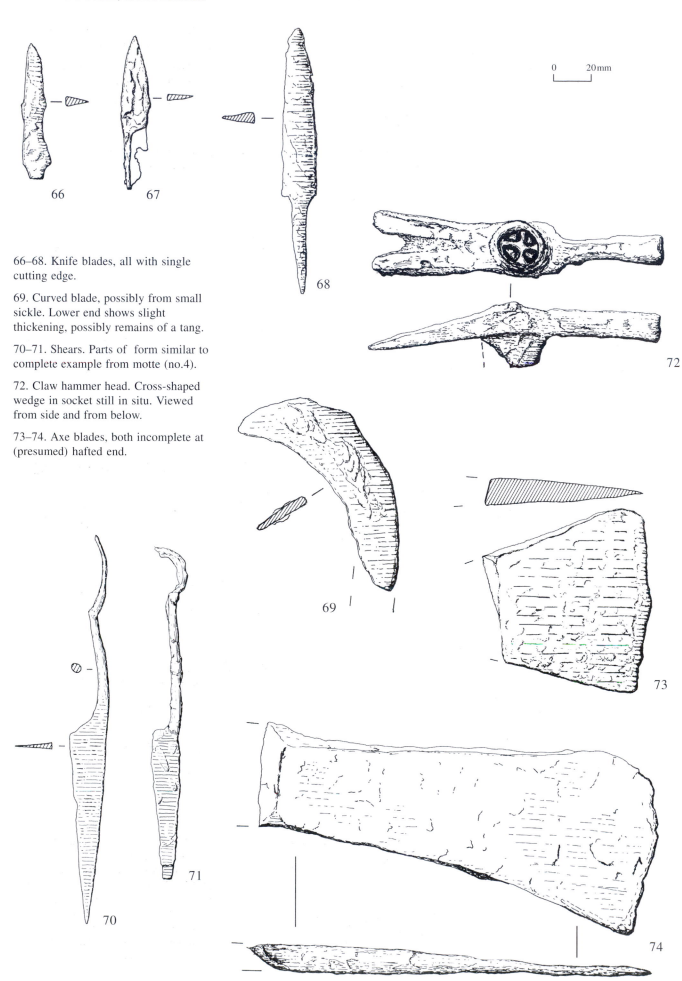

66–68. Knife blades, all with single cutting edge.

69. Curved blade, possibly from small sickle. Lower end shows slight thickening, possibly remains of a tang.

70–71. Shears. Parts of form similar to complete example from motte (no.4).

72. Claw hammer head. Cross-shaped wedge in socket still in situ. Viewed from side and from below.

73–74. Axe blades, both incomplete at (presumed) hafted end.

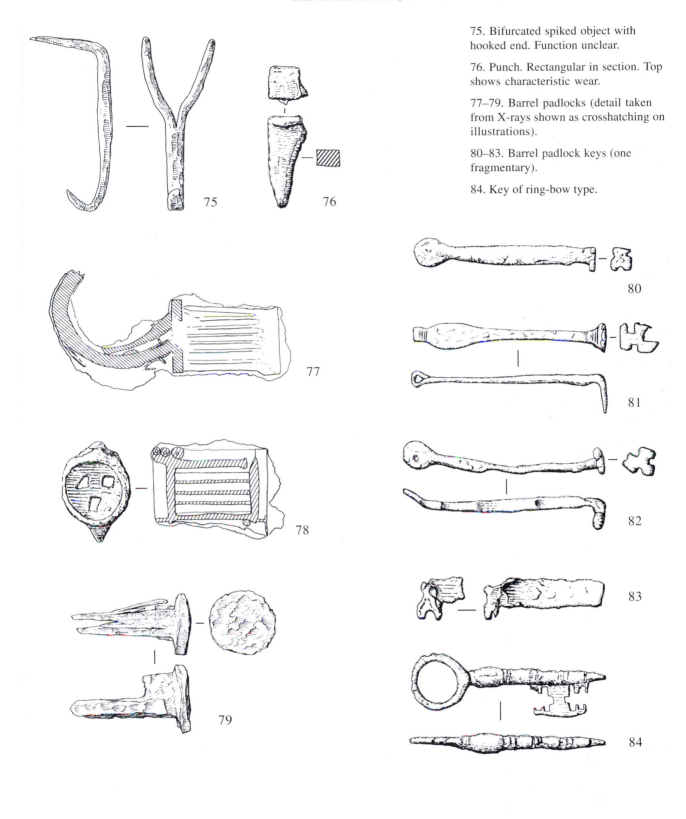

75. Bifurcated spiked object with hooked end. Function unclear.

76. Punch. Rectangular in section. Top shows characteristic wear.

77–79. Barrel padlocks (detail taken from X-rays shown as crosshatching on illustrations).

80–83. Barrel padlock keys (one fragmentary).

84. Key of ring-bow type.

85–96. Miscellaneous iron fittings including staples, nails, handle fragment (with heavily corroded twisted profile), large pin with hooked end, two examples of figure-of-eight shaped hasps, pierced fitting with looped terminal and staple at one end, and a small punch (?) with quadrangular section and pointed end.

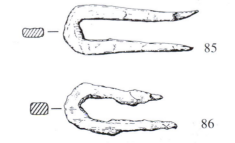

0   20mm

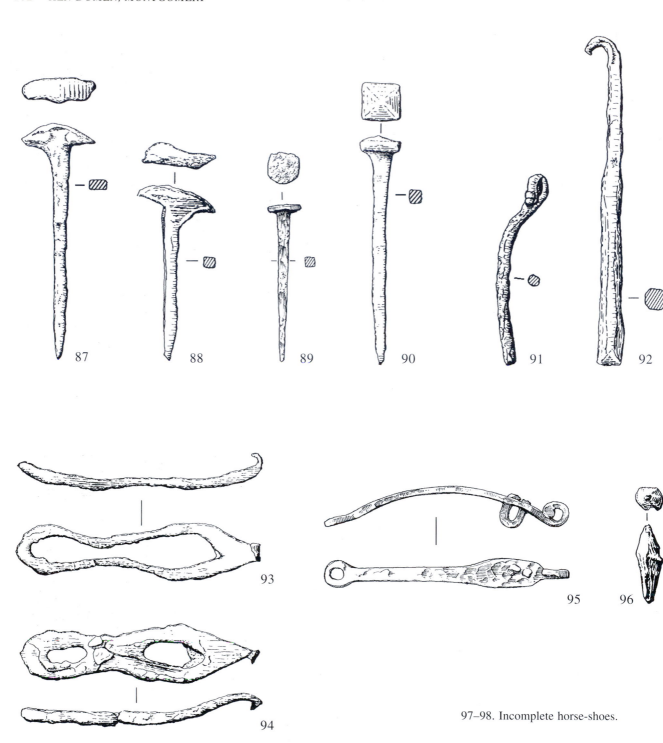

87   88   89   90   91   92

93

95   96

94

97–98. Incomplete horse-shoes.

0   20mm

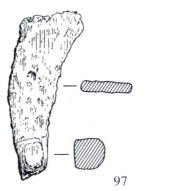

97

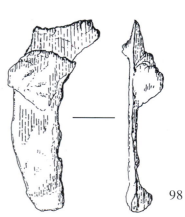

98

Fig. 5.6: **Copper Alloy Objects**

99. Needle, with part of eye surviving.

100. Tweezers.

101. Finger ring with blue glass 'stone': late twelfth–early thirteenth century style (identification by J. Cherry, British Museum).

102. Large buckle with gilded decoration and triangular bow. Traces of leather survive on reverse. Three rivets.

103. Square buckle hinged to rectangular and very thin (and corroded) bronze plate. Latter riveted in each corner. Plate decorated in quadrants of a cross and edges decorated as for buckle itself.

104. Square buckle with elongated and semi-circular end. Decoration similar to no. 103. Pin missing.

105. Small rectangular buckle continuous (no hinge) with very narrow and elongated plate riveted in two places. Buckle end has separate roller. Fragment of pin survives.

106. Small D-shaped buckle hinged to rectangular, double-sided plate with five rivets. Pin missing.

107. Pair of identical strap ends (one only illustrated) with two rivets. Leather preserved within. Finely incised decoration.

108. Double-looped strap distributor (similar to no. 37 from motte). This example has preserved double pin of iron.

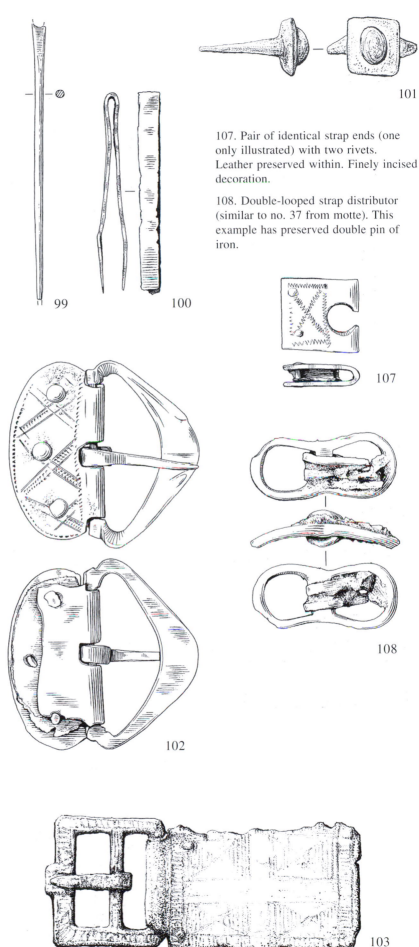

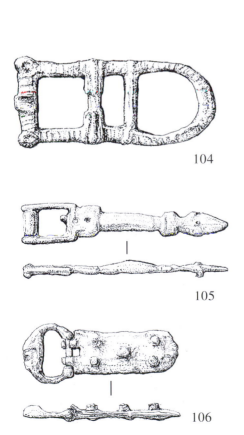

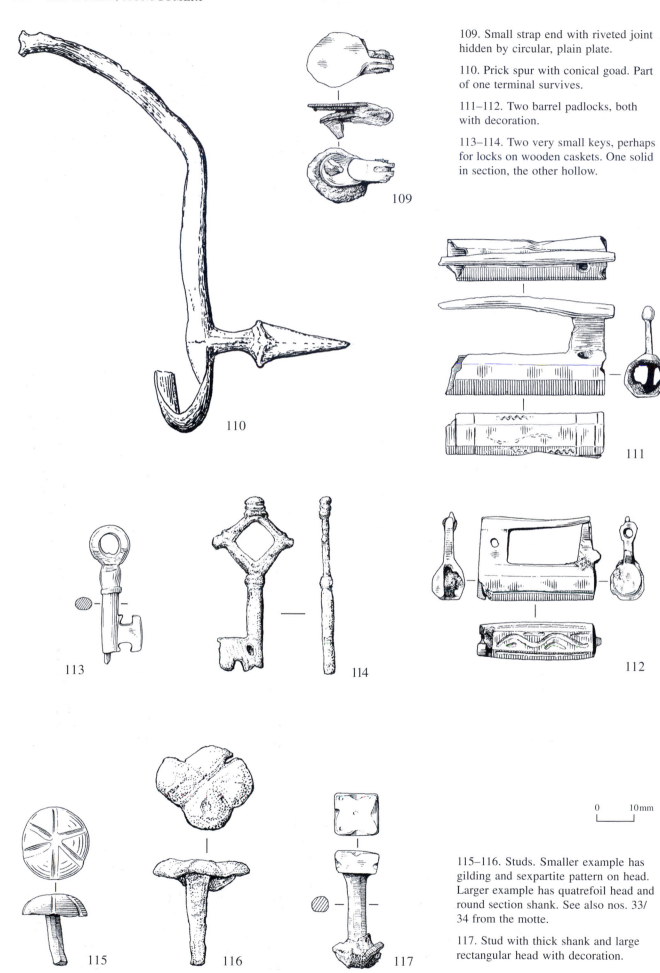

109. Small strap end with riveted joint hidden by circular, plain plate.

110. Prick spur with conical goad. Part of one terminal survives.

111–112. Two barrel padlocks, both with decoration.

113–114. Two very small keys, perhaps for locks on wooden caskets. One solid in section, the other hollow.

109

110

111

113

114

112

0   10mm

115–116. Studs. Smaller example has gilding and sexpartite pattern on head. Larger example has quatrefoil head and round section shank. See also nos. 33/34 from the motte.

117. Stud with thick shank and large rectangular head with decoration.

115   116   117

118. Gilded U-sectioned binding strip, with rivet holes (incomplete) at ends.

119. Possible binding strip with rivet hole in spade-end.

120. Binding, arms with spade ends (one with rivet hole, *cf.* 119), riveted at bifurcation.

121. Multi-branched binding, arms with rivet holes.

122. Binding with decorative perforations, some possibly also for attachment.

123. Gilded fitting with two lobes, ends of which are perforated. Incised decoration at junction of lobes.

124. Part of (apothecary's ?) balance. Beam comprising two hinged arms, one surviving almost whole length (with broken suspension ring), the other broken at centre joint.

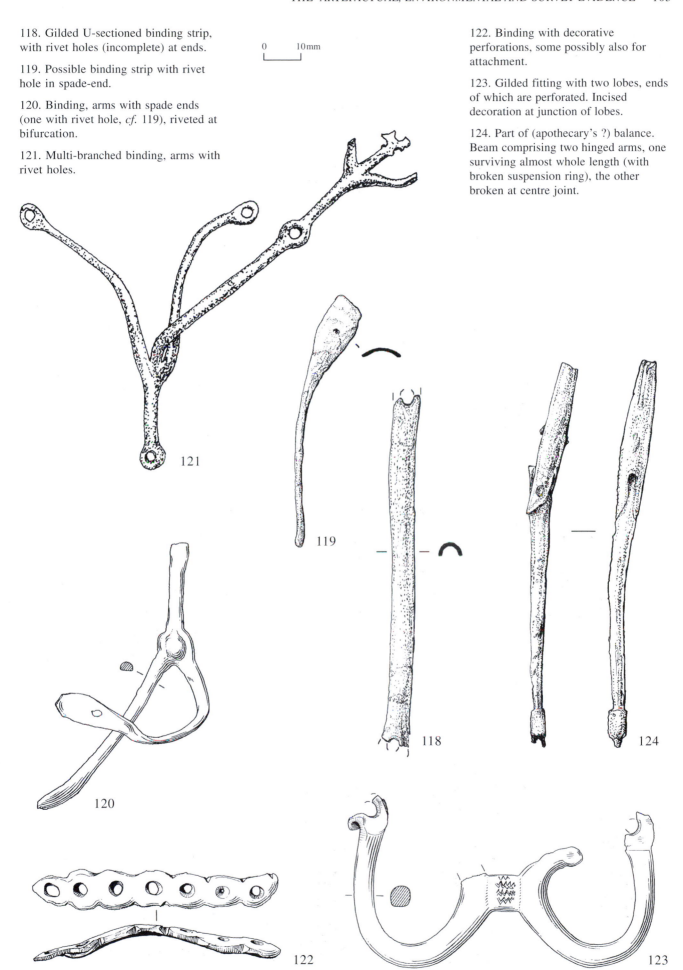

0   10mm

125. Decorative (incomplete) hinge plate with rivets.

126. Incomplete bronze ring.

127. Small gilded rectangular object with central raised area. Possible (pilgrim's ?) badge. Top edge extends into perforated lug for attachment.

128. Tapered ferrule, folded from a single sheet down long axis and again at closed (narrow) end.

129. Narrow strip with one rivet hole at one end and possible fragments of (double ?) rings at other end.

Fig. 5.7: **Lead Objects**

130. Plumb-bob ? of tapered polygonal profile. Evidence for suspension lost (damaged ends).

131. Decorated lead sheet (raised diagonals between raised double borders). Perhaps from a vessel. Other fragments of undecorated sheet not illustrated.

132–133. Two small lead weights, possibly fishing accessories?

134. Washer ?

135. Disc, hollow longitudinally through a thickened mid-rib. Pendant seal ?

A total weight of 2.5kg of lead waste was recovered from widely scattered contexts in the bailey. How far this was a by-product of manufacture of lead objects on site, or how far simply the result of melting of lead objects in accidental fires, is not known. Fragments were also found on the motte (see non-ferrous category in report on motte metalwork).

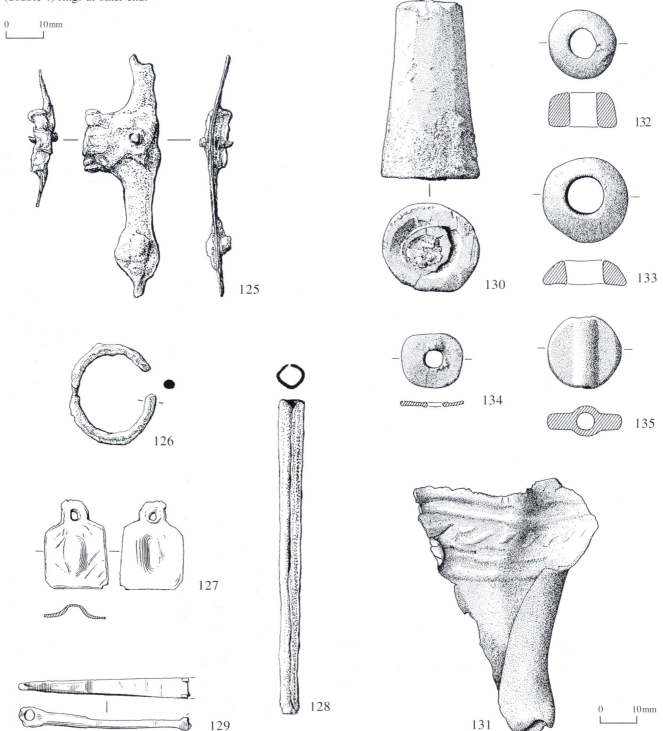

Fig. 5.8: **Bone Objects**

136. Bone gaming counter, central dot and incised circles with ring/dot ornament around perimeter.

137. Bone gaming counter, incised concentric circles in centre, ring/dot ornament around perimeter.

138. Perforated object (toggle ?) one end broken, other end with chop marks; neat perforation through centre.

139. Fragment of comb with two iron fixings surviving. Teeth perhaps deliberately cut back for secondary use of object (NB this item was found on the motte).

In addition to the objects listed, fragments of antler tine, exhibiting cut marks, may be the by-products of bone artefact manufacture.

The paucity of bone objects is notable. This may reflect the poor preservation of bone throughout most of the excavated contexts: except where better preserved in a pit or other discrete deposit, the animal bone from food waste was generally very eroded (see Browne, below).

Fig. 5.9: **Stone Objects**

140. Spindle whorl; soft stone, perhaps a mudstone.

141. Spindle whorl; radial lines on both upper and lower surfaces.

142. Broken spindle whorl, incomplete central perforation. From pebble surface 1111, either early castle or pre-castle.

143. Counter (?), shaped and polished to uniform dimensions.

144. Whetstone, square in section. Perforation at one end and groove in adjacent end face, presumably if in conjunction providing means of attachment to a handle or perhaps the remains of an earlier perforation.

145. Fragment of square section artefact, identification impossible.

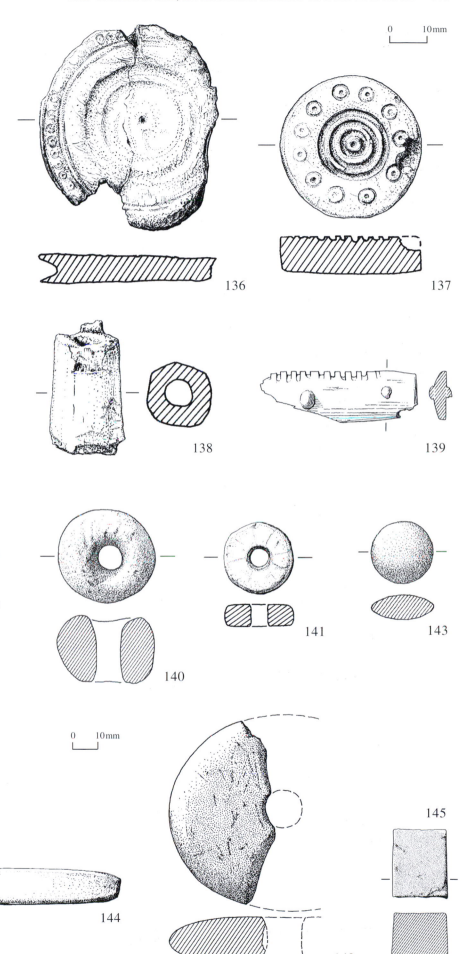

146. Incomplete vessel made from a non-local fossiliferous limestone, heavily polished externally and internally. Either a high quality domestic mortar or a vessel for liturgical use.

147. Incomplete vessel made from a coarse non-local fossiliferous limestone. The internal face shows deliberate damage in the floor of the vessel. The positions of two protruding pedestal feet are indicated by their deliberate removal (which may indicate a secondary use of the object). The rim originally had two opposing protruberances, one of which survives, aligned at a right angle to the pedestal feet. Vessels of this form have a long history as domestic mortars, but are also found as holy water stoups in churches. It is interesting therefore that the object was found in a post-hole of the possible chapel site in the north-west sector of the bailey (see Barker & Higham 1982, 38, 45).

Coin (identification by Dr J.Kent)

148. Cut halfpenny. A late issue of John or an early one of Henry III, 1215–1218. Moneyer: (RA)VF, known from several mints. Found, unstratified, near the edge of pit VII (1/27) in its filled and floored form when it was covered by building of phase Z. (Not illustrated).

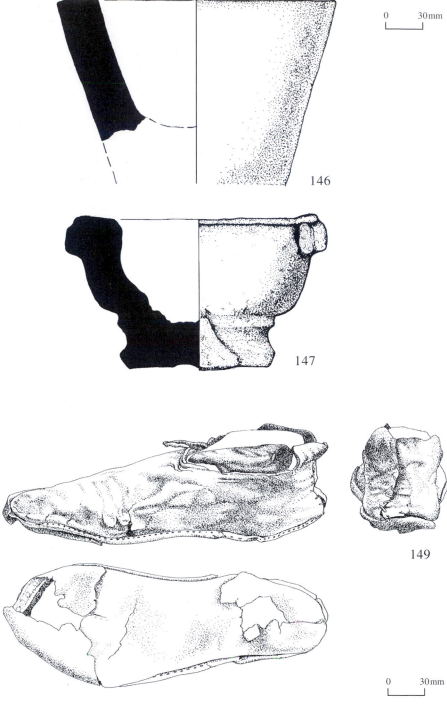

Fig. 5.10: Leather

149. Almost complete shoe, from pit 1/ 27 (see Barker & Higham 1982, 46–47).

In addition, from the same context, came leather fragments (not illustrated) including off cuts and repairs, revealing leather working within the castle.

Fig. 5.11: Worked Daub

Large quantities of clay were discovered, normally in very small pieces, which seemed to be constructional material rather than simply the boulder clay (and its derivatives) of which the site in general is composed. It was either fired, or very hard and clean, and sometimes bore imprints or was deliberately shaped in some way. Some of it may have come from clay floors or hearths, but, given the number of buildings excavated *in situ* these were not numerous. The firing of many pieces may have resulted from the burning of structures to which they belonged at, or after, their destruction. Very hard fired pieces were sometimes difficult to distinguish from fragments of Roman tile, which also occurred on the site (see below). Given the varied origin of this material, and the risk of including some which is not specifically artefactual, no attempt has been made to quantify the total recovered in excavation. Subsequent sorting, however, produced about 3kg which bore signs of working or impressions. Some of it had impressions of wattling and some had smoothed surfaces, presumably the external faces of wall-cladding. This material, in general, simply adds to the view, expressed at various points in the 1982 and present reports, that many of the buildings at Hen Domen were clay-clad and not simply timber.

150. One fragment is illustrated here, in section, from the site of Building LIV. It is of interest because (a) it is not fired and therefore must be a piece of building material in its original form, (b) it contains a very clear impression of a wattle, and (c) it contains a layer of charcoal whose even thickness may suggest it was a deliberate inclusion in the wall-cladding. Further material, which may also be burned wall-cladding has been noted in the report on the metallurgical slags (see Juleff, below).

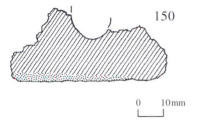

150

0   10mm

Iron Nails

In this category are included timber and horseshoe nails. They occurred as whole examples, incomplete examples and fragments which were of an appropriate size for tentative identification as one or other type of nails. But in the last category are fragments which may actually have been parts of other objects, and it is sometimes also impossible to distinguish fragments of timber nails from those of horseshoe nails. Quantification and detailed break down of this data would therefore be of limited value and has not been attempted. X-ray analysis of the material would be necessary to take study further and this was not felt justified by its intrinsic interest. Comments made here are based on visual examination only.

The overall weight recorded, of all types and fragments, was approx. 17kg, with only 2kg coming from the motte top, with its restricted area and more limited building sequence. The evidence occurred in all periods of the site, except that (as with other categories of artefact evidence) very little was associated with the earliest occupation. The weighed sample also included unstratified material, which undoubtedly includes some post-medieval examples—the site has presumably had a succession of fences and other minor structures, built by generations of farmers, since its abandonment.

The objects were scattered fairly evenly in all parts of the site excavated between 1960 and 1992. Much of the evidence, however, given the movement of clay and other deposits which must have accompanied the frequent re-buildings which excavation has demonstrated, was presumably discovered in places other than where it had been originally used. Distributional studies therefore seem inappropriate for publication, though in the early years of excavation in the north-east sector of the bailey distribution plots of this (and other types of) evidence were compiled in an attempt to maximize use of data. The motte produced a few horseshoe nails, presumably lost in the bailey and re-deposited on the motte. It seems unlikely that horses were regularly taken to the motte top given the steepness of the climb (as well as the possibility of access to the bridges through the buildings at their foot). The space in front of the buildings on the motte, where any horse must have stood, was in any case very restricted.

The occurrence of timber nails on the site is hardly surprising. Considerable quantities must have been needed in the construction of the numerous timber buildings and other, minor structures. But there was presumably also much use of timber pegs in jointing, for which the evidence has not survived (but see below, discussion of wooden objects, where pegs occur in the manufacture of a tub, and also Barker & Higham 1982, 41, where a preserved piece of bailey palisade was of pegged construction).

The appearance of horses within the castle should not surprise us, as they were a valued commodity in medieval society and would have merited protection. But we do not know whether they were corralled in the small open space in the centre of the bailey or stabled in a building in its (unexcavated) southern half. We have assumed that the bent examples are so shaped because they had been used and that straight examples are unused. If this is correct, the presence of unused examples within the bailey suggests that horses were actually shod there. We do not know where the various types of nail were manufactured. But smithying on, or very close to, the site is attested by slag evidence (see Juleff, below) and it is possible that these and other simple items were made here for immediate consumption.

In addition to repeating types identified from the motte, examples excavated in the bailey also included larger forms, some of which are listed and illustrated above.

Residual Finds

The following objects are of pre-castle origin, but were excavated in medieval contexts within the castle. None is illustrated here.

Prehistoric Flint

The following comments have been provided by Dr Linda Hurcombe.

The plano-convex knife and button scraper represent later prehistoric flintwork traditions. Another fragment is probably of mesolithic origin.

151. Small button scraper, 19mm x 17mm x 5mm, made by removing a squat flake with a thin butt and flat bulb of percussion from a core face which has been lightly trimmed. Finely flaked on the distal dorsal surface although the scars on the left dorsal surface are both more abrupt and irregular, suggesting they are due to subsequent damage. Approximately 50% of the dorsal surface is cortex. From layer 12 within large pit 1/27.

152. Small plano-convex knife, 45mm x 22mm x 6mm. The small butt is of cortex and the fine, invasive flaking on the dorsal surface has created slightly rounded sides with a distal point. The edges appear to have secondary working or edge damage in the form of small, undercut step fractures especially on the right dorsal edge. From 12/20, a post-hole in the early stages of excavation in the north-west sector.

153. Medial section of a blade with two parallel dorsal ridges. The bulb has been removed and the fractured edge abruptly re-touched, whilst the distal break is an oblique snap fracture. The two sides show abrupt retouch on the left dorsal edge and a slightly more acute and irregular touch on the right edge with a few scars on the ventral edge. From layer 3 within cistern 828.

154. Fragment of flint from a small, probably Mesolithic core, measuring 26mm x 10mm x 5mm. Best described as a longitudinally split blade with twisted profile typical of the bi-polar technique. There is some damage but no retouch. From tail of rampart clay (904).

155. Object with one worked edge, 33mm long but incomplete; perhaps part of a fabricator. From upper levels in north-west sector of bailey.

Metalwork

156. Pennanular bronze brooch. Found on rampart crest in north-east sector of bailey immediately beneath the topsoil.

157. Bronze axe. Found in north-west sector of bailey immediately beneath the topsoil.

Roman Finds

The Roman fort at Forden Gaer, to the north-west of Hen Domen, must have provided an accessible source of useful materials during the middle ages. Ploughing around (and eventually within) it would have produced a regular supply of objects, valuable either as re-cyclable raw material or as re-usable artefacts, to the medieval population of the area. Dr Valerie Maxfield has provided the following comments:

158. A total of some 10kg of fragments of Roman tile was found in various contexts throughout the bailey. In their more or less complete form these may have been useful domestic objects for the castle's occupants, providing smooth and hard working surfaces. The more complete pieces included parts of floor tiles, roof tiles and flue tiles. A possible context for their original use may have been a bath-house outside the fort.

159. Piece of worked sandstone (fragment of millstone?), found in the upper levels of the north-east sector of the bailey.

160. Two fragments of one stone mortarium, and various fragments of another, found in the upper levels of the north-west sector of the bailey.

161. Glass melon bead, found in the upper levels of the north-east sector of the bailey.

162. One roof-slate, with perforation for nail.

WOODEN OBJECTS

by Seán Goddard, Sue Rouillard; species identifications by Richard Brunning

The excavations at Hen Domen have been carried out in predominantly dry environments. It appears that most of the archaeological deposits on the site are dry, with two exceptional areas. First, where individual features in the bailey interior have reached the underlying water table, the lowest parts of their fills are waterlogged. Second, the inner ditch of the bailey defences is still waterlogged, to surface level, at the north-east and south-east corners of the site. A base timber from the earliest motte bridge, environmental evidence from a very deep pit at the western end of the bailey, and part of the bailey palisade (from the western waterlogged extremity of the northern ditch) were discussed in the earlier excavation report (Barker & Higham 1982, 41, 46–47, 51–71). During the excavation of the north-east sector of the bailey, in 1983, further sections were cut across the adjacent bailey ditch in order to increase our understanding of the castle's defences (see Chapter 3). It was also thought likely that, by locating two of these sections in the waterlogged area, interesting artefactual evidence might be recovered. In the event, this section produced several well-preserved wooden objects which are described below together with one object recovered in the 1960s (from Pit 1/27—see Barker and Higham 1982, 46–47) but not previously published.

Despite their small number, the importance of these objects is great. First, together with the items published in 1982, they give us direct glimpses of the wooden environment of the castle's occupants—an environment which otherwise we see only at one remove through the ghost evidence of post-holes and similar features. Since our overall theme has been the demonstration of a *timber* castle, it is notable (as visitors often observed) how little timber was actually to be seen during so many years of excavation. The fragments of building timber and the roofing shingle go a little way towards putting flesh on the excavated skeleton. Second, these items remind us of the archaeological potential of the, albeit limited, wet environments in the site. If the waterlogged bailey ditches to the north and south of the main entrance were to be fully excavated they might produce a very interesting array of evidence shedding light on daily life in this high-status residence. In any future, fully resourced excavation at Hen Domen, a strong case could be made for total examination of the wet ditch areas in an attempt to balance the otherwise overwhelmingly 'dry' archaeology. Third, evaluation of these objects makes us think hard about the limitations of the archaeological record. This is particularly the case with the stave-built tub. Because it is physically impressive and unique among our finds, it is tempting to regard it as a high-quality object. In one sense, it is such, because it was manufactured with great skill. On the other hand, the fact that it seems to have been discarded in the ditch, and not recovered for repair and re-use, may reveal that the occupants of Hen Domen had access to an abundant supply of quality wooden goods which are scarcely visible in the available archaeological evidence at all. Finally, the dendrochronological analysis of this tub provided unexpected data prompting a reconsideration of our assumptions about the history of the castle's defences (see Chapter 3). The tub is shown partly exposed during its excavation (fig. 7.8).

We have not described and illustrated every fragment of wood recovered from these ditches, which included many pieces of unworked tree branches and other non-artefactual material. We have included one good example of a worked stake-end, since this illuminates the many stake-holes excavated on the site. Other, unillustrated examples had been burned, suggesting old building material was used as a source of firewood.

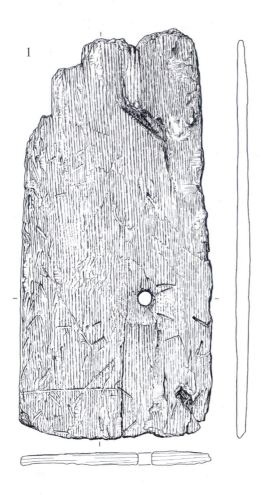

1

Note that in the accompanying illustrations, solid toning in the sections depicts wood whose structure was not identifiable and line shading depicts rays in the wood (unless specifically stated to be growth rings). All individual artefacts reproduced at 25%.

Fig. 5.12: **Wooden Objects**

1. Roof Shingle (oak). From ditch section C, context 13. Length 430mm (damage to top end), width 202mm (right edge worn), depth 14mm; single, undamaged perforation, diameter 13mm. Very straight-grained, bottom edge chamfered. Some insect damage visible.

2. Cone (beech). From ditch section C, context 13. Length 55mm, max. width 49mm, diameter at top 43mm. Shaped to a rounded point at one end, other end flat. Many small chop marks visible. Function uncertain—perhaps a bung for a wooden vessel?

2

3

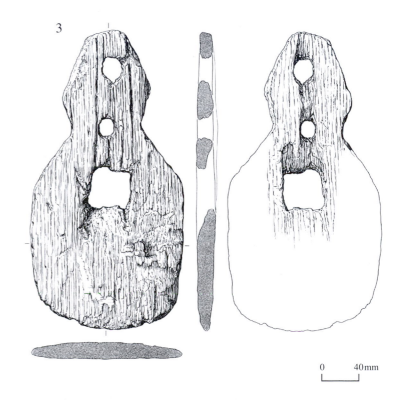

0   40mm

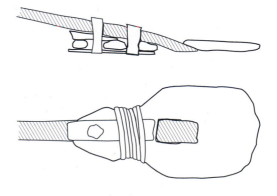

3. Shovel blade (oak). From ditch section C, context 11. Length 315mm, width 160mm, depth 18mm. Two peg holes, the less eroded 14mm diameter. Rectangular slot for shaft, surviving width 43mm. This well-preserved example conforms to the type published by Morris (1980, where ten examples from the tenth to fourteenth centuries are discussed), in which a shaft (perhaps of ash?) was inserted into the slot, pegged twice and probably bound around the narrow neck of the blade. This example, however, has a further detail: a shallow indentation on the underside of the blade which suggests that the two pegs were set into a short baton. The angle at which the shaft and blade met strongly suggests that a wedge, perhaps itself pierced by one of the pegs, would have been inserted between shaft and upper surface of the blade. There is no evidence for a metal shoe on the blade end, which, together with the sharply sloping shoulders of the blade (unsuitable for foot pressure), indicates that the implement was a shovel, for moving loose material, rather than a spade for cutting. Such an implement might have a variety of applications in agricultural, building, industrial or domestic contexts. A suggested reconstruction is illustrated. A wedge has been inserted, in this reconstruction, between the blade and haft. This is suggested by the narrow slot in the blade top and its insertion would make the implement's parts less likely to become loose during use.

4. Perforated implement (hazel). From ditch section C, context 13. Length 85mm, diameter of end 68mm, perforation diameter 30mm. This could be half a mallet head (with perforation for shaft) but the face is smooth and shows no evidence of repeated impact. Another possibility is that the perforation held one end of a wooden roller or narrow pole in an implement where rotation was required. It could also be part of a fence-rail or even a fragment of a piece of domestic furniture.

4

5. Stake end (willow). From ditch section C, context 13. Length 806mm, thickness 55mm. In two pieces. Detail of pointed end illustrated.

6. Three pieces of flat/almost flat wooden strips. From ditch section C, context 13. Perhaps building materials or parts of unidentifiable objects. Not illustrated.

   (a) Oak—in four fragments: length 178mm, width 64mm, thickness 10mm.

   (b) Oak—length 470mm, width 55mm, thickness 20mm. Top end appears to be chamfered.

   (c) Unidentified species—in four fragments: length 385mm, width 42mm, thickness 10mm. Split from a piece of roundwood. Possible peg hole (7mm diameter) at 150mm from top end.

7. Three pieces of roundwood. From ditch section C, context 13. Not illustrated.

   (a) Field maple—length 110mm, diameter 28mm. One end chopped (in three blows).

   (b) Field maple—length 86mm, diameter 20mm. Both ends chopped flat (in at least three blows).

   (c) Hazel—roundwood cut to sub-rectangular profile. Overall widths 74mm x 44mm; length 116mm. Bottom end broken, but top end shows incomplete cut (at an angle) with torn edge.

8. Five split wood pieces (species not identified). From ditch section C, context 13. Not illustrated.

   (i) Pieces (a) and (b) have pointed ends.

   (ii) Pieces (a), (b), (c) and (d) have comparable widths (30mm– 40mm).

   (iii) the section of piece (e) shows growth rings.

5

9. Stave from a small tub. From pit 1/27, context 6 in north-west quadrant of bailey (see Barker and Higham 1982, 46–47). Height 178mm, top diameter 55mm, bottom diameter 35mm. Wall thickness 5mm (top), 7mm (bottom). A small domestic vessel, perhaps for kitchen use (butter?).

0   40mm

9

10. Stave-built tub. From ditch section A, context 7.

This fine object seems to have fallen or been thrown from the bailey rampart into the ditch, where it lay on its side and was crushed partly by the initial impact and partly by the weight of subsequent deposition. It was made wholly of oak and is of stave construction, held together by four oak straps with no trace of corking or pitch. The tub, which was in very good condition and showed no signs of wear or damage before abandonment, was constructed of sixteen staves and had inwardly sloping sides. Two of the staves were longer and perforated with a hole. The estimated maximum capacity of the vessel is 15.5 galls (*c.*71 litres). Measurements are given below in metric form. But the internal base diameter and height of the tub are approx. 1ft 6in and the longer (handle) staves are approx. 2ft. This may have been how its maker construed it. For a general history of barrels, tubs and casks, to whose craft tradition this tub belongs, see Kilby 1971.

The staves were radially split, probably finished with an adze working diagonally across the grain, as wood-working marks could clearly be seen on many of the staves. Sixteen in total, the staves have an average height of 470mm (excluding the handle staves) and widths ranging from 62mm to 130mm, with, in most cases, a width taper of approx. 6mm from bottom to top. Thickness of the staves also tapers from bottom to top, with base average of 19mm and top average of 12mm. A square rebate for the base, average 11mm wide, was cut approximately 40mm from the bottom of each stave. On two of the staves (10.24 and 10.26) there are striations across the grain close to the rebate suggesting possible saw marks: the method of creating the rebate was apparently to make saw cuts first and then chisel the slot out. The staves were also chamfered inwardly on both their top and bottom edges. The two longer staves (10.1 and 10.25, at max. 600mm) had

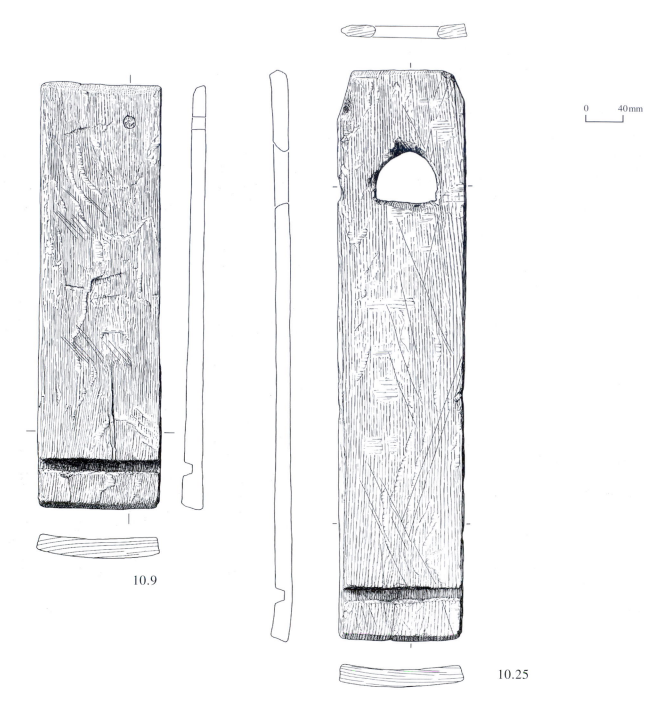

10.9

10.25

identical shaped holes, creating handles, cut into them, 53mm high by 61mm wide and worked mainly from the inner side of the tub. Similar tool marks could be seen on both and the surfaces had been well finished and smoothed. The bottoms of these handle holes lie just above the top of the tub rim. Staves 10.9 and 10.29 had identical small perforations near to their top edges. That in 10.29 was empty while that in 10.9 was filled with wood and made flush with the surface of the stave.

The base was made from two radially split pieces, butt-joined and pegged/dowelled with two pegs, as indicated in the accompanying illustration by dashed lines. It had an additional pegged batten holding the two halves together which was pegged in five places from the inside of the tub, through the base and into the batten. The exposed heads of the pegs were in extremely good condition, showing no wear or damage. The outer edge of the base was chamfered to facilitate a good fit with the staves.

The taller, handled staves (10.1 and 10.25) were positioned opposite one another in line with the batten on the underside of the base, while similarly broad staves (10.9 and 10.29) were placed at right angles to the handles and spanned the butt-join on the base. These four staves appear to have been deliberately so placed at the outset and other staves filled around them. Staves 10.9 and 10.29 each have a perforation although this does not appear to have been necessary for the construction of the vessel. Dendrochronological study has identified staves 10.9 and 10.29 as having come from the same tree yet not matching the rest of the tub staves. This suggests that timber was stored in a carpenter's work shop for re-use (Morgan, see below). Such an explanation might account for the two small perforations with no apparent function. Such broad straight-grained wood would be unlikely to have been discarded and the small holes intended for their original use could easily be filled so that the timber was suitable for the tub.

The staves, made from slow-grown, straight-grained oak, were held together by four tightly fitting straps, also made of oak (10.28). But the timber required to take the stress necessary for bending around the tub was, in contrast, fast-grown coppiced material, as indicated here by the widely spaced growth rings. The width of the annual growth rings is occasionally as little as *c*.1.4mm (in some of the later wood) but most of the pieces average approx. 4.0mm with a few up to approx. 4.8mm (in the more early growth). Each strap runs around the tub and overlaps with ends shaped to a blunt point. They were secured on the overlap by three small wooden pegs driven through holes made in the strap while the strap was held in position. Straps numbered 1 to 4 from the base up measure, including the overlap, between 1,940mm (strap 4) and 2,110mm (strap 2) in length. Their average width is 70mm and average thickness 6mm. The uppermost strap (4) runs in the opposite direction from the other three and has an additional third layer of wood 185mm long to bulk out and tighten it. The additional piece is located beneath the pegs spanning staves 26–27 and perforated to accommodate the two end pegs of the strap.

All the small wooden pegs for the straps and the base batten were carefully made and fairly uniform in size. They have square heads with corners removed with approximate dimensions of 10mm diameter and 25mm height.

This study and eventual reconstruction was made possible by careful dismantling during excavation and on-site recording. Locating the position of each strap was made possible by retaining associations of strap fragments and appropriate staves during excavation and removal. Although most of the strapping was quite fragmentary it was possible to re-assemble the pieces so that each strap, and eventually the whole tub, was reconstructed. See over page.

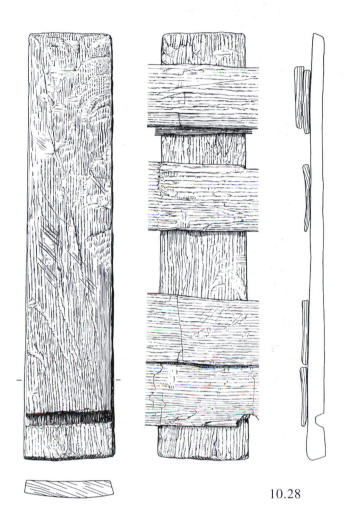

10.28

0   40mm

strap 4

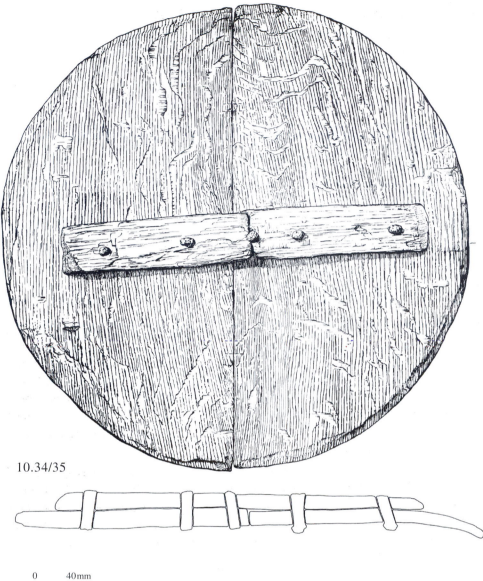

10.34/35

0　　　40mm

Tubs similar to the specimen from Hen Domen have been excavated elsewhere, for example in London where one has been published from Billingsgate (Rhodes 1980). They also appear in medieval pictorial sources. They could no doubt be put to all manner of domestic purposes—storage, carriage, washing and perhaps agricultural and industrial purposes as well. Though the circumstances of the Hen Domen discovery suggested that the tub had fallen into the ditch, the possibility must also be borne in mind that it had performed its function *in* the wet environment of the ditch.

This tub was subjected to dendrochronological analysis by Ruth Morgan (Sheffield University). The implications of the results for the chronology of the bailey defences were discussed above (Chapter 3) and the analysis itself follows.

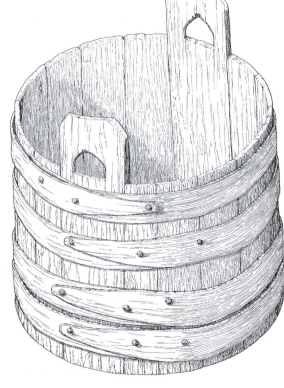

TREE-RING DATING OF THE HEN DOMEN TUB

by Ruth A. Morgan

In 1982 a stave-built tub of oak was discovered in the bailey ditch at Hen Domen, and the wood was examined in Exeter early in 1983 to assess its potential for tree-ring dating. Its position in the ditch suggested a twelfth or thirteenth-century date, but the greater accuracy available from successful tree-ring dating could be applied also to the associated contents of the ditch. However, at this early stage, it was necessary to take into consideration the possible drawbacks and disadvantages of attempting to date an object such as a tub, and to balance these against the requirements of conservation and museum display.

Tree-ring dating is based on the premise that trees growing at the same time will produce a similar pattern of wide and narrow annual rings; having built up a record of this pattern, in which each ring is allocated a calendar year, it is possible to match and date series of rings of unknown age. The method can now be applied with great success to building timber (see Baillie 1982; Hillam 1981 and 1983; Laxton *et al.* 1983 for example) because we can usually assume that the trees used were grown locally and compare the pattern with other local chronologies. There have been fewer achievements in the dating of movable objects of oak, such as furniture, the panels of paintings and the staves of barrels and tubs (only a few reports deal with these, e.g. Fletcher, 1976; Bauch *et al.* 1974), for several reasons:—

1. The source of the trees cut down to make the object is unknown. Timber was extensively imported, especially from the Baltic, and transported around the country even in early medieval times (Salzman 1952). Barrels may be made in France and imported full of wine. Such movement makes tree-ring comparisons difficult and results sometimes unexpected (e.g. Siebenlist-Kerner 1978). The geographical extent of reference chronologies varies and while good matches can be found sometimes over great distances, other chronologies from adjacent areas fail to match.

2. While wide-ringed oak was selected for building timber because of its greater strength, very narrow-ringed oak was selected for staves and panels from very aged and slow-grown trees. The wood for staves needed to be both pliable and impervious, and slow growth supplied the correct qualities (Kilby 1971). However, series of very narrow rings are not always ideal for cross-matching, owing to difficulties of resolving all the ring boundaries and the lack of year-to-year variation, or sensitivity.

3. Because of the effort involved in selecting and preparing staves and panels, they were not discarded when a barrel or other object was dismantled, but stored for future use. Thus re-use and repair were frequent, complicating interpretation of any tree-ring results.

4. The preparation and trimming of staves during manufacture was very thorough, usually removing all trace of the outer sapwood of the tree which could decay and lead to holes. However, the presence of sapwood indicates proximity to the bark of the tree and thus to the year in which it was felled; even one sapwood ring enables the felling date to be estimated to within 10–55 years (Hillam *et al.* 1987). With no trace of sapwood, an unknown amount of heartwood is lost, and the date of the last measured ring can only be regarded as a *terminus post quem*.

With all these factors in mind, it was considered worthwhile to proceed with analysis of the Hen Domen tub in the hope of dating, despite the need to saw some pieces in half. With eventual display in mind, the damage was kept to a minimum (Morgan *et al.* 1981).

Method of Analysis

Two wide planks formed the base of the tub; these and fifteen of the widest staves were transported to the dendrochronology laboratory at Sheffield University in a rigid container filled with water. In order to measure the rings, a transverse surface must be cleaned, and the two base planks, each a semi-circle, had to be sawn in half to provide a suitable edge. The staves could be examined at one end. Each piece of wood was wrapped in polythene to prevent drying out, and deep-frozen for several days; the transverse surface was then firm enough to clean with a Stanley Surform plane while the wood was supported in a vice. Thus only a few millimetres of wood need be removed from the edge to give a clear surface with every growth ring visible.

Since it was not possible to take thin sections from the tub components, the ring-widths could not be measured on the Sheffield equipment (a Bannister travelling stage linked to an Apple II micro-computer); instead a ×10 hand lens containing a 0.1mm scale was used and the ring-widths were typed on to the Apple for comparisons and the construction of mean curves.

Table 12: Tree-ring details of the Hen Domen tub staves

Stave number	No. of rings	Dimensions mm	Average ring-width mm
10/1 handle	75	130 × 20	1.77
10/2	77	90 × 15	1.23
10/5	59	100 × 13	1.79
10/8*	35	75 × 20	wide rings
10/9	110	130 × 15	1.12
10/10	58	95 × 20	1.70
10/23	60 +	85 × 20	1.41
10/24*	30	65 × 16	
10/26	48	80 × 20	1.60
10/27	64	95 × 20	1.53
10/28	60	95 × 20	1.50
10/29	125 (89 measured)	130 × 20	1.02
10/30	63	95 × 17	1.47
10/31	54	90 × 20	1.65
10/32	55	95 × 16	1.80
10/34 base	106	245 × 20	2.34
10/35 base	108	245 × 20	2.35

ring widths not measured

The ring-widths are plotted as a graph or curve clearly showing the variations and enabling cross-matching to be done by overlaying the curves and moving them along against each other until a position of good fit is found. The quality of any match can be assessed using the CROS program (Baillie & Pilcher 1973) which calculates a Student's *t* value for each position of overlap; a value in excess of 3.5 may be significant and can be checked visually.

The Tub and its Dating

The samples examined at Sheffield consisted of fifteen staves, one of which was a handle (10/1), and two base planks (10/34 and 10/35). The staves varied in width from 62mm to 130mm while the base planks were 245mm wide (table 12); thickness at the base of the staves ranged from 13mm to 20mm. The staves were 470mm long on average. The number of rings within each stave depended on the average ring-width and on stave width; only two staves had too few rings for measurement (10/08 and 10/24), while the others had between 48 and about 125 rings (stave 10/29 was cracked enabling only 89 rings to be measured). Average ring-widths were about 1.0–1.1mm for 10/9 and 10/29, about 1.5–1.8mm for the other staves and 2.3mm for the base planks (see table 12). The wood was thus wider-ringed than much oak used for barrel staves examined at Sheffield, commonly with average ring-widths below 1mm.

Visual comparison of the curves from each sample soon showed that many of the staves probably came from the same tree or at least the same source, since their ring-width patterns were almost identical.. Ten of the staves were cross-matched (fig.5.14, 10/1 to 10/26) spanning 100 years. The two base planks also provided an almost identical growth pattern over 117 years, but in view of the higher average ring-width it is thought that they originated in a different tree from that of the staves. A

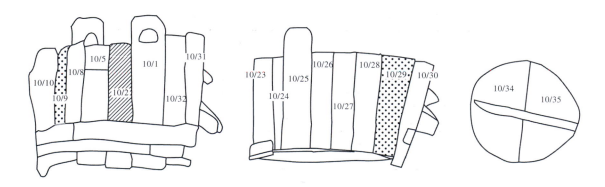

Fig. 5.13: Sketch of the Hen Domen tub. All numbered staves were examined dendrochronologically and dated, except for 10/9 and 10/29 (same tree) and 10/2

Table 13: Mean ring-width values (0.1mm) for the Hen Domen chronology, AD 931–1049; N = no. of staves involved per decade

	0	1	2	3	4	5	6	7	8	9	N
930		23	23	12	16	12	13	15	21	16	4
940	21	24	23	13	28	27	29	31	32	24	9
950	34	10	11	17	18	19	11	13	14	22	12
960	15	16	13	22	14	13	16	20	19	15	12
970	19	14	11	14	14	20	18	26	16	23	12
980	31	15	25	24	17	19	22	20	14	17	10
990	15	17	14	14	18	12	11	15	12	19	8
1000	22	14	15	19	25	18	18	15	22	17	5
1010	16	15	18	26	15	20	12	14	15	15	3
1020	16	16	24	16	7	7	6	9	11	9	3
1030	15	10	9	9	10	8	7	16	14	11	2
1040	11	13	23	18	17	17	15	14	12	12	1

faster-grown tree may have been deliberately selected to provide the qualities needed for the base of the tub.

Thus twelve curves were cross-matched into a chronology of 119 years and a mean curve was created by averaging the data (table 13). Three curves still remained to be matched, 10/2, 10/9 and 10/29, and they were then compared to the mean curve; it is often possible to slot less obvious matches into place at this second stage. However, 10/2 still showed no similarities; 10/9 and 10/29 came from the same tree and have the longest ring series, but their pattern also showed no indication of matching with the mean curve. These three staves are therefore assumed to represent either re-used pieces stored in the cooper's workshop, or replacement staves put in during a subsequent repair. Staves 10/9 and 10/29 both have holes near the top which serve no apparent function and do not occur on other staves. Subsequent attempts to find an absolute date for these staves also failed, so it is not known whether they span an earlier or later period than the tub staves themselves (fig. 5.13).

The 119-year mean curve was compared with available reference chronologies from various parts of the British Isles, initially from the west and south-west on the assumption that the tub was made locally. No confirmation could be found of the date suggested archaeologically, but as the cross-matching was extended to include the south-east, north and Ireland, a consistent date of AD 1049 emerged; Student's *t* values are given in table 14. The mean curve was thus found to span AD

Table 14: Hen Domen chronology AD 931–1049
Dating of the chronology was confirmed by consistently high student's t values when compared to various reference chronologies

reference chronology	student's t value
Dublin (Baillie 1977)	4.3
Lincoln (Laxton *et al.* pers. comm.)	5.1
REF 6 (Fletcher 1977)	4.8
Coppergate, York (Hillam pers.comm.)	5.7
British mean (Baillie & Pilcher, pers. comm.)	5.7
Carlisle (Baillie & Pilcher, pers. comm.)	4.4
Trier, Germany (Hollstein, 1980)	2.9

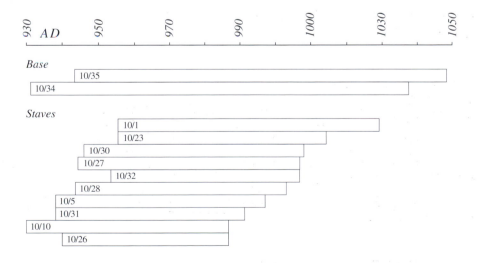

Fig. 5.14: Bar diagram showing the years spanned by the rings of each stave. None had any sapwood

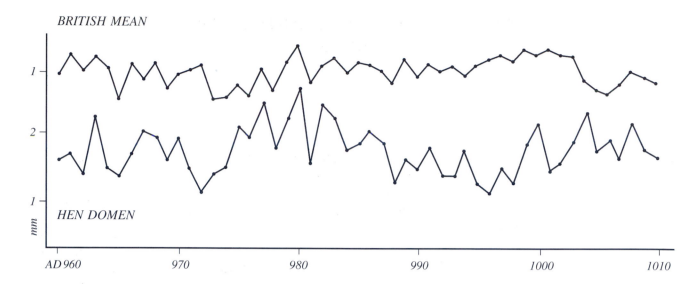

Fig. 5.15: Part of the Hen Domen ring width curve compared to the British mean curve between AD 960 and 1010. The latter has been converted to indices

931 to 1049. The highest *t* values are geographically widespread, the maximum of 5.7 being with a composite chronology for the entire British Isles (fig. 5.15). There is no indication in the matches of the origin of the trees used to make the tub, other than that they are British; no chronologies for the Hen Domen area extend back as far as the eleventh century.

No trace of sapwood was found on the staves, so it is impossible to give a close estimate of when the trees were felled and the tub made. Allowance must be made for 10–55 sapwood rings and an unknown amount of lost heartwood, as well as a few years' seasoning before use. So felling must have taken place at some time during or after AD 1059–1104. The tub was possibly in use in the last years of the eleventh century or the early twelfth century, but equally the staves could have originated from the inner wood of a tree felled later.

Discussion

Stave-built buckets and tubs have a long tradition going back at least to the Iron Age, but are found infrequently enough to merit careful recording of all their features, in particular the wood species used, size and capacity, and the method of construction. The Hen Domen tub is two-handled and held together by at least four oak straps; its capacity is estimated to be about 71 litres or 15.5 gallons (Seán Goddard, Exeter University, pers. comm). As such, it resembles the dolly tub in size, and might have been used for a variety of purposes, both domestic (washing) or industrial (brewing, cheese-making, dyeing, etc.).

Even if tree-ring dating can only give a *terminus post quem* to well-trimmed staves of oak, the value of recording ring-width patterns is worth the effort. The main potential lies in ascertaining similarities in pattern which may indicate the source of the trees used by the cooper in making the tub, and in showing which staves are original and which represent repairs. The more tubs and barrels that can be examined, the more informative the dendrochronologist can be.

Acknowledgement: this work was carried out in the HBMC Dendrochronology Laboratory at Sheffield University.

METALLURGICAL SLAGS AND OTHER DEBRIS
by Dr Gill Juleff

The excavations in and around the bailey at Hen Domen yielded a small quantity of metallurgical slags and other finds identified as possible industrial debris. This body of material was assessed with the aim of determining what activities relating to metal production and processing were operating on the site and whether the slags warranted further detailed investigation.

The Material

The assemblage examined, comprising 125 separately recorded bags of material, represents the total sample of industrial debris retrieved from the excavations. The largest component of the assemblage (tables 15 and 16) derives from within the bailey. These excavated contexts cover approx. 50% of the area of the bailey. The remainder of the material was retrieved from a single context, the fill of cutting E, which relates to an 'extra' earthwork outside the bailey to the north-east of the site (table 17). Two further slags were recovered, one from a narrow section extended outside the northern defences and the other from cutting A, between the inner and outer ramparts (table 15). Reference should be made to figs 0.2 and 3.17 for the location of these cuttings.

Examination Procedure

As this exercise was intended as a general assessment, not a detailed investigation, the principal technique used was visual examination. Artefacts were first identified as either slags (metallurgical slags and debris associated with metallurgical processes) or non-slags (material perhaps of unknown origin but not derived from metallurgical processes). These two groups were then examined and recorded separately, except where slags and non-slags occurred together in the same finds bag, in which instance all the material was recorded with the slags. In the case of the slags, the degree of completeness of each individual find was recorded, as well as its weight, overall dimensions and morphological characteristics, including shape and density. These details, along with more precise identifications of the type of slag, are given in tables 15 and 17. The non-slags recorded in table 16 were not weighed or measured.

Slags and Non-slags from Contexts within the Bailey (tables 15 and 16)

Although thirty-one separate slag finds were recorded the total weight of slag from within the bailey is only 4 kg. This, combined with the fact that the majority occur as fragments, with only eight finds being complete, and that the material was sparsely distributed over a wide area with no localized concentrations evident, suggests that most of it had been redeposited. The worn surfaces of many of the fragments also supports the likelihood of redeposition. Although a hard, dense material, slag is also brittle and easily fractured, particularly when exposed to physical trampling. The degree of wear of many of the fragments might indicate that they had been incorporated at some time in material used to fill pathways.

Despite the probable secondary nature of the deposition of these slags, the majority of them appeared to be smithing slags of consistent quality. The more complete forms include plano-convex cakes of varying sizes, some with charcoal impressions in their surfaces. The sample could be regarded as 'background noise' to be expected on a settlement site, given that iron smithing for the manufacture and repair of iron tools was a common activity. The consistent quality of the slag may indicate that it derived from a single smithy but the location of a smithy within the bailey is not indicated by any depositional concentration (see below).

The material of the non-slags from within the bailey (table 16) could not be positively identified by visual examination alone. The discoloration and fragmentary condition of the material suggests it has undergone some alteration, possibly through intense heating. One possible interpretation is that it represents a building material which has been subjected to high-temperature destruction burning. The relatively large quantity of this material suggests it warrants further investigation and explanation. Other material of relevance is commented on under 'worked daub' (see above). It is notable that virtually all the material listed here came from the uppermost archaeological layer beneath the turf-topsoil in the north-east quadrant of the bailey. If it is derived from building material (clay wall-cladding?) it may have come from the structures described in this and other reports as phase Z.

Table 15: Slags from contexts within the bailey

Year	Grid	Con	No	Ind	Id	Comp	Wt (g)	Diam (cm)	Depth (cm)	Notes
HD 75	G 42/47	F828	1		slag	comp	1000	14×11.5	6	smi. cake
HD 71	G 53		2	1	slag	comp	100	8×6	3	smi. cake, worn surface, pl-c
				2	slag	frag	<25	3	1	smi. slag
	G 59	L1/2	2	1(x3) 2	slag	comp	250	8	3.5	pl-c smi. cake w. poss. hearth wall attachment, good example org/inorg?
				2	non-slag	frag				
HD 76	G 60		1		slag	comp	400	11×10	5	smi. cake, pl-c irregular shape, worn?
	G 62	II	1		slag	comp	250	10×8	3.5	pl-c smi. cake, ovoid, charcoal imp. on upper surface, worn
HD 86	northern defences		1		slag	comp	850	11	4.5	pl-c smi. cake, good example, not worn
HD 82	ditch 1	2	1		slag	comp/frag	350	9	4.5	large smi. cake frag, pl-c, vitri. on upper surface
HD 70	G 46a	L 1/2	2	1	slag	comp?	100	9.5×7	2.5	smi. cake, irregular shape
				2	slag	frag	<5	1.5	1	smi. slag
HD 80	F 828	7	1		slag	frag	<25	3	1	vitri., non-diagnostic
HD ?	G 14	I	1		slag	frag	100	6	2.5	smi. slag?, upper surface v. smooth
	G 47		2	1	slag	frag	<5	1.5	1	smi. slag ?
				2	Fe	frag	<5	1.5	1	non-magnetic
HD 70	G 5	15a	1		slag	frag	<5			slag/vitri., v. small, non-diagnostic
HD 70	G 52a	L 1/2	6	1	slag	frag	<10	3	2	smi. slag?, w. vitri., poss. org/inorg? coated w. slag org/inorg?
				5	non-slag	frag				
HD 71	G 53	II i 8	1		slag	frag	25	5×4	1.5	smi. cake frag, pl-c, worn surface
HD 76	G 55		1		slag	frag	100	4	4	smi. cake frag, newly fractured but worn surface
HD 73	G 56	3	1		slag	frag	<25	3×2	2	smi. slag, worn surface
HD 70	G 59a	L1/2	1		slag	frag	<10	2	1	smi. slag, worn surface
	G 60		2	1	slag	frag	25	3	2	smi. slag, v. worn, redepos
				2	slag	frag	25	3	2	*as above*
	G 60		1		slag	frag	100	7×5	2.5	smi. cake frag, v. worn surface, pl-c
HD 74	G 60	III	1		slag	frag	<25	5	2	smi. slag, worn surface
HD 74	G 60	III	1		slag	frag	<5	0.5	0.5	vitri. dribble, non-diagnostic
HD 75	G 61	III	3	1	slag	frag	25	5	3.5	smi. slag w. vitri.
				2	slag	frag	<10	1	1	glassy, poss. hearth lining
				3	slag	frag	<5	<1	<1	dribble, non-diagnostic
HD 76	G 62	F 766	1		slag	frag	100	6×4	2	smi. slag, worn surface
HD 75	G 64	F 838	1		slag	frag	<10	2	1	glassy, poss. hearth lining
HD 72	G 66	2	1		slag	frag	25	4	2.5	small smi. cake frag, worn surface
HD 76	G 70		1		slag	frag	100	6	2.5	smi. cake frag, worn, magnetic, dense
HD 71	G 48	II 1	1		Pb	frag				corroded lead
HD 76	G 63		multi		Pb	frag	250			v. corroded frag of Pb, no form, ex-artifact?
HD 75	G 59	II	3	1-3	Fe	frag	<1	<1	0.5	min. Fe, poss. ex-artifact

Total entries			37				4,345g	
Total slag			31				4,090g	
		slag entries = comp				8		
		slag entries = frag				23		

Notes and abbreviations

Year	from bag label	Fe	iron	min.	mineralised
Grid	from bag label	Pb	lead	org/inorg?	organic or inorganic
Con	context, from bag label	non-slag	not metallurgical slag	poss.	possibly
No	number of artifacts	frag	fragment	redepos.	redeposited
Ind	individual artifact	comp	complete	surf.	surface
Id	identification	smi.	smithing	vitri.	vitrification/vitrified, glass formation
Comp	degree of completeness	pl-c	plano-convex		
Wt	weight (g)	c-c	convex-convex	v.	very
Diam	diameter (cm)	dest.	destruction	w.	with
Depth	thickness (cm)	imp.	impressions		

Table 16: Non-slags from contexts within the bailey

Year	Grid	Con	No	ID	Comp.	Wt	Diam	Depth	Notes
HD 70	G 40a/b	L 1/2	5	non-slag	frag				org/inorg?, low density, laminar structure, siliceous, occ. surf. vitri., black-grey-orange-yellow, bitumen dest. burning?
	G 40c	L 1/2	1	non-slag	frag				org/inorg?
	G 40d	L 1/2	4+	non-slag	frag				org/inorg?
	G 41a/b	L 1/2	4	non-slag	frag				org/inorg?
	G 41d	L 1/2	1	non-slag	frag				org/inorg?
	G 42a/b	L 1/2	3	non-slag	frag				org/inorg?
	G 43b	L 1/2	2	non-slag	frag				org/inorg?
HD 70	G 46a	L 1/2	3	non-slag	frag				org/inorg?
HD 70	G 46b	L 1/2	2	non-slag	frag				org/inorg?
HD 70	G 46c	L 1/2	3	non-slag	frag				org/inorg?
HD 70	G 46d	L 1/2	6+	non-slag	frag				org/inorg?
HD 70	G 47b	L 1/2	2	non-slag	frag				org/inorg?
HD 70	G 47c	L 1/2	8	non-slag	frag				org/inorg?
HD 70	G 47d	L 1/2	5	non-slag	frag				org/inorg?
HD 70	G 48a	L 1/2	4	non-slag	frag				org/inorg?
HD 70	G 48b	L 1/2	2	non-slag	frag				org/inorg?
HD 70	G 48c	L 1/2	7	non-slag	frag				org/inorg?
HD 70	G 49a	L 1/2	6+	non-slag	frag				org/inorg?
HD 70	G 49b	L 1/2	9+	non-slag	frag				org/inorg?
HD 70	G 49d	L 1/2	3	non-slag	frag				org/inorg?
HD 70	G 50c	L 1/2	1	non-slag	frag				org/inorg?
HD 70	G 52b	L 1/2	8	non-slag	frag				org/inorg?
HD 70	G 52c	L 1/2	2	non-slag	frag				org/inorg?
HD 70	G 53b	L 1/2	8+	non-slag	frag				org/inorg?
HD 70	G 53d	L 1/2	3	non-slag	frag				org/inorg?
HD 70	G 54a	L 1/2	11+	non-slag	frag				org/inorg?
HD 70	G 54b	L 1/2	1	non-slag	frag				org/inorg?
HD 70	G 54c	L 1/2	2	non-slag	frag				org/inorg?
HD 70	G 54d	L 1/2	7+	non-slag	frag				org/inorg?
HD 70	G 55a	L 1/2	1	non-slag	frag				org/inorg?
HD 70	G 55d	L 1/2	1	non-slag	frag				org/inorg?
HD 70	G 56a	L 1/2	1	non-slag	frag				org/inorg?
HD 70	G 56b	L 1/2	9+	non-slag	frag				org/inorg?
HD 70	G 56c	L 1/2	1	non-slag	frag				org/inorg?
HD 70	G 56d	L 1/2	7+	non-slag	frag				org/inorg?
HD 70	G 58a	L 1/2	2	non-slag	frag				org/inorg?
HD 70	G 58b	L 1/2	1	non-slag	frag				org/inorg?
HD 70	G 58d	L 1/2	1	non-slag	frag				org/inorg?
HD 70	G 59b	L 1/2	1	non-slag	frag				org/inorg?
HD 70	G 59b	L 1/2	2	non-slag	frag				org/inorg?
HD 70	G 59c	L 1/2	3	non-slag	frag				org/inorg?
HD 70	G 60a	L 1/2	9+	non-slag	frag				org/inorg?
HD 70	G 60b	L 1/2	5+	non-slag	frag				org/inorg?
HD 70	G 60c	L 1/2	4	non-slag	frag				org/inorg?
HD 70	G 60d	L 1/2	3	non-slag	frag				org/inorg?
HD 70	G 61a	L 1/2	1	non-slag	frag				org/inorg?
HD 70	G 61d	L 1/2	6+	non-slag	frag				org/inorg?
HD 70	G 62a	L 1/2	6+	non-slag	frag				org/inorg?
HD 70	G 62b	L 1/2	2	non-slag	frag				org/inorg?
HD 70	G 62c	L 1/2	4	non-slag	frag				org/inorg?
HD 70	G 62d	L 1/2	2	non-slag	frag				org/inorg?
HD 70	G 63	L 1/2	3	non-slag	frag				org/inorg?
HD 70	G 64	L 1/2	2	non-slag	frag				org/inorg?
HD 70	G 65	I	2	non-slag	frag				org/inorg?
HD 70	G 65b	L 1/2	6	non-slag	frag				org/inorg?
HD 70	G 68a	L 1/2	2	non-slag	frag				org/inorg?
HD 70	G 71	L 1/2	1	non-slag	frag				org/inorg?
HD 70	G67b	L 1/2	2	non-slag	frag				org/inorg?
HD 70	G 67a	L 1/2	1	non-slag	frag				org/inorg?, poss. hearth lining
HD 76	G 42	F 1020	1	non-slag	frag				burnt daub?
HD 73	G 48	3	1	non-slag	frag	<5	2	1	poss. burnt mortar?
HD 76	G 42	F 1019	1	non-slag	frag	<10	4	1.5	Fe, poss. ex-artifact
HD 77		F1057/1	4+	geological	frag	<5			small stone, Fe staining
HD 77	G 55	III	1	geological?	frag	<10			poss. ex-artifact or Fe nodule
HD 70	G 56c	1/2	1	geological	frag				small stone, Fe staining

| *Total entries* | | | 64 | | | | | | |

Slags from Cutting E (table 17)

In contrast to the fragmented nature and sparse distribution of the slags from within the bailey, the completeness and concentrated occurrence of the slags from the ditch in cutting E indicates primary deposition, probably in close proximity with an operational smithy. Of a total of twenty-four finds, twenty are complete and only four are fragmented. In this case the total weight of the sample, which derives from a single context, is almost 7kg.

The slags of this group fall into two types. The first type consists of relatively dense, heterogeneous slags typical of smithing. While these slags vary in size and shape, many tend to be sub-conical or wedge-shaped, rather than the more common plano-convex shape of the slags such as those from within the bailey. Many have small stones adhering to their outer surfaces, suggesting that they may have been discarded while they were still warm and slightly soft. However, none of the slags have been washed and the adhering material may not be associated.

The second type comprises lightweight, low density slags which are glassy in texture. These slags vary in shape in the same manner as the first type, indicating that they were also formed in smithing-hearth operations, but their texture suggests that they may relate to practices using higher temperatures or the use of particular fluxes or perhaps different starting materials, e.g. bloomery iron smelted under special conditions. This variation in slag type could be interpreted as indicating a well-established smithy where a range of operations were carried out.

Table 17: Slags from Cutting E

Con	Ind	Id	Comp	Wt (g)	Diam (cm)	Depth (cm)	Notes
Ditch 3	1	slag	comp	1000	16.5×13.5	7.5	smi. cake, c-c w. comp edges, w/o charcoal imp., w. small stones adhering to unwashed surface, poss. discarded when warm?
	2	slag	comp	750	11×9	6.5	smi. cake, pl-c w. slight side protrusions, texture as for 1
	3	slag	comp?	500	12.5	6	smi. cake, irregular shape w. convex bottom, upper surface vitrified and smooth
	4	slag	comp	500	12×9	7	smi. cake, pl-c, slag texture as for 3 fluid and glassy, low density
	5	slag	comp	300	10.5×8.5	6.5	smi. cake, c-c, low density, some charcoal imp. and adhering small stones
	6	slag	comp	400	10×9	5.5	smi. cake, pl-c in section otherwise irregular, texture as for 1, dense
	7	slag	comp	400	11	7.5	smi. cake?, v. irregular shape, 'fingers' of fluid slag, low density, charcoal imp., adhering grey clay, poss. hearth lining
	8	slag	comp?	350	10×6	3	smi. cake, charcoal imp., dense
	9	slag	comp?	400	11×6.5	3.5	half smi. cake, pl-c, dense
	10	slag	comp	250	7	2.5	small smi. cake, charcoal imp., upper surface vitrified, glassy texture, low density
	11	slag	comp?	250	12×8	4	smi. cake?, irregular shape, v. glassy and fluid, low density, vesicular, charcoal imp. adhering grey clay, poss. hearth lining
	12	slag	comp?	250	10	4	smi. cake?, irregular shape, texture and density as for 11, upper surface glassy, lower surface dense, quartz inclusions
	13	slag	comp?	100	10×5.5	2.5	smi. cake?, irregular shape, texture as for 11, quartz inclusions
	14	slag	comp	14-24 total wt 1500	7×4.5	3.5	smi. cake, irregular wedge-shape, charcoal imp., dense
	15	slag	comp		6	2	smi. cake, concave-convex, smooth upper surface, dense
	16	slag	comp		6×4.5	1.5	smi. cake, irregular shape, dense
	17	slag	comp		5	4	smi. cake, irregular shape, dense
	18	slag	comp		9×4.5	4	smi. cake, wedge-shaped, dense
	19	slag	comp		8×6	4	smi. cake, irregular shape, dense
	20	slag	comp		8×6	3.5	smi. cake, wedge-shaped, glassy texture, low density
	21	slag	frag		7.5	2.5	quarter smi. cake, pl-c, dense
	22	slag	frag		4×3	2	smi. cake, irregular shape, dense
	23	slag	frag		7×4.5	2.5	hearth lining, external surface vitri., v. lightweight, vitri. depth 1.5cm, clay has fine texture and orange-yellow oxidised colour
	24	slag	frag		5.5	1.5	hearth lining/smi. cake?, irregular shape, charcoal imp., glassy texture, low density

Total weight			6,950g		
Total entries = comp	20				
Total entries = frag	4				

Total weight of slag, 5.15 and 5.17	11,040g

Comments

The total slag sample from the excavations is approximately 11kg. This is not an especially large sample and over a third of it derives from secondary deposition. However, the overall assemblage, including the primary deposit of intact smithing slags from cutting E, does indicate that iron smithing was taking place at the site. The sample from within the bailey is too fragmentary and sparsely distributed to warrant further investigation. The sample from cutting E represents a coherent body of material which would be worthy of further detailed examination as part of an investigation into the technological practices of the medieval period. None of the slags examined indicate that smelting was carried out at the site and it can be assumed that smelted iron was being imported onto the site from elsewhere.

THE ANIMAL BONES
by Sue Browne

The Material

The subject of this report is 3,306 fragments of mammal, bird and fish bone, and a more or less complete pig skeleton, from selected contexts excavated at Hen Domen between 1961 and 1985. The bone comes from the bailey ditches; the motte ditch; the excavation on the side of the motte which revealed the bridges; and, inside the bailey, the buried soil pre-dating the construction of the castle (context 1083), the possible cistern (containing context 828) behind the rampart, the large pit (context 1/27) at the west end of the bailey and a very small and shallow pit (1272—not illustrated in the structural plans published in this report) on the rampart. Apart from a few fragments recovered from the buried soil, all the bone was deposited during the period of the castle's life, i.e. between the eleventh and the thirteenth centuries.

Most of the bone was retrieved and sorted by hand, but layers 9–18 of the deep pit (context 1/27) were wet-sieved. The bone from these layers includes some bird species not present in the rest of the assemblage, and the only fish bone, but it is uncertain whether this is due entirely to the different methods of recovery as it is likely that differential survival in the lower (waterlogged) layers of the pit is also a factor, especially as it is possible that the fill accumulated fairly rapidly (see below). Furthermore, the precise function of this pit is not known and it may be that different patterns of deposition are involved as well. Other environmental evidence from this pit has already been published (Barker & Higham 1982, 60–71). The recovery rate in the hand-dug samples seems to be reasonably high as they contain small elements such as petrous temporal bones and unfused epiphyses.

On the whole, the bone from the contexts selected for examination is very well preserved (unlike the bone from the many layers within the bailey generally, which was not), although much fragmented by butchering activities. A few fragments are burnt and many have been chewed by carnivores. Some bones from the bailey ditches, the motte ditch and pit 1/27 are eroded or a paler colour than the rest—probably the depositional history of these fragments differs slightly from that of the rest of the bone. There is considerable variation in the colour and degree of preservation of a small group of unstratified bones from pit 1/27, suggesting that at least some of

them are derived from a variety of sources, and this group, although included in the overall totals, is excluded from the more detailed analysis of the pit assemblage. The pig skeleton from context 1272 is friable and shows much recent damage.

The Analyses

All the bone submitted is listed in table 18, from which it can be seen that 86% of the total came from one pit (context 1/27). Because the functions of this pit and of the suggested cistern (context 828) are, strictly, uncertain and it is not known to what extent the bones deposited in these contexts are typical of the food remains from the site as a whole, the total for each of the selected contexts is shown separately. Inevitably the overall results for the selected contexts are biased by the presence of such a large amount of bone from one context. The original intention was to compare and contrast the samples from (a) the bailey ditches, (b) the possible cistern (context 828) and (c) the large pit (context 1/27), but in the event only the sample from the pit is large enough to warrant detailed analysis. However, at least part of all three assemblages may well have been deposited contemporaneously. The sample from the ditches was probably deposited between the eleventh and the thirteenth centuries, context 828 is eleventh to twelfth-century in date, and pit 1/27 was dug and used in the mid to later periods of the castle's life. No meaningful chronological distinctions can therefore be made between the materials studied.

The Methods

The bone was identified using reference material in the writer's possession and tentative identifications were checked at the Natural History Museum. I am grateful to Mr Graham Cowles (Department of Ornithology, Tring) and Dr Juliet Jewell (Department of Zoology, London) for allowing me to use the Collections in their care and for helpful discussion as well.

Undiagnostic fragments of mammal bone are grouped according to their size and a distinction is made between '*Bos*/horse-sized' bones, which may include bones from large deer, and bones which are from either *Bos* or large deer ('B/D') but not from horse. Because the total number of horse bones is very low (see table 18), bones in the '*Bos*/horse-sized' group are perhaps more likely

Table 18: Hen Domen bone fragment count

Taxon/size	Bailey ditches	Motte ditch	F1083	Cistern F828	Pit F1/27	u/s F1/27	Pit F1272	Total*
Bos	33	6	2	19	103	15		178
BHs	13	10		6	285	45		359
B/D		3		1	36	9		49
Horse	8	1			8	3		20
Pig	35	10	7	4	525	38	skeleton	619
Ps		1			146	13		160
Sheep/Goat	8				6			14
Sh/Gs	2	3		3	165	10		183
Dog	16				4			20
Cat	2			1		1		4
Red deer		1			27	6		34
Rs					1			1
Roe deer	3	1		1	23	3		31
Hare					6	1		7
Squirrel					1			1
Fowl	2	1			20			23
Fs		1			47	1		49
Goose	2				8			10
Gs					35			35
Other/b					33			33
Indet./m	1				22	2		25
Indet./b					10	2		12
Indet./f					1			1
Unid.	55	19	9	152	1156	47+		1438
Total	180	57	18	187	2668	196	skeleton	3306

* total not counting pig skeleton

The unidentified total from unstratified deposits in pit 1/27 does not include many minute crumbs and splinters of bone.

Key

BHs	Bos/horse-sized		Fs	Fowl-sized
B/D	Bos or deer		Gs	Goose-sized
Ps	Pig-sized		/m	mammal
Sh/Gs	Sheep/Goat-sized		/b	bird
Rs	Red deer-sized		/f	fish

to be from cattle (or large deer) than from horse. Similarly, the scarcity of certainly-identified sheep/goat bones suggests that at least some of the 'sheep/goat-sized' bones are from roe deer. It is also possible that the 'pig-sized' group includes a few deer bones. Undiagnostic fragments of bird bone are recorded in a similar way. Most of the fowl bones from this site are from small birds approximately the same size as pheasant (from which species a single bone was identified), and chicken-like bones which are incomplete and lack diagnostic features enabling them to be distinguished certainly from pheasant are recorded as 'fowl-sized', although probably most of them are indeed from fowl. Bones in the 'goose-sized' category are all within the size range for greylag goose (*Anser anser*) and are likely to be from this species (if they are from goose).

The bone is quantified numerically for all the selected contexts and as representing a minimum number of individuals from pit 1/27. The minimum number of individuals present has not been calculated for the whole assemblage at this stage.

Age estimation is based on data published by Grant (1982) and Silver (1969). Skeletal maturation in animals of Norman date may not have occurred at precisely the same age as it does in present-day animals and any reference to the chronological age of an animal is intended as a guideline only.

Measurements were taken following the method outlined by von den Driesch (1976) and are listed in table 25.

Domestic/Wild Ratio

In all, 1,821 fragments were identified to species level or placed in one of the size categories mentioned above. A large proportion of the assemblage is small, undiagnostic fragments of chopped-up long-bone shafts and this is reflected in the low identification rate (56%). The calculation of the relative proportions of the remains of domestic and wild animals is complicated by the presence of many fragments which cannot be assigned with certainty to either. Alternative figures, counting all the *Bos*/deer bones as (a) cattle and (b) large deer, all the sheep/goat-sized bones as (a) sheep/goat and (b) roe deer, and all the goose bones of greylag size as from (a) domestic and (b) wild birds, are shown in table 19. How many of the *Bos*/horse-sized bones are from large deer is unknown. All the pig remains are thought to be from domestic animals—no measurable bone (or tooth) is large enough to be from wild pig and although the mandibular canine teeth of the (male) pig skeleton from context 1272 are very large, the dimensions of the third molars are well below the range for wild boar. The goshawk bones are counted with the wild species although this bird may have been kept in captivity (see below). Probably the real proportion of the remains of domestic animals in the assemblage is between 79% and 94%.

Table 19: Alternative figures for the frequency of domestic taxa in the mammal and bird bone, counting the Bos/deer and sheep/ goat-sized bones as a) all cattle or sheep/goat and b) all deer; the fowl-sized bones as fowl; and the goose-sized bones as goose and as a) all domestic and b) all wild, except for those too large to be from wild Anser anser. The bone from F1083 is excluded.

Number of fragments

		Domestic	Wild
Mammals			
	a)	1597	74
	b)	1365	306
Birds			
	a)	117	33
	b)	85	65
Total (n = 1821)			
	a)1714 (94.1%)	107	
	b)1450 (79.6%)	371	

Species Representation

The bones of pig predominate in the assemblage (see table 18), followed by the remains of cattle. Deer bones are more numerous than the remains of the other domestic species and sheep/goat bones are remarkably sparse (over twice as many roe deer bones were identified). The remains of domestic fowl are more plentiful than the remains of goose, and the goshawk bones are probably the partial skeleton of a single bird. Horse bones are rare in the assemblage, a few bones from dog and cat were recovered, and the presence of rodents is indicated by their tooth marks on some of the bones. Some bones from small wild mammals and wild birds, and a single fish bone, were recovered from pit 1/27.

Butchery and Other Activities

The favourable burial conditions have preserved many of the chopped bones in 'fresh' condition. Numerous clean, unsplintered edges were seen bearing a sheen left on them by the metal implement with which they were cut. Most of the dissection and dismemberment of the carcases appears to have been carried out with bladed implements, but saw marks are clearly visible on a long-bone shaft fragment of *Bos*/horse size (which also has a straight-edged cut through the thickness of the cortex, indicating the use of a heavy blade).

Chop and cut marks were seen on 12.7% of the bone from the six large to medium-sized mammals or from one of the four size categories for undiagnostic fragments of mammal bone. This rather low overall percentage conceals considerable variation between species, since 27.5% of the cattle bones are chopped but only 4.8% of the pig bones. However, many of the pig bones have been chewed by carnivores, and perhaps their activities have destroyed some of the butchery evidence on the slightly less well preserved bones of this species. Most frequently, slanting chop marks were recorded on long-bone shafts, which have often been reduced to very small fragments. Joints which have been severed (in cattle, horse, pig and red deer) include the elbow (distal humerus and proximal radio-ulna) and the hock (astragalus and calcaneum). Pelves which have been chopped through the pubis (cattle, pig and red deer) or through the ilium (cattle) and cut edges seen on the femur in the region of the greater trochanter (cattle, horse and pig) are probably connected with the separation of the hind limbs from the rest of the carcase. Vertebrae are chopped longitudinally to one side of the median line (in the thoracic vertebra, through the costal articulations) or at right angles to the long axis. Ribs of all sizes are chopped across the long axis or through the articulation. Some cranial fragments from pig have cut edges just in front of the maxillary premolars or along the sagittal line and a bovine mandible has been severed from the ramus immediately behind the third molar. Only one bird bone, a fowl-sized tibiotarsus with a few shallow cut marks on the distal end of the shaft just above the articulation with the meatless tarso-metatarsus, bears knife marks.

Part of a bovine cranium, including portions of the frontal and temporal bones, is chopped through just in front of the horn core and there is a cluster of small and shallow cut marks on the surface of the bone in the region of the chopped edge, possibly connected with removal of the horn for use by a horn-worker. (No horn cores were recovered from the selected contexts.) The distal end of a dog humerus from pit 1/27 has been chopped off and there is a line of short, parallel cut marks on the posterior aspect of the shaft just above the chopped edge.

A small, oval sliver of bone has been removed from the shaft of a cat femur, also from pit 1/27. In both cases, these cuts may have been made during removal of the skin. A few pieces of 'worked' bone and antler were recovered. A roe deer tine cut from the beam has been whittled away all round just above the tip, making it into a long, slender point and the lowest tine has been sliced off part of a roe deer antler (in which one tine has failed to develop normally). The tip of a tine cut from an antler of red-deer size has the marks of a saw with rather irregular teeth on the cut surface and is smooth and polished at the tip. A bovine radius shaft fragment (unfused distally) from pit 1/27 has V-shaped notches cut out of it which are reminiscent of Romano-British and Iron Age artefacts from Oving (Browne 1985, 238) and Danebury (Cunliffe & Poole 1991, 354–7) but there is no aspect of this bone which distinguishes it as being residual.

Gnawing by Other Animals

The marks of gnawing by carnivores were seen on 19.1% of the bone from the large and medium-sized mammals. Dogs were present on the site and, if they were allowed to roam freely, were probably responsible for most of the chewing (also, bones may have been fed to them deliberately). But wild carnivores (foxes and wolves) may have been attracted, too, by the smell of the bone waste in the ditches. The destructive action of these animals cannot be quantified but probably many of the missing articular ends of long-bones—and indeed many bones—have been consumed (or carried off) by them. A few bird bones appear to have been chewed by a smaller carnivore, perhaps a cat, and a few bones have been gnawed by rodents.

Pathology

There is no skeletal evidence of serious disease in any of the animals represented by the bones from the selected contexts. A few bones were recovered (all from pit 1/27) showing minor pathological conditions - healed fractures in two ribs, infection or inflammation in leg and foot bones from pig and oral disease in a pig mandible in which the first and second molars are worn down to the roots and there is periodontal disease around the exposed roots of the first molar, which is probably in the process of being lost.

The Assemblage from Pit 1/27

Because it was decided (for the reasons mentioned above) to regard the bone from the different contexts as separate assemblages, and because only pit 1/27 yielded a sufficiently large sample to justify a detailed examination, the rest of this report concentrates on the assemblage from this pit, although much of what follows applies also to the bone from the other selected contexts.

If the bone from another context provides additional information, it is discussed below under the relevant heading. Details of the bone recovered from each layer in pit 1/27 are shown in table 20.

Minimum Number of Individuals

The minimum number of individuals represented by the bone from the pit is shown in table 21. The remains of many more pigs than cattle were recovered but the figure for pigs includes eight very young piglets and as one ox provides about as much meat as three to four pigs, the weight of meat represented by the bones of the two species is approximately equal.

Skeletal Representation

The number of different anatomical elements from the large and medium-sized mammals is shown in table 22. Bones of the head and feet from all six species are present and fragments of pig jaws are numerous, possibly a deposit of butchering waste. Not surprisingly, evidence of butchery is more common on the meat-bearing bones, particularly those of the larger species, than on the relatively meatless extremities and very few of the major long-bones have survived intact. The only complete cattle bones are tarsals, phalanges and an atlas (1st cervical vertebra), while a few complete or almost complete meat-bearing bones from pig (all from immature animals) were recovered, as well as a number of metapodials and phalanges. (The bones, mostly complete, from very young piglets are excluded from table 22). Many very small pieces of chopped-up long-bones were recovered; some were identified positively as fragments of cattle bones and most of the rest are from animals the size of cattle. The different degree of fragmentation in different skeletal elements introduces an unavoidable bias into a simple numerical quantification (as in table 22) but nevertheless it is clear that many if not all of the pigs came onto the site alive (for slaughter at the castle) or as whole carcases and that this also applies to at least some of the cattle. Presumably the deer were brought back after a day's hunting as bones from all parts of the body including jaws and teeth, as well as antlers broken from the skull, were recovered from pit 1/27 and from the ditches. Whether sheep/goats and horses provided meat for human consumption is not known. The single upper limb bone from a sheep/goat bears no butchery marks while the four from horse have all been chopped.

Mammals

Cattle

The cattle bones are from a minimum of six animals. Two of them are represented by calcanea with the *tuber calcis* unfused (in present-day cattle, fusion occurs between the age of 3 and 3.5 years) and three immature

Table 20: Bones recovered (number of fragments) from pit 1/27

Taxon/ size	3	4A	6	7	8	8(p)	10	11	12	12a	12b	12c	12d	12e	12f	12g	12h	12x	13	14	15	18	Total	u/s
Bos		3	2	43	13	2	2	2	8	1	2	9		6		2	1		2	2		3	103	13
BHs				87	33	8	15	5	36	1		50		13		5		1	11	17		1	285	45
B/D	1			6	6	2	1		4		2	4		5			1		3	1			36	9
Horse			3	4																1			8	3
Pig		1	1	72	22	3	44	11	96	4	2	92	5	6		13	1	96	18	16	17		525	38
Ps				26	11		8	3	23	2		40	4	1		18	5	2		3			146	13
Sheep/Goat		1		2				1	1					1									6	
Sh/Gs				28	19		14	5	21		3	26		5		29			11	1	12	165	166	
Dog					1							2						1					4	cat 1
Red deer	1			11					2		1	4	1			1			4		1		27	8
Rs														1								1		
Roe deer				7	1			1	2		1	8	1			1			1				23	3
Hare				5	1																		6	1
Squirrel														1									1	
Fowl				1	4	1			1			5				2			4			2	20	
Fs				3	2		10		8			6		2		9	1		1	1		3	47	1
Goose				2	2		2		1									1					8	
Gs				3	3	1	1	2	15			6				1	1	1	1				35	
gamebirds						1												1					2	
waterfowl & waders			1									10		1									12	
Goshawk & Gos-s																19							19	
Indet./m								1				15				1	1		4				22	2
Indet./b											1	6	1						1				10	2
Indet./f																					1		1	
Total id.	1	5	7	302	120	17	99	31	219	8	11	283	14	42		101	11	101	62	42	20	16	1512	149
Total unid.		8	64	39	2	52	20	199	19	10	414	26	80	2	99	12	9	63	27	3	8		1156	47+
Total from each layer	1	13	7	366	159	19	151	51	418	27	21	697	40	122	2	200	23	110	125	69	23	24	2668	196

Key as in Table 1.

u/s = unstratified.

Bones from 'layer 8, probably pit' are listed under 8(p).

Bones supplied separately from bulk environmental samples of layer 12 are listed under 12x.

Table 21: Minimum number of individuals from pit 1/27 (stratified bone only).

Bos	6
Pig	23
Sheep/Goat	1
Horse	1
Dog	1
Red deer	3
Roe deer	2
Hare	1
Squirrel	1
Fowl	4
Goose	2
Bittern	1
Mallard	1
Goshawk	1
Partridge	1
Pheasant	1
Woodcock	1

Table 22: Anatomical elements (number of fragments) recovered from large and medium-sized mammals: a) meat-bearing bones, excluding pig fibula (n=23) and b) meatless bones. The number of distal radii and distal tibiae included in the total for a) is shown in brackets alongside.

Element	Bos	Pig	Red deer	Roe deer	Sheep/Goat	Horse
(a)						
Scapula	11	13	3	1		
Humerus	8	15		2		
Radius	9 (2)	13	1	1	1	1
Ulna	5	10	2			1
Vert+ribs	2	12				1
Pelvis	8	6	6	2		
Femur	11	8	3			1
Tibia	7 (3)	10 (1)	5 (2)	1		1
Total	**61**	**87**	**20**	**7**	**1**	**5**
(b)						
Skull	9	86	2	4	1	1
Loose teeth	8	67	2	2	2	1
Tarsals	17	3	2			
Metapodials	5	21	2	7	2	
Phalanges	3	26		1		1
Total	**42**	**203**	**8**	**14**	**5**	**3**

metapodial shafts could all be from the same calf. The rest of the bones are from adult animals.

There is no evidence of the sex of any of the animals and the sample is too small and fragmented to evaluate the extent of variation in the size of the long-bones, although a few bones from apparently adult animals are noticeably small.

Pig

The pig bones represent at least twenty-three animals, including eight very young piglets which probably died at around the time of birth or soon after. Most of the other pigs were skeletally immature when they died: epiphyseal union is not completed in any of the late-fusing bones which were recovered and only five of the thirteen scorable mandibular third molars, and two of the eight scorable maxillary third molars, are fully erupted and in wear. The eight left and eight right scorable mandibles are between Mandible Wear Stages (MWS) 16 and 46 (*cf.* Grant 1982, 91–108) and they are listed in table 23 with the sex indicated if this is known. The degree of wear on the left maxillary molars in two male jaws is probably equivalent to MWS 17 and 39.

Table 23: Mandible Wear Stage (numerical value) of pig jaws (Grant, 1982).
(e = estimated because toothrow is incomplete
M = male and F = female).

Left mandibles	Right mandibles
	e 16-17
17	17 (F)
18-19 (F)	e 17-21 (F)
21-2	19
e 21-2 (F)	e 21-5 (M)
25	23-4 (F)
28-31	28-36
36 (F)	e 36
45-6	

Jaw fragments with the canine tooth *in situ* (or the socket undamaged, if the tooth was lost post mortem) indicate that the remains of nine females and four males are present. The few older animals were probably kept for breeding purposes and the presence on the site of the bones of very young, perhaps newborn piglets suggests that breeding sows were kept very near the bailey at farrowing time at least, if not at other times of the year.

The pig skeleton from context 1272 is of interest because burials of complete animals are recovered relatively rarely from archaeological sites (see fig. 7.6). Unfortunately, the bones are friable and much fragmented and few are measurable, so they provide only limited information about this animal of Norman date. It is an adult male, with the maxillary third molars lightly worn (these being the only dental remains from which its age may be assessed). In present-day pigs, the third molar erupts when the animal is aged between 17 and 22 months. The canine teeth are very large but almost certainly it is a domestic animal because of the modest size of the third molars and the measurable postcranial bones (table 25). Apparently its flesh was not eaten, as there are no cut marks on the bones. Its burial in a pit apart from the locations where food remains were deposited seems to confirm this. Perhaps it died of a disease, or in circumstances which made its flesh unpalatable. There is no skeletal evidence of the cause of death.

Sheep/Goat

The few sheep/goat bones may all be from one animal aged, in present-day terms, about two years old.

Horse

Horse, too, is represented by only a few bones which may all be from the same (adult) animal.

Dogs and Cats

Dogs and cats were present on the site. Three limb bones from a large dog, which may have been skinned (see above), and part of a cranium were recovered from the pit. Although the limb bones are only slightly, if at all, smaller than the bones from a very small wolf in the Collection of the Natural History Museum, the cranium (with a carnassial tooth *in situ*) is definitely from domestic dog. There is no way of telling whether the cranium and the limb bones are from the same animal, but the remains of large hunting dogs have been recovered from deposits of Saxon and early medieval date at Thetford and Canterbury (see table 24 for a comparison of the measurements) and probably the Hen Domen bones, also, are from a hunting dog rather than a wolf. The dog bones from the bailey ditch are from two smaller animals. The remains of certainly two and possibly three small (domestic) cats were recovered from unstratified deposits in the pit, the bailey ditch and context 828.

Table 24: Measurements, in millimetres, of (a) dog bones from pit 1/27 and comparative material in the BM(NH), (b) wolf, 1846.6.18.4, (c) hunting dog from deposits of c.1200 AD at Watling Street, Canterbury, 82.347, and (d) dog from Saxon deposits at Thetford, 1969.676.

Element		(a) Left	(a) Right	(b)	(c)	(d)
Scapula,	HS	148.3		142.0		
	SLC	27.8	27.9	31.2	34.2	
	GLP	33.2	33.7	35.8	38.3	
Humerus, Dp			47.7	50.9	53.6	47.5

Red Deer (Cervus elaphus) and Roe Deer (Capreolus capreolus).

The bones of large deer are from three adult and one immature red deer. The sex of the adult animals is unknown because no skull fragments include the frontal bone and the only piece of antler which is not from roe deer is a worked tine, which could be from a shed antler. All the measurable bones are well outside the range for fallow deer *Dama dama* from Okehampton castle (Maltby 1982, table 15) and all the unmeasurable bones, including a metatarsal from an immature animal, are too large (or too long) to be from fallow deer on the basis of the comparative material seen. It is generally thought that fallow deer were introduced to this country after the Norman Conquest, but it seems that they were not widespread until some time later and their bones are not recorded in any number at Okehampton before the fourteenth century. In view of the early date of the Hen Domen deposits, the apparent absence of this species is not surprising. One adult (male) and one immature roe deer are represented by the bones from the pit and an unshed antler from another adult roebuck came from the bailey ditch.

Other Species

The few hare *Lepus* sp. bones are all from an adult animal and one bone from red squirrel *Sciurus vulgaris* was identified.

Birds

Fowl

The remains of at least four adult fowl were recovered from the pit, and if the fowl-sized bones are all from fowl, they add one immature bird to the total. Most of the bones are from small birds about the size of jungle fowl *Gallus gallus*. The three left tarsometatarsi are unspurred, i.e. from hens. Broken femur shafts were checked for the presence of medullary bone (which indicates that a hen is in an egg-laying cycle, or about to start laying), which was seen in only two fragments of femur (probably the same bone) from the motte ditch.

Goose

All the goose bones are probably from greylag goose *Anser anser*. The remains of at least two adult birds are present, but whether or not they were domestic geese is uncertain. Most of the bones are from the wings and are the same size as in the wild greylag female, but three leg bones are too large to be from a wild greylag male and presumably these are from a domestic bird since there is no record of the larger Canada goose *Branta canadansis* in Britain until the seventeenth century at the earliest (Cowles, pers. comm.). If, as is thought likely, all the goose-sized bones are also from greylag goose, they add three more adult birds to the total.

Other Species

Other species identified are bittern *Botaurus stellaris*, represented by foot and lower leg bones, mallard *Anas platyrhynchos*, a number of bones from goshawk *Accipiter gentilis*, probably all from the same bird, partridge *Perdix perdix*, pheasant *Phasianus colchicus*

Table 25: Metrical data (measurements in millimetres). The bones from context 1272 (marked *) all belong to the same animal; 'e' = estimated.

Mammals: postcranial bones

	Bone	GL	Bp	DC	DPA	SD	DD	Bd
Cattle								
MDI/L13	R m/c	187.0	50.2			25.8	19.0	51.6
F1/27 u/s	R m/c							52.5
OBD Sect 1	R m/t	196.5				20.7	20.2	46.6
F 828/7	R m/t	205.0				24.6	22.8	47.0
F 828/7	R m/t							51.5
Sheep								
HDD1 F6	L m/c	119.5				12.2	8.3	23.1
Roe deer								
HDD2 F4	L m/c	158.0						20.7
F1/27 L7	L m/c	164.0	19.5					20.3
Pig								
F1272	*R hum	190.0						
F1272	*L hum	190.0						
F1/27 L7	R rad		28.5					
F1/27 L7	L rad		28.4					
F1/27 L8	R rad		27.5					
F1/27 L12	R rad		29.6					
F1/27 u/s	L rad		27.1					
F1272	*L rad		30.1					
F1/27 L7	R ul				38.2			
F1272	*R ul				40.8			
F1272	*L ul				39.6			
F1272	*R fem	58.9		27.3				
F1272	*L fem							49.0

Mammals: teeth

	Tooth	L	B/GB
Pig			
F1/27 L7	L mand. M3	32.4	14.0
F1/27 L12	L mand. M3	27.0	12.8
F1/27 L14	R mand. M3	32.8	15.9
F1/27 L14	L mand. M3	30.6	13.8
F1/27 u/s	R mand. M3	26.8e	14.2
F1/27 L7	L max. M3	32.3	15.1
F1/27 L8	L max. M3	31.6e	18.6
F1272	*R max. M3	31.7	18.1
F1272	*L max. M3	30.6	18.1
Dog			
F1/27 LB	R max. M1	19.9	10.7

Birds

	Bone	GL	Bd
Fowl			
F1/27 L8	R hum	61.3	
F1/27 L8(p)	R fem	68.9	13.4
F1/27 L10	L fem		13.5
F1/27 L12	L fem	73.5	13.9
F1/27 L12c	R fem	71.0e	14.0
F1/27 L13	R fem	68.5	
HDD5 F13	R tibt	106.0	11.3
F1/27 L10	L tibt		10.7
F1/27 L18	L tibt		9.8
HDD5 F13	R tm/t	71.9	
F1/27 L8	L tm/t	69.8	
F1/27 L8	L tm/t	66.0	
Goose			
F1/27 L10	R fem	83.0	21.5
HDD5 F12	L tibt	145.8	

Key to measurements (following von den Driesch, 1976)

GL	*Greatest length*	DD	*(Smallest) depth of the diaphysis*
Bp	*(Greatest) breadth of the proximal end*	Bd	*(Greatest) breadth of the distal end*
DC	*(Greatest) depth of the* Caput femoris	L	*Length*
DPA	*Depth across the* Processus anconaeus	GB	*Greatest breadth*
SD	*Smallest breadth of the diaphysis*		

and woodcock *Scolopax rusticola*. A rather diffuse pale green stain was noticed on the surface of some of the goshawk bones, possibly due to their having been near a metal object at some stage. The goshawk is a rare bird in Britain now but a few pairs do still breed here and it may have been more common in Norman times. Its presence in archaeological deposits at Hen Domen arouses suspicions that this was a bird which was kept in captivity and used for hawking. A few very small fragments of eggshell were recovered from the bulk environmental samples. The species concerned is/are indeterminate.

Fish

One small fragment of a head bone was recovered from the floated samples. The species is indeterminate.

Discussion of the Bone from Selected Contexts

The assemblage from the selected contexts is unusual in that the proportion of sheep/goat bones is so low: less than 2% of the identified bones. It is difficult to evaluate the significance of this because so many of the sheep/goat-sized fragments are not identifiable certainly to species level, but at Okehampton sheep (or goat) bones are 22% of the identified assemblage from pre-1300 deposits (Maltby 1982, 114–35). This raises questions which cannot be answered without a sizeable sample of bone from contexts more closely associated with the kitchen and dining quarters. Did the occupants of Hen Domen eat very little mutton and lamb (and goat's flesh), or were the bones of sheep/goats simply not deposited in the selected contexts discussed in this report? It is uncertain to what extent taphonomic processes are involved, but there are some indications that at least part of the assemblage from pit 1/27, which yielded 86% of the bone examined, was not a primary deposit. About 20% of the bone, including some from the lowest level, has been chewed, and taking into account the great depth of the pit, presumably these bones were accessible to carnivores before being deposited there. On the other hand, the very good preservation of most of the bone and the 'fresh'-looking chop marks indicate that it was not lying around on the surface of the ground for any length of time. (Bones which have been butchered *and* gnawed are not infrequent, so it is not simply a case of butchering refuse having been put straight into the pit.) Also, the number of loose teeth (table 22) is low (a high percentage is usually interpreted as indicating disturbed

and/or derived assemblages), especially if in the case of pig most of them have dropped out of the empty sockets in the numerous jaw fragments during post-excavation handling of the bone. No conjoining fragments, nor diaphyses to which unfused epiphyses belong, were seen among the bones recovered from the *same* layer and the only elements which appear to have been articulated when they were deposited are the bittern's foot bones, but there may have been differential 'sinking' of bones after deposition; there was not time to investigate this possibility by looking for conjoining fragments from different layers. As the function of this deep pit is, strictly, unknown and the bone assemblage recovered from it may not be a representative sample of the food remains from this site, it would be unwise to draw any conclusions from it at this stage. However, the recovery of bones from all parts of the body indicate that at least some of the cattle and pigs were slaughtered at or near the castle and the remains of a number of very young piglets, and the mature boar from context 1272, suggest that breeding pigs were kept nearby.

The documentary record for and general historical assumption of hunting (Barker & Higham 1982, Chapter III) are supplemented by the recovery of the remains of red deer, roe deer and hare, and probably by the bones of a large dog which may well have been used for hunting. The bones of fallow deer and rabbit, both generally thought to be post-Norman introductions to this country, are absent from the selected contexts. The recovery of a partial skeleton of a goshawk is interesting because of the possibility that it was a captive bird used in falconry.

Summary

The bone assemblage from the selected contexts is unusual in that the number of sheep/goat bones is very low, but the significance of this is uncertain because a large proportion of the bone is from one deep pit, the original (or intended) function of which is unknown and which may not have contained a representative sample of the food remains of the site. The presence of breeding pigs very near or even within the castle is suggested by the remains of a number of very young piglets in the bailey ditch and the deep pit and a mature domestic boar buried separately in a pit in the rampart. Wild species recorded include red deer, roe deer and hare, but not fallow deer or rabbit. Further indications of hunting, and hawking, activities are probably provided by some bones from a large dog and the partial skeleton of a goshawk.

GEOPHYSICAL SURVEY OF
THE UNEXCAVATED (SOUTHERN) HALF OF THE BAILEY
by Peter Barker, C.Eng. MICE. MIWEM. MIFA.

In order to assess the archaeological potential of the southern half of the bailey, geophysical surveys were carried out by Stratascan (Geophysical & Specialist Survey Services) in March and August 1991. These included magnetometry, resistivity and ground-probing radar surveys. The methods employed and the recorded data are described in a full report deposited with the excavation archive, CADW and the Clwyd–Powys Archaeological Trust. What follows is a brief account of the work, the main results and their archaeological implications.

The magnetometer readings were taken at 0.5m centres along traverses 1.0m apart. The resistivity readings were taken at 1.0m centres along traverses 1.0m apart. The radar scans were carried out along traverses 1.0m apart on a parallel grid and data collected at 16 scans per second (approximately 40 scans per metre). The magnetometer and resistivity surveys achieved a depth of penetration between 0.5m and 1.0m. The ground-probing radar scans achieved a depth of up to 1.7m. The extent of the surveys in the south-west corner of the bailey was limited by the excavation site huts. The resistivity and magnetometry surveys were carried out to the eastern limit of the bailey, but the radar survey did not reach so far.

Where the surveys extended into the excavated part of the bailey, recorded anomalies presumably relate to backfilled features and variations in the backfill material itself. In the unexcavated area, the resistivity survey revealed a band of lower resistance, broadly parallel with the line of the southern defences, suggesting deeper stratigraphic deposits at the tail of the rampart. This is precisely the pattern of evidence encountered in the excavation of the northern half of the bailey. The survey also revealed the southern extent of the large building picked up by the ground-probing radar (see below).

The magnetometer survey produced numerous and widespread reactions. These were probably created by burnt clay and buried iron objects, which were frequently encountered in excavation of the area to the north. Some areas of stronger magnetic anomalies were also encountered.

The ground-probing radar survey produced anomalies which, beyond reasonable doubt, represent the southern extent of Building LIa (and its successor LIb), a large structure adjacent to the motte ditch belonging to the early (and middle) phase of the castle's construction. Other anomalies are probably the southward continuation of the post-holes immediately to the east of this, representing its enlargement (as Building LIb). This survey also identified other features which may represent structures, including a possible building platform opposite that carrying Building XLVIII in phase X.

Simplified plans showing the extent of the features suggested by the surveys are shown in fig. 5.16 whose upper portion illustrates the magnetometry and resistivity surveys and whose lower portion illustrates the ground-probing survey.

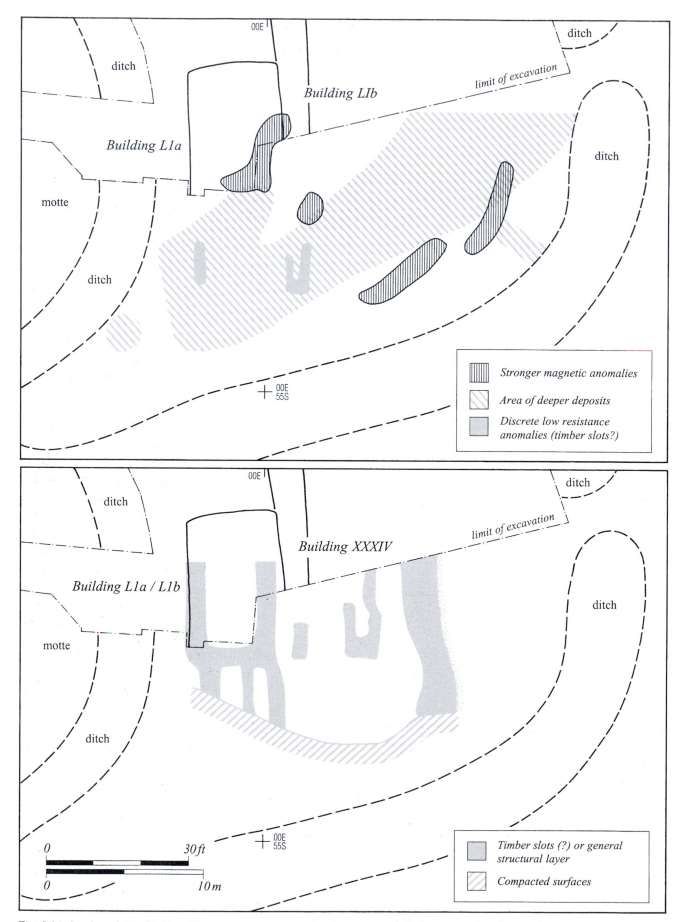

Fig. 5.16: Southern half of bailey. Above: magnetometry and resistivity survey. Below: ground-probing radar survey

SURVEY OF THE PRE-CASTLE PLOUGH-SOIL SURFACE

by Jonathan Freeman

In 1968 and 1969, two portions of the pre-Norman agricultural landscape at this motte and bailey site (established *circa* 1070) were examined:—

a) one portion excavated and surveyed where it had been preserved beneath the castle rampart in the north-west quarter of the bailey and was therefore demonstrably pre-castle;

b) a second portion, in the field outside the castle, which seemed to be a continuation of the excavated portion since it was cut through by the castle's outer defences.

Both portions were characterized by narrow ridging and, in the excavated portion, marks found in the underlying boulder clay were further evidence of ploughing. Another feature in the excavated area, running at a different alignment from the adjacent plough-ridges, was identified as possibly part of a headland separating two parts of the field system. The soil proved devoid of artefactual evidence except for a few abraded sherds of Roman pottery. Analysis of a small amount of pollen surviving in the buried soil in the excavated area suggested an abandoned arable environment (very little tree or grass pollen but lots of pollen from weeds of cultivation and bracken) in which cultivation had stopped a decade or two prior to the construction of the castle. The documentary evidence was also consistent with an abandoned arable theory: the castle was built in the 1070s by Roger de Montgomery and Domesday Book (1086) reveals that at some time before 1066 Edward the Confessor had granted this part of the English–Welsh border to three *thegns* for use as a hunting chase. It was not, however, possible to identify the pre-Norman settlement to which this arable field system had belonged, the nearest Domesday names (*Staurecote and Horseforde*) being too far away. Perhaps it was part of the settlement, whose name is unrecorded, of which a hollow way and building platforms can be seen to the west of the castle (see Chapters 1 and 2). The 1968–69 excavations also revealed a building which pre-dated the buried soil and which therefore cannot be part of the settlement in question.

When this evidence was published (Barker & Lawson 1971) it was emphasized that dated examples of agricultural land surfaces from the early middle ages are extremely rare in the British Isles and western Europe.

The origins of ridge and furrow cultivation (and of the ploughs capable of creating it) are also a matter of some controversy, to which dated evidence such as this clearly makes an important contribution. The field system recorded at Hen Domen was therefore of great interest, especially as a mixture of data—excavated, documentary and environmental—pointed to a coherent conclusion.

When the excavation of the castle proceeded, from 1970 onwards, to explore the north-eastern quarter of the bailey, it was anticipated that further evidence of this pre-castle land surface would be discovered beneath the rampart in due course and that the evidence would be broadly similar to that discovered in 1968–69. Because the post-1970 excavation proceeded slowly, and because the area now under examination was twice as large as that examined in 1960–69, many seasons of work passed before the pre-castle levels were reached, in the late 1980s. As the rampart was gradually removed, the buried soil exposed beneath was progressively covered with a layer of polythene and spoil so that it could eventually be examined in its entirety. This was achieved in 1988, when the whole surface was cleaned and surveyed, with readings taken on a grid of 0.2m intervals. A hand-drawn contour survey was produced with contours at 0.05m intervals. During the subsequent removal of the soil, samples were taken for environmental analysis (by Astrid Caseldine, University of Wales and CADW) and the deposit was washed and sorted on-site in a search for artefactual and other evidence. As in 1968–69, removal of the buried soil also revealed evidence of still earlier occupation, here in the form of the post-holes of a small building at the eastern end of the area examined (see Chapter 2).

There were considerable contrasts between the results obtained from the two excavated areas. The second area examined contained no sealed artefactual evidence, though a few animal bone and pottery fragments were found where the surface of the buried soil emerged at the extreme tail of the rampart. These, however, seem to have been deposited during the castle period rather than earlier. The environmental samples taken proved devoid of pollen or other remains. These results, though disappointing, were not wholly unexpected. The artefactual evidence from the first area examined had been very little anyway. The earlier pollen analyst (Dr P.D. Moore, University of London) had commented in

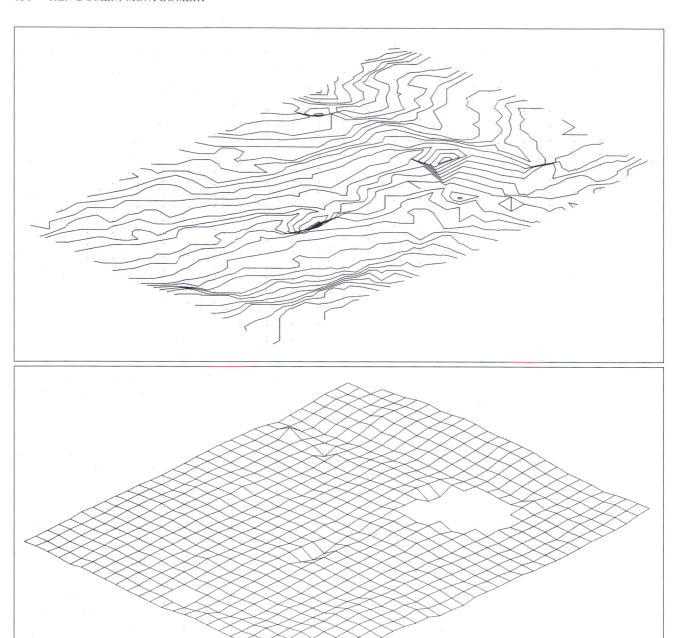

Fig. 5.17: Computer manipulation of sample survey area, viewed from south-west.
Above: isometric view of contour survey. Below: three dimensional mesh

the 1971 publication that the survival of pollen in buried plough soils is rare, the aeration created by ploughing encouraging its decomposition. The pollen sample recovered in 1968–69 was therefore something of a bonus. It is, nevertheless, interesting that this accident of survival occurred in one part of the excavation but not the other.

Perhaps more surprising, however, was the visual contrast between the two areas. Where the first area had clear evidence of ridges, the surface of the second area seemed much more amorphous, the only features apparent to the naked eye being two very low banks. When the soil was removed, some plough-marks were

discovered at the western and eastern extremities of the area, though their direction did not correspond with any ridges visible to the naked eye. Neither did the section through the soil, which was eventually visible at the bottom of the longitudinal section of the rampart, show evidence of undulation which might imply ridges (as had certainly been the case in the area excavated earlier and published in 1971). This last observation, however, would not in itself deny the possible existence of ridging since this might have been running parallel to the section rather than into it. These apparent contrasts were certainly not the result of a change in excavation method between the two areas examined. Indeed, with the demonstrable interest of the first area in mind, enormous care was taken in the exposure, cleaning and surveying of the soil surface in the north-eastern quarter.

The evidence recovered and observed *in situ* suggested that the castle was built on top of the junction of two contrasting areas of agricultural use, one an arable area ploughed in ridges, the other used for some other purpose and with part of a field boundary or other feature running through it. Two observations are important in commenting upon this apparent difference. First, it was noted in the 1968–69 work that the excavated area contained a feature running not parallel to the observed ridges and that this might represent a headland at the edge of a ploughed area (above, fig.2.6). Within this excavated area there may, therefore, have been the start of a second part of this field system which was exposed more extensively in the subsequent excavation. There is, however, a further complication. In 1969, when the removal of the lower part of the bailey rampart and the examination of the soil took place, the weather was consistently very hot and dry: the work was extremely arduous and the workforce quite small. In order to have a coherent set of data by the end of this annual season, a portion of rampart at the eastern end of the excavated area was left *in situ*. When excavation of the north-eastern quarter of the bailey began in 1970 this unexcavated piece of rampart, a few metres wide, was bypassed. It is, in retrospect, most unfortunate that this decision was made, since it created a separation between the pre-castle evidence in the two areas under consideration. The explanation of the contrast between them almost certainly lies in the unexcavated area. This is an excellent example of a fundamental methodological lesson: portions of an excavated area left unexamined will always present problems of interpretation, whether they consist of a narrow baulk or, as in this case, a larger area. It is, ironically, the only part of the northern half of the bailey to have been left unexcavated.

The issue has another dimension. Had the excavation started in the north-east quarter of the bailey it might, on the basis of the surface indications visible in the buried soil exposed there, have been concluded that this deposit was of little interest, a conclusion which would have been supported by the negative results of environmental sampling. It is possible that the excavation might not even have bothered to remove all of this deposit, in which case the plan of the pre-soil building surviving at the eastern end of the area may never have been discovered. Had the excavation then moved on to the north-western quarter of the bailey, the pre-castle levels would have been approached with a quite erroneous assumption about their potential interest, or lack thereof. Crucial evidence about the overall development of the site upon which the castle was eventually built might therefore

never have been recovered. Another fundamental methodological lesson is apparent here: all parts of a site should be treated as of potentially equal value and only thorough excavation will reveal which parts contain more or less evidence.

While indicating that the pre-castle land surface had contrasting functions/characters at the point where the castle was built, the contrast between the two areas also suggested that further analysis of the data might be worthwhile. In the 1971 publication, computer-enhanced presentation of the survey of the field outside the castle had proved very useful. The ridges and furrows were graphically demonstrated through a three-dimensional plot in which the vertical scale of the ground features was magnified. Further analysis of the newly-excavated surface, therefore, had two aims:—

a) to establish whether the observed features (i.e. the two low banks) could be more graphically illustrated;

b) to establish whether subtleties in the surface which might not have been apparent to the naked eye (or from the manually produced contours) could be elicited from the survey data.

Subsequent to the completion of the excavation (in 1992), two further analyses of the survey data of the soil surface in the north-eastern part of the bailey were conducted.

The first analysis was carried out in 1994, by Mike Rouillard: a second manual interpolation of the 0.05m contour lines (originally drawn up on-site when the survey was carried out) was made in order to see whether any further evidence could be observed. This exercise (which is the basis of the survey here published as fig. 2.7) made some refinements of the earlier effort but indicated no new conclusions overall: the main features apparent were still the two banks referred to above. Computer storage of the survey data was then commenced using the programme UNIMAP but difficulties were experienced with this programme and the exercise was abandoned.

The second analysis was conducted in 1996, by Jonathan Freeman, under the supervision of Seán Goddard and Mike Rouillard: computer analysis of a sample from the middle of the area under scrutiny. Survey data (comprising approx. 800 readings) from a rectangle covering approx. 7.0m x 5.0m was entered into the survey programme PENMAP. The process involved calculating for each survey point: a reduced level (the surface in question being always below the site bench mark) as well as easting (X co-ordinate) and northing (Y co-ordinate) readings, a total of *approx* 2,400 entries. This information was then manipulated so that three separate contour survey print-outs of the sample area were created, with contours interpolated at 0.01m,

0.025m and 0.05m intervals. As in the case of the second manual interpolation, this exercise simply reinforced the impressions we already had gained and is not illustrated.

The data stored in the PENMAP programme was then transferred to AUTOCAD and this programme was used to create print-outs showing isometric views of the data viewed from the south-west, north-west, north-east and south-east. These showed the features already observed more graphically than had any of the two-dimensional depictions. In addition to the features already observed, this method of analysis also revealed the presence of one or two features which had not been obvious on the ground and which were only hinted at in the manual interpolation and its PENMAP equivalent, notably a gulley/bank running parallel to the northern edge of the excavated area.

As a final stage of this preliminary analysis, the data was re-worked in PENMAP so that it could be manipulated in AUTOCAD not as a collection of contours but as a three-dimensional mesh viewed from the south-west (fig. 5.17, lower). This image (whose counterparts from other directions could easily be generated) should be compared with fig. 5.17, upper. It is interesting that although they have much in common, the feature near the northern edge of the area, referred to above, is less obvious on the mesh image than it is on the contour image. Creating the mesh image, however, permitted the removal of spurious contours created by PENMAP in the south-east corner of the sample area where the buried soil had actually been destroyed by the castle's subsequent development. The site surveyors had left this point blank in their coverage of readings, but we were unable to find a way of making this gap apparent in the PENMAP manipulation: the latter insisted on running contours across the gap.

It should be noted that all the images so far produced contain the survey data in its original form: no exaggerations of any of the dimensions have been introduced. The result of the sample exercise described here suggests that computer manipulation of the rest of the survey data would be worthwhile. While it would be unlikely to reveal new major features, it might highlight further subtleties in this preserved agricultural surface of early date.

As the final stage of analysis of the sample area, the PENMAP data was given to the Exeter office of the (then) Royal Commission on Historical Monuments (England). The data was processed by Philip Newman using KEY TERRA-FIRMA programme in an AUTOCAD environment. A Digital Ground Model was then produced in which the 0.05cm contour interval was retained, but for contrast with the images generated previously, the vertical scale was doubled. This image further emphasized the two banks observed earlier and has been reproduced above in Chapter 2 (fig. 2.8). Similar vertical exaggeration was employed to good effect in publication of the first part of the pre-castle field to be examined (Barker & Lawson 1971). Vertical exaggeration, however, has the potential drawback (as noted by Susan Lafflin in her processing of the data published in 1971) of hiding from view features which lie behind those in the foreground. This problem did not emerge, however, in the exercise here illustrated. Thanks are due to Philip Newman for his contribution to this part of the analysis.

CHAPTER 6

LANDSCAPE HISTORY AND FIELDWORK AROUND MONTGOMERY

During the later 1970s and early 1980s, when much emphasis was placed upon the training of volunteers in excavation techniques, we also looked more systematically at the surrounding landscape as a whole. This examination extended our earlier observations of the immediate context of the site (Barker & Higham 1982, 5–7) to other areas and provided our volunteers with a basic exercise in interpreting the surrounding palimpsest. It is an enormously rich landscape, which it had originally been our intention to study and publish in some depth. In the event, there has been neither time nor resources for us to achieve this. Recording of a putative settlement site immediately to the west of the motte at Hen Domen has been discussed above (Chapter 2). We

have confined ourselves here to a report on two further specific pieces of field recording (at Sarkley and Lymore) and to a discussion of Old Montgomery's environs. One of us (RAH), supported by a small British Academy grant, also spent several weeks in Montgomery in 1981, collating data held in the Clywd–Powys Sites and Monuments Record and other repositories, examining material in the National Library of Wales, as well as doing further field examination in the parish itself. This exercise contributed in various ways to this chapter and our general thoughts about the landscape of Montgomery. The context of the site at Hen Domen has already been discussed in print (Barker & Higham 1982, 5–7 and above, Chapter 1) and the published map of its

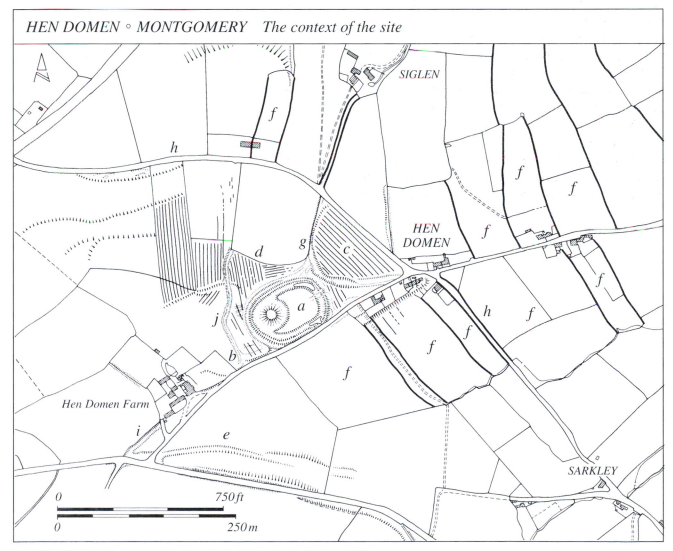

Fig. 6.1: The immediate context of the site (after Barker & Higham 1982)

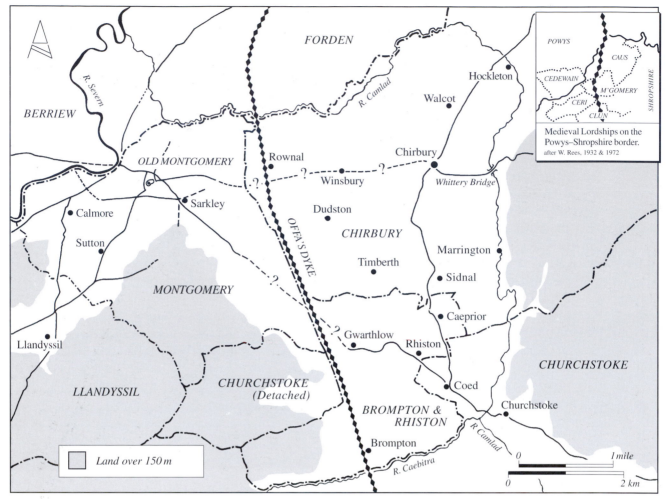

Fig. 6.2: The wider landscape setting of Old Montgomery

immediate environment is reproduced here as fig. 6.1. It should be noted that the plough-ridging shown on this map arises from survey carried out at various times, but that aerial photographs taken by C.R. Musson suggest more extensive remains of ridge and furrow in the immediate vicinity.

We were not, of course, the only ones to be attracted by this landscape and others have also carried out and published valuable work. The Clywd–Powys Archaeological Trust has been active in the area, and important evidence has been recovered by them through aerial photography and excavation of parts of the *vicus* and of a probable post-Roman hall outside the Roman fort at Forden Gaer (Crew 1980; Blockley *et al.* 1990). Other, as yet unpublished work by the Trust includes the excavation of a medieval tenement in the former borough of Montgomery and the discovery of a circular earthwork, 20.0m in diameter, within the hillfort at Ffridd Faldwyn (Gibson 1992). The University of Wales has carried out an interesting piece of fieldwork on the well-preserved earthworks in Lymore Park (Arnold & Reilly 1986). Another piece of fieldwork on Offa's Dyke and an adjacent field system by P.A. Barker and C.R. Musson gave rise to a survey by the Royal Commission on the

Historical Monuments (England). The controversial results of this work have been published, with commentaries by the various participants (Everson *et al.* 1991). J.K. Knight's excavation of Montgomery Castle, on behalf of CADW, has now been published in various instalments (Knight 1990–91, 1992, 1993, 1994). C.J. Arnold has also published (1990) a general survey of the county's archaeology, from prehistory to the later middle ages. Most recent in this series of local studies is an examination of part of Montgomery's town defences (Jones & Britnell 1998), a subject first studied some sixty years earlier by Bryan St J. O'Neil.

(Old) Montgomery *circa* 1200: a tentative reconstruction of the landscape around the caput of a marcher lordship

Two maps (figs 6.2 and 6.3) illustrate, in very general terms, the environment of Old Montgomery. One map extends east of Offa's Dyke and shows the medieval lordships and eventual parishes. The other shows in more detail the landscape of Old Montgomery itself. The latter had been the western extremity of the marcher lordship which was created after 1102 on the demise of the earldom of Shrewsbury and which also included the

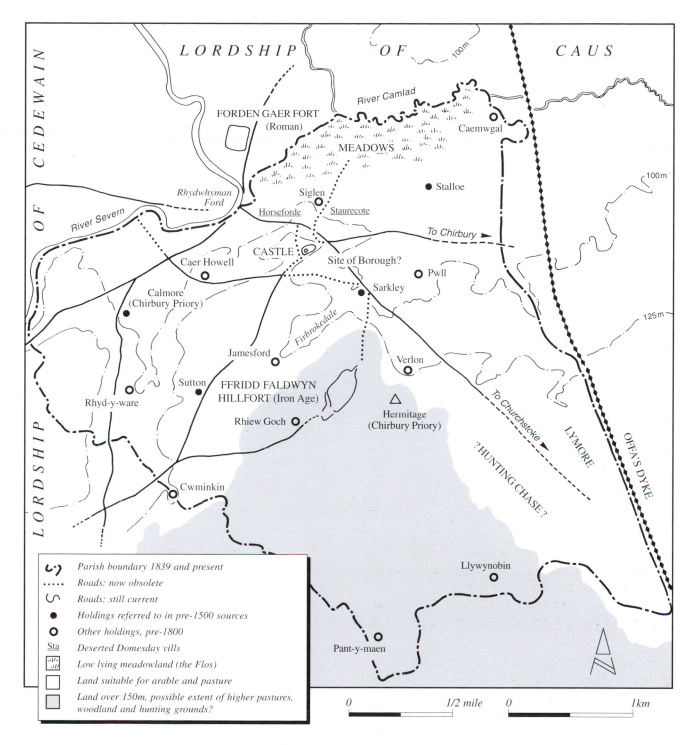

Fig. 6.3: The environs of Old Montgomery

territory around Chirbury. The lordship was given by Henry I to the family of de Boulers, whose ancestors may have come originally from Flanders (Warlop 1975–76). In the late eleventh century, this had been part of the Welsh borderlands of the earls of Shrewsbury, the first of whom, Roger de Montgomery, established the castle and gave it his own, Norman, name. Domesday Book described a *castellarium*, comprising twenty-two vills and about fifty hides of land, which extended far beyond this map (see Barker & Higham 1982, fig. 7). With the disappearance of the de Boulers, who had no

direct male heirs in the early thirteenth century, the lordship passed to the English king. In 1223, the new castle was founded by Henry III, and a new town, New Montgomery, quickly followed: the first (known) significant nucleation of settlement and population in the immediate vicinity since the decline of the Roman fort and its *vicus* at Forden Gaer. A new parish was then carved out of the large ecclesiatical territory dependent on Chirbury, and it is this which is covered in the more detailed of the two maps. Like most western Shropshire parishes, Chirbury contained a number of townships (as

it still did in the nineteenth century), and perhaps the land which became the parish of Montgomery had formerly constituted one or more of these. The area west of Offa's Dyke retained its marcher status and was eventually included in the new Welsh county of Montgomery in 1536. To the east, Chirbury was absorbed at the same time in the English county of Shropshire (see Morgan 1981 on the administrative history of region).

The more detailed map (6.3) is based on information from modern Ordnance Survey maps, on evidence from the first edition 1 inch : 1 mile Ordnance Survey map and the Tithe Map, on fieldwork in the present landscape and on a variety of medieval documentary sources (those not quoted fully here will be found in Barker & Higham 1982, Chapters I, II, III). Some features can be placed on the map with confidence, even though their exact location or extent may be uncertain. Others are much more hypothetical. Fig. 6.4 is an aerial view of part of this landscape, showing New Montgomery in the foreground. Ffridd Faldwyn is in the centre and Hen Domen in the distance (top right).

Roads

We do not know exactly how many of today's roads existed in the twelfth century, nor how many of today's footpaths may represent former roads. Some roads of

medieval date have since disappeared, such as the lane from Sarkley to Rownal, just over the Chirbury border, mentioned in 1481 (Powis Schedule, no. 16244). In figs 6.2 and 6.3, roads which were built at any time after the foundation of New Montgomery have been removed, leaving a network centred on the old castle and other settlements in the western part of the parish. This was the heart of Montgomery before its south-eastward shift after 1223. Virtually all roads shown are still in use, though it is unlikely that their twelfth-century courses were exactly as today. They would have been affected in detail by the late medieval developments suggested below: the replacement of hamlets by farms and open fields by enclosures. The route running north into the Corbet lordship of Caus and south-west into the Welsh lordship of Cedewain was originally of Roman origin, though when the Roman course was replaced by the present one is not known. There must have been a road to Chirbury, the parochial centre, and another to Churchstoke, which, like Montgomery, was still part of Chirbury parish and where a daughter church of Chirbury's minster had been established before the time of Domesday. It is not clear where exactly these roads left the present parish: surviving footpaths running eastward towards Winsbury and south-eastward through Lymore towards Rhiston and Gwarthlow may be relics of these routes. Noble's suggestion (1983, 78) that a

Fig. 6.4: Aerial view (by P.A. Barker), showing New Montgomery (foreground), Ffridd Faldwyn (centre) and Hen Domen (top right)

gap in Offa's Dyke near Rownal marks the course of the Old Montgomery–Chirbury road is a good one. Further south, Lymore Park creates an interruption in a route from Churchstoke, through Brompton and Rhiston, then Gwarthlow, whose eventual continuation is the road to the Severn. This road, running to the ford at Rhydwhyman, was probably very ancient, perhaps prehistoric in origin and with a Roman phase of use too: there was a succession of military camps at Brompton. At Rhydwhyman, the English and Welsh met for negotiation down to the late thirteenth century. A footpath, which eventually joins a road into the heart of Cedewain, may represent the continuation of this road on the Welsh side. Rhydwhyman was clearly a crossing with a long history and perhaps some symbolic significance: its use was essential to reach (what is now) Berriew and the area beyond. Another (and simpler) way to travel into or from other parts of Wales was via the route, established in Roman times, south-westward along the Severn.

The roads running towards the entrances of the Iron Age hillfort on Ffridd Faldwyn are presumably prehistoric in origin. The one on the south has continued to modern times, whereas that on the north was abandoned at some point. The hollow way which marked its former course, near Sarkley, was filled in quite recently (see below). In the middle ages, these roads would have provided access to high pasture and hunting territory. The date of another early road, running to the river west of Hen Domen, near Caer Howell Farm, is not known. The map suggests a gradual westward shift in crossing points, first at Rhydwhyman, then here near Caer Howell, finally at the present road bridge (not shown on map) in the nineteenth century. The intersection of roads at the castle of Old Montgomery itself is very puzzling, since none leads directly into the bailey entrance. It is impossible to be certain whether all the hollow ways in the vicinity of the site were in use at this time. One to the immediate west of the site (*j* on fig. 6.1), associated with the pre-Norman fields on which the castle was built, may already have been out of use (Barker & Higham 1982, 6–7 and above Chapter 2).

Land use

The extent of various land-uses suggested can only be approximate, though the overall pattern seems fairly clear. The former existence of open fields is suggested by existing landscape evidence: the reversed-S shape boundaries of some fields, whose shapes reflect enclosure of former open field strips; and medieval ridge and furrow surviving in various parts of the parish when our fieldwork was conducted (e.g. in several parts of Lymore Park, just north of Montgomery town at SO223973 and near Sutton at SO205969). Documentary evidence points to the same

conclusion: open field terminology survived to the nineteenth century, being recorded on the Tithe Map in such terms as *maes*, *cae* and *erw* in Welsh, and *quillet* and *furlong* in English. The Tithe Map also recorded enclosed strips which have since been absorbed in larger fields, and there are thirteenth and fourteenth-century references to parcels of land in open fields, normally described as acres in a *campus*. The places which are specifically mentioned in such references include *Horseforde* (near Rhydwhyman), Sarkley, Sutton, Calmore, and there are other references simply to the field of Montgomery. Parts of this were designated the 'old field' or the 'field of old Montgomery', and this area was said to be at Sutton and Calmore (see Barker & Higham 1982, 11, for grants to Chirbury priory of land in the old field; other references to open field parcels in Powis Schedule, nos 16233, 16246, 16260, 16261, 16263, 16264, 16266, 16267, 16273). The accumulated evidence, of course, reflects developments over many centuries and it is not possible to produce a map showing details which are exclusively pre-1200. The Maes Kerry, or Kerry Field, for example, revealed by Tithe Map field-names on the high ground immediately south of New Montgomery, is likely to be a thirteenth-century development. Perhaps it was this, or another new development, which made the more northerly land already cultivated into 'the old field' (above). There was certainly woodland clearance and assarting in the vicinity of New Montgomery in 1224–25, because it was the subject of specific instruction (Knight 1992, 107). This must have greatly changed the character of this part of the landscape, though it was probably inspired as much by the need for the new castle's security as by agrarian development. Nevertheless, creation of the new town is unlikely to have brought a total agrarian re-organization of the new parish, and it may be assumed that much of the land then cultivated had also been worked in the twelfth century. The main arable-pasture belt seems to have followed an arc running from the south-west, up to the old castle, and thence eastwards. Field boundaries of reversed 'S' shape near Hen Domen itself (marked *f* on fig. 6.1) may reflect the later enclosure of open field strips in use during the life of Old Montgomery. Whether this arable-pasture area was completely cleared, or whether it contained pockets of managed woodland, we cannot say. Domesday Book referred to four ploughlands in Roger de Montgomery's demesne and two in Roger Corbet's (below), suggesting that, as elsewhere in the region, at least part of the countryside was organised in open fields by the late eleventh century. Development of open fields seems to have been more the result of best exploitation of suitable topography than of particularly 'English' or 'Norman' practice, since evidence of open fields in suitable terrain is plentiful in eastern Montgomeryshire generally

(Sylvester 1955). On the other hand, the possible contribution of 'infield–outfield' systems to the agrarian organisation of the area should also be borne in mind.

The area near the River Camlad is still known as the Flos, an English name first recorded in the fourteenth century (e.g. Powis Schedule, no. 16254—*Fouleslos*) meaning marshy ground. Meadow and common pasture were mentioned lying by the Camlad in 1369–70 (Powis Schedule, no. 16271) and the burgesses of Montgomery had meadow and pasture here until the area was enclosed in the late eighteenth century (Pryce 1912). Ffridd is the Welsh word for upland open pasture and the de Boulers family may be associated with it in the name Ffridd Faldwyn (the first and last lords were called Baldwin). There was perhaps a practice of transhumance here in the medieval economy, and the two roads illustrated (discussed above) would certainly have been convenient for this. In the seventeenth century, the Ffridd was part of the manorial demesne and was used as a deer park, like Lymore, by the Herbert family (Smith 1963). The de Boulers, too, may well have hunted on this higher ground. Lymore was known by this name (*Leymore*) not later than the fourteenth century (Rees 1932). It was eventually emparked and a grand house built here for the Herbert family. The park is referred to by name from the mid- seventeenth century (Smith 1963, *passim*) but was enclosed perhaps a century earlier. The northern edge of the paled area is shown on John Speed's depiction of Montgomery in his *Atlas* of 1614, and the Herberts had been constables of Montgomery castle since the mid-sixteenth century. In an account of royal holdings in the Montgomery area made in 1364–65, reference was made to the 'wood of Oldecastell and Leymore' (PRO, Ministers' Accounts, List & Index, no. V, 488; *Montgomeryshire Collections*, i, 1868, 473). In this context, given the known later association of the Ffridd and Lymore in the Herbert period, the 'old castle' was presumably the hillfort at Ffridd Faldwyn rather than Old Montgomery (Hen Domen).

It has been tentatively suggested on the accompanying map that, centuries earlier, Lymore and the Ffridd may also have been a hunting chase of the de Boulers lords. But the history of part of this area was clearly very complex, since there survive in Lymore Park extensive remains of earthworks and fields ploughed in ridge and furrow. Their date is unknown: one possibility is that the area was a field of New Montgomery before its later emparkment. Another is that the area included one of the vills recorded as waste in Domesday Book and which later disappeared completely (Higham & Barker 1982, 8; Arnold & Reilly 1986). Nor can it safely be assumed that all the ridge and furrow (and other features) within the park pre-date its formal creation. It has been shown (Stamper 1988) that in the later middle ages emparked

areas could contain mixed land-use, with woodland, pasture and arable together, and hunting pursued throughout, as landlords diversified their manorial economies. Such parks also anticipated the less functional and more 'general amenity' parks of later centuries—which may well have applied at Lymore. The difficulty of determining even the general extent of woodland and arable at a much earlier date is illustrated by the debate surrounding one aspect of the interpretation of Offa's Dyke. Fox (1955) argued that straight stretches of the Dyke reflected open country, where surveyors had clear lines of sight, but that sinuous stretches reflected wooded country where visibility was limited. But Noble (1983) has criticized Fox's analysis of the Dyke's form as well as pointing out the limitations of the theory on other grounds.

The origins of this landscape lie rooted in prehistory, and its exploitation was no doubt already well developed in pre-Norman times. The presence of the Iron Age hillfort at Ffridd Faldwyn (O'Neil 1942–43) demonstrates wider rural settlement from an early date; there was a *vicus* outside the Roman fort at Forden Gaer and part of a post-Roman timber hall has recently been discovered there (Blockley *et al.* 1990); part of a pre-Norman field system was discovered at Hen Domen (Barker & Lawson 1971) and this itself sealed buildings of still earlier date (above, Chapter 2). The pre-English, Celtic estate which occupied this territory may have contained equivalents of the classic elements of the medieval Welsh landscape: a lord's residence (*llys*); nucleated settlements of bondmen who worked the lord's demesne (*tir bwrdd*); dispersed settlements (*trevi*) of freemen with their own land; the upland settlement (*hafod*) for the summer pasture, and so on (Jones 1989; Owen 1989). Its natural boundaries may have been: the Camlad valley to the north; the junction of low and high ground on the east (where the Camlad flows through Marrington Dingle); the Caebitra valley on the south; the River Severn on the north-west; and within the high land to the south-west. Most of the settlement features of this putative estate have been obscured by later landscape and naming developments. Chirbury, however, despite its English name, could well be pre-English. When fortified as a *burh* (*Cyricbyrig*) in 915 it may have been chosen because it was already a place of administrative or ecclesiastical importance: a newly established church site of *burh* status is more likely to have produced a *minster* place-name than a *cirice* place-name by this date (Gelling 1990, 80–81). Although the plan of Chirbury has some indications of rectilinear planning, its site is not naturally defensible and no traces of a defensive perimeter have ever been convincingly demonstrated. Perhaps Aethelflaed simply built a palisade, without earthworks, around a place that was already recognized as the centre of the territory. Indeed, the origins of land organization in the area must have had much earlier origins, perhaps in the pre-Roman Iron Age when Ffridd Faldwyn became a hilltop settlement extending over 10 acres. It has been suggested (Jones 1960) that large prehistoric estates underlie the administrative units which later emerge as English hundreds, and Chirbury hundred could be one such case. Whatever the underlying Celtic settlement pattern may have been, it was eventually overlain with a new framework—or at least a framework with new, English names. The outline of this framework may have been the places with Old English *tun* names, many of which were to become the township names of Chirbury and the other adjacent parishes (see Barker & Higham 1982, 9, fig. 7). It has been suggested that the use of the *tun* element was common in the mid-eighth century as a designation for the individual units of which the larger, pre-English estates had been composed (Gelling 1989, 197–99). Interestingly, the English hundred which was known as Chirbury from the twelfth century was known at the time of Domesday as *Witentreu*. The name is still found, in Whittery Wood and Whittery Bridge, a mile to the east of Chirbury, on the River Camlad. It has been observed that Old English 'tree' place-names often occurred near boundaries and were compounded with personal names. They may represent meeting-places and perhaps the personal names were those of some important owner of the estate in question (Gelling 1984, 211–22). The survival of Whittery as a name may support the suggestion (above) that the Camlad was the eastern boundary of the original territory, though Chirbury was later to stretch further east. Although *Witentreu* looks tantalizingly like 'tree of the Witan', if the suggested personal name explanation of 'Hwita's tree' (Gelling 1984, 213) is correct it may reveal the name of the first English owner of this estate at the time of its putative eighth-century re-organization.

Domesday Book described the area as an agricultural landscape which had become waste at some time before 1066, perhaps as a result of intermittent English–Welsh warfare. Edward the Confessor had given the territory as a hunting ground to three English *thegns*, Sewar, Oslac and Azor. The Norman settlement brought partial economic recovery, still in progress in 1086. At that date the eight vills held by Roger of Montgomery's tenant, Roger Corbet, were recovered and viable. But the thirteen vills of the *castellarium* retained by the earl himself were still waste in 1086 (Barker & Higham 1982, 8). Perhaps this indicates that the castle's founder also used the area as a hunting chase, like his English predecessors, but Domesday Book's mention of four ploughlands in Roger de Montgomery's demesne (as well as two in Roger Corbet's) indicates at least some agricultural revival. Domesday is silent on other details of land resource, but

by the twelfth century all forms of land-use, including arable, pasture, meadow, waste, woodland, and hunting chases, must have been available to sustain the de Boulers lords and their tenants. In addition, the Rivers Severn and Camlad would have provided fisheries and mill sites whose number and location are unknown. There are thirteenth-century references to mills, perhaps of earlier origin, on both rivers in the immediate vicinity of Montgomery, and recently a mill site of unknown date has been discovered in Lymore Park on a tributary stream of the Camlad (Everson *et al.* 1991). However, distinguishing mills of earlier date from those which are known to have been created after the foundation of New Montgomery is not easy: there is documentary evidence for a new, thirteenth-century water-mill as well as a (in fact, *the* earliest documented in Wales) windmill built *circa* 1230 on the high ground between the new castle and Town Hill (Barton 1997). Analysis by James Greig of the contents of a deep pit in the castle bailey at Hen Domen, perhaps a failed well (full data in Barker & Higham 1982, 60–71), revealed preserved plant remains (seeds and/or pollen) in some quantity. These included species whose natural habitats were arable fields, hedgerows, meadows, marshes and woodland. Particular tree species were seen in remains of birch, hazel, oak and willow. Arable crop remains were mainly wheat, with some barley, and weeds of cultivation were plentiful, including types made rare by modern, improved agriculture. Otherwise, the range of species observed would not be out of place in modern Wales, though the evidence preserved in one archaeological context is not necessarily wholly representative of the twelfth–century environment.

Settlements

The origin of individual rural settlements in the parish, now represented by farms and cottages, is impossible to define exactly. Nor can we be sure that, even when a property existed in the middle ages, the present farm occupies exactly the same site as its predecessor. Evidence elsewhere in Wales suggests that (as in parts of England) in the later middle ages an ancient pattern of hamlets with open fields began to evolve into a new pattern of discrete, consolidated farms with enclosed fields (Griffiths 1989), a process which culminated, in this part of the Welsh borderlands, in private acts of enclosure in the late eighteenth and early nineteenth centuries (Sylvester 1955). The single dots which represent farms on the accompanying maps (figs 6.2 and 6.3) may, therefore, be very misleading as precise indicators of the nature of medieval settlement.

West of Offa's Dyke, in addition to the castle named Montgomery, Domesday Book mentions *Staurecote* and *Horseforde*, though both subsequently disappeared as named places. Their approximate locations, shown on the map, are based on field-names (Horsewell and Starecote) from the Tithe Map and other sources and there is also a late thirteenth-century reference to *Horsefordeshul* (Powis Schedule, no. 16264). But other places may be just as early, even though not mentioned by name in 1086, and some may also have disappeared without leaving any documented trace at all. *Horseforde* was presumably also the English name for the adjacent ford known in Welsh as Rhydwyman, a crossing wide enough for horse-traffic and therefore military use. English place-names on the Shropshire border west of Offa's Dyke (whether or not they happen to appear in Domesday Book) have three possible explanations. They may represent Mercian lands lost to the Welsh when the Dyke was built at the end of the eighth century. They may represent Welsh land conquered and colonised by the English between *circa* 800 and 1066. But it is a third explanation, first published by Noble (1983), which currently finds most favour (Gelling 1989, 199–201). They probably represent English naming of settlements arising from the consolidation of Mercian power in the seventh–eighth centuries, the estates to which they belonged being later truncated by the Dyke. The western limits of these estates continued as before and their integrity was not destroyed by the building of the Dyke. The latter functioned as a defensible line, within English land, from which the border territory could be monitored. The limits of these estates are probably represented by the parish and township boundaries, known from later evidence, and which for most of the Dyke's length are not coincident with it. This hypothesis (see Noble 1983, 71–79, for discussion of this particular area) certainly makes sense at Montgomery: it would explain why the land between the Dyke and the Severn was part of an English hundred described in Domesday Book; why the vills in the Domesday *castellarium* of Old Montgomery were situated on both sides of the Dyke (and why it had been possible for this land to be held by three English *thegns* before 1066); why the de Boulers lordship extended on both sides of the Dyke; and why, until the establishment of New Montgomery parish after 1223, the land around Old Montgomery was part of a large parish, whose centre (Chirbury) lay east of the Dyke. In other words, the River Severn had been the true border between the English and Welsh in the pre-Norman period, and Roger de Montgomery's *castellarium* and Baldwin de Boulers's marcher lordship were also created out of what was English land, rather than out of land conquered from the Welsh. Some of its population may, however, have been of Welsh origin (below). In the days of our training excavation at Hen Domen, we would often describe the area between the Dyke and the Severn as a 'no-man's land' on our field excursions. This notion,

though drawn from more modern military analogies and not strictly correct, perhaps nevertheless conveys something of its early character. Paradoxically, the stretch of Offa's Dyke near Montgomery became a more significant *territorial* division only in later times—when it became a parochial boundary in the thirteenth century and then a national and county boundary in the sixteenth, dividing English Shropshire from Welsh Montgomeryshire. In earlier centuries, territories, variously defined, had straddled it.

Calmore and Sutton, not far from the castle of Old Montgomery, were first recorded in thirteenth century charters, as *Caldemore* and *Subbedune* (Barker & Higham 1982, 11). Sutton was still spelt *Subdon* in 1648 (Powis Schedule, no. 12951) and perhaps contains the element 'dun' (hill) since it is situated below Ffridd Faldwyn. The earliest recorded form of Sarkley is *Salkley*, mentioned in 1481 in reference to a field next to a stream called Fyrbroke running through *Fyrbroke Dale*, presumably the small, steep-sided valley whose upper parts were filled in when the new road from Montgomery was built in the nineteenth century (Powis Schedule, nos 16244, 16246). The derivation of the name is obscure, but one possibility is an Anglo-Welsh compound containing an earlier Celtic name ('Sark') for the stream on which it stands (Ekwall 1960, 404) with Old English *leah* (clearing). The creation of an English pronunciation of a Welsh name is also seen at New Montgomery, where the names Arthur Street and Arthur Gate, which were employed by the early fourteenth century, derive from the name Gorddwr, the land north of the Camlad, lying between the Severn and the Long Mountain (R. Morgan, pers. comm.). This was technically part of the lordship of Caus but was disputed between the Corbets and the princes of Powys in the thirteenth century and had a Welsh name (Morgan 1981, 38–44). In general, however, Welsh settlement names were not rationalized into English ones in the Shropshire–Welsh borderlands: they were either replaced by English names or carefully preserved in Welsh (Dr M. Gelling, pers. comm.). Field-names and agrarian terminology, however, were subject to linguistic fusion (Sylvester 1955).

Old Montgomery castle was the chief residence of the lords and the administrative centre for the whole lordship, which comprised a compact area of land (illustrated on our maps) and outlying properties scattered further east in Shropshire (see Barker & Higham 1982, Chapter III, for details). South-west of Old Montgomery, Calmore became a grange farm of the de Boulers' priory at Chirbury (settled there by 1198 after an unsuccessful start at Snead, near Churchstoke, earlier in the decade). Robert de Boulers, the priory's founder, made the original grant of lands in Chirbury and Montgomery, together with mills at Walcot and Churchstoke (VCH, II, 59–62; for what follows see the references given in Barker & Higham 1982, Chapter III). The priory's holdings were later enlarged, between 1235 and 1270, through gifts and sales of adjacent parcels of land near Sutton, by the burgesses of New Montgomery, to become the grange at Calmore, which by 1291 comprised over 30 acres. That they had land to dispose of there suggests that some of the newly created burgesses were inhabitants of Old Montgomery rather than immigrants. Robert also gave the priory the site for a hermitage on land which was eventually to be occupied by the new town and castle. The priory later received other lands in compensation for this in the thirteenth century. Stalloe (*Stanlawe* in thirteenth-century spelling) was a tenant's holding by serjeanty, for which the service of an armed man was owed at Old Montgomery castle in time of war for three weeks. Similar services, as well as provision of victuals and hunting attendants, were owed for other holdings to the east of Offa's Dyke (fig. 6.2), at Winsbury, Timberth, Brompton and Rhiston. Some of these tenants had their own little mottes—an interesting example of castle-building at a relatively humble social level—as surviving (or recently destroyed) at Hockleton, Winsbury, Dudston and Gwarthlow.

The absence (by name) of Sutton, Sarkley and Calmore from Domesday Book may suggest that the four ploughlands which Earl Roger held in demesne at Montgomery were, in part, distributed among them. House platforms by a hollow way immediately west of Old Montgomery castle presumably also represent a settlement site, though their date is unknown (above Chapter 2). Nor is it known whether this is the settlement to which the abandoned field system upon which the castle was built had belonged. In 1086, two ploughlands were also held at Montgomery by Roger Corbet, the earl's tenant. These probably coincided with *Staurecote* and *Horseforde*, which he held of Earl Roger. With the reorganization of the western edge of the former earldom, after 1102, the area around these two Corbet vills, immediately adjacent to the castle, became de Boulers property and the de Boulers/Corbet boundary was settled on a line, later to become the Montgomery/Forden parish boundary, following a stream from Rhydwhyman to the Camlad. *Staurecote* and *Horseforde* subsequently disappeared as identifiable holdings. Later evidence, however, suggests basic continuity in the overall extent of the demesne. A survey of Montgomery made in 1249 (*Cal. Inq. Misc.,* vol. I (PRO), no. 70) recorded six carucates of demesne land at Montgomery (that is, demesne of the lordship which was now in royal hands), a total which corresponds exactly with the four ploughs of Earl Roger's demesne together with the two ploughs of Roger Corbet's demesne mentioned in Domesday

Book's description of Montgomery in 1086.

There is some documentary evidence (Barker & Higham 1982, 12) that the de Boulers were fostering the growth of a borough at Montgomery by the end of the twelfth century: men from Shrewsbury and Ludlow had established the right to come here to trade. Its location is not known, though the crossroads immediately east of the castle, where the hamlet of Hen Domen now sits, seems an obvious place. Perhaps burgage tenements were, or would have been, created out of strips in the adjacent open fields? The short earthwork north-east of the castle bailey may also have been related (above, Chapter 3). Our 1982 discussion of this first borough can now be supplemented by the recent discovery of a reference to a burgage here in 1201. This belonged to Chirbury priory and was mentioned in a confirmation of the priory's possessions by Pope Innocent III (Migne, *Patrologia Latina,* vol.214, col. 944. We are grateful to James Lawson for this reference). If the priory had a burgage there were presumably also others. Whatever developments were taking place by *circa* 1200 were presumably halted in the years 1207–23, when Montgomery was successively in the hands of various royal guardians and the Welsh. That the name Old Montgomery did not become established here, being replaced by the descriptive Welsh phrase Hen Domen, meaning 'old mound', must indicate that these developments were very limited. It is not clear whether the present hamlet of Hen Domen represents continuous survival of a small medieval nucleation or a separate post-medieval growth. Although speculative, it is quite possible that, had the de Boulers occupation of the lordship not come to an end, their efforts to attract trade would have resulted in the formal establishment of a small 'new town' alongside their castle, a pairing common elsewhere in the twelfth and thirteenth centuries.

Land Organization: 'Anglo-Norman' and 'Welsh'

Limiting the discussion to places referred to in medieval (pre-1500) written sources may be misleading: other properties may also have had early origins. Nor do we know whether the area was organized along wholly English manorial lines, or whether elements of Welsh land tenure, involving settlements of freemen and bondmen, survived through the middle ages. This is, however, more than likely: a survey made in 1540 shows that five vills, which had originally belonged to the Domesday *castellarium* of Montgomery but which later passed into the Corbet lands to the north, were still held by Welsh bond tenure at that late date. One of them was Thornbury, immediately north of Old Montgomery castle, a township of Forden parish with an English name (presumably the *burh* where thorns grow—i.e. Forden

Gaer) but obviously of Welsh origin (Whitfield 1951–53; Jones 1960). Also relevant, and very near Chirbury, is the name Walcot—a vill mentioned in Domesday Book whose name specifically means 'cottages of the British' (Gelling 1990, 297–98) and must indicate a survival of native, Welsh-speaking population. The Corbet lands certainly had Welsh-speakers amongst their population, for they were mentioned in an inquisition of 1246 (*Cal. Inq. Misc.*, vol. I (PRO), no. 35). The demesne of Old Montgomery itself could originally have been worked by bondmen living in the Sutton–Calmore–Sarkley area, though by the thirteenth century, when records begin to survive for these areas (see above), the land-holders there had English names. Then, as now, Montgomery was a border land. Even to its east, around Chirbury, Welsh language and culture was alive in the sixteenth century (Morgan 1981, 22), though how far this represented continuity from the early middle ages is not clear: Welsh field and other names on the English side of the border may also have arisen from later immigration of Welsh speakers (Foxall 1980, 68–70; see also Morgan 1997). Late Welsh names for such places as Chirbury and Marrington were also recorded in the sixteenth–seventeenth centuries, though these Welsh names had no etymological connection with the English names (Gelling 1990, 297–98). Vestiges of Welsh culture still remain east of Offa's Dyke in the modern map, in place-names such as Caeprior and Coed Farm, south of Chirbury. But most names in this area, such as Winsbury, Rownal, Sidnal, Dudston, Timberth and Gwarthlow, are solidly English with no obvious Welsh name antecedents. The consolidation of Mercian power in the eighth century, culminating in the building of Offa's Dyke, seems to have brought with it a thoroughly English administration and consequent re-naming process (Gelling 1989, 197–98). Shropshire as a whole is notable for its low survival of British names, witness to 'a drastic re-naming of settlements and landscape features after the area became part of the kingdom of Mercia' (Gelling 1990, xiii). Unfortunately, the transformation of names from one language to another in the area under discussion is hidden by the paucity of early sources: only Chirbury itself is named in any source earlier than Domesday Book. Another complication arises from the contrasting history of English and Welsh place-name formation. In English, place-names became fossilized in the middle ages, whereas in Welsh they remained part of the living language and continued to evolve with it. Unless a Welsh name contains an independently datable element it is very difficult to know how old it is (Dr M. Gelling, pers. comm.). Domesday Book mentions Welsh population in the western parts of Shropshire (though not specifically at Montgomery) but how many other Welsh people were anonymously included in the Domesday slave population of the area is a difficult issue (Gwynne 1971–72).

The western boundary of Montgomery was a river with a Celtic name (Severn), but the Camlad, which formed part of its northern boundary, was known in the middle ages by a name (*Kemlet*) which may have been a hybrid of English and Welsh (Morgan 1997, 20). This river also has the distinction of being the only one to flow from England into Wales. Some of the existing Welsh farms in Montgomery parish—Cae(r) Howell, Cwminkin, Pwll, Rhiew Goch, Llwynobin and Caemwgal—are probably creations of more recent times, and their earliest documentary references are of post-medieval date. But their earliest documented appearances could possibly disguise medieval (or even earlier) origins, and the occupants of some of these places may have been among the de Boulers' tenants. It has been suggested that the 600ft/200m contour often marked the Englishry/Welshry distinction in a marcher lordship (Owen 1989). If the present distribution of Welsh names is at all meaningful, the distinction in this particular lordship, however, was not a simple lowland/highland one, for the distribution of Welsh names is too general. On the other hand, the map may simply be telling us that farms with Welsh names in the lowland of Montgomery are post-medieval creations, irrelevant to the medieval Welshry. In any case, distinctions within the population were as much social and legal as physical: the twelfth-century courts of the lordship, which we hear from later records were held at the castle (Barker & Higham 1982, 19), were for the tenants of such places as Stalloe (and Winsbury and Timberth immediately east of the Dyke) who owed feudal service; any Welsh tenantry were presumably administered separately through another court.

Speculation about the Welsh population in the landscape is limited by the general absence of early dating evidence for settlements with Welsh names. One case, however, may be revealing and it is all the more interesting for being a lowland settlement. It is notable that the northern half of the parish boundary on the east follows not Offa's Dyke but a tributary stream of the Camlad: by the thirteenth century, when the boundary was created, this stream was presumably recognized as the demarcation between two townships in the (then) parish of Chirbury. At the extreme north, the new parish boundary took in a small eastward bulge of land. Part of its shape may reflect a change in the course of the Camlad: the Forden–Chirbury boundary has just such a deviation a little way to the east, and presumably the boundary originally followed the course of the river. But the bulge also accommodates the land of an adjacent farm, Caemwgal, and it is possible that this settlement, whose name contains a Welsh word for open field (*cae*), is at least as old as the parish boundary, though the earliest reference to it is sixteenth-century.

Conclusion

This exercise in landscape history has been necessarily limited in scope: it contains, for example, no input from field-walking, which might have produced datable artefactual evidence (though little of the area is much ploughed), nor from environmental sampling (except that recovered from Hen Domen itself). Nor have we attempted to depict the evolution of the current field boundaries through comparisons of Ordnance Survey, Tithe and the limited earlier map evidence. Such an exercise would, in any case, mainly reveal aspects of post-thirteenth-century evolution rather than the preceding century which is the object of our study. We have, instead, simply suggested a broad outline of probable land-use, communications and settlement in the period of Hen Domen's occupation. Although no doubt inaccurate in many respects, and certainly more empty than the real environment must have been, the tentative map of Old Montgomery presented (fig. 6.3) illustrates how generally different the landscape of *circa* 1200 was from that of today (*cf.* the reproduction of the 1:25,000 map in fig. 6.5). The present landscape is more obviously the creation of later centuries: the thirteenth century, which brought the new castle, town and church as well as roads to serve them; the later middle ages, which brought piecemeal enclosures and emparkment; the eighteenth and nineteenth centuries, which brought a rebuilding of the town, turnpike roads, final land enclosures and a railway. Nevertheless, the eleventh and twelfth centuries made crucial contributions to the palimpsest which this landscape presents to its modern reader, not the least of which was the name Montgomery, imported from Normandy and given in turn to two castles, a borough, a marcher lordship and a Welsh county.

Some authors would no doubt have presented an account of this landscape as one of a 'territory' with a succession of 'central places': Ffridd Faldwyn, Forden Gaer, Chirbury, Hen Domen and finally New Montgomery. This notion is useful as long as we recognize its limitations. First, the territory itself was not constant: within historic times, known variants are the pre- and post-Conquest hundred of Chirbury, the *castellarium* of Domesday Book, the twelfth-century lordship and the thirteenth-century parish. We have no way of knowing how the territory attached to Ffridd Faldwyn in earlier times may have evolved, even though the topography suggests reasonable boundaries (above). Second, the functions and social contexts of these places were not constant: Ffridd Faldwyn was a fortified community, Forden Gaer was a fort in a much wider military network, Old Montgomery was a castle belonging to powerful individuals, whereas the *burh* at Chirbury and the castle and town at New Montgomery were royal establishments. Third, any overall interpretation of this area construed in 'central place' terms is weakened by our ignorance of some important points about the early middle ages: particularly, how long after the Roman period occupation of the *vicus* area outside Forden Gaer may have continued, whether Ffridd Faldwyn had any post-Roman occupation, and precisely what role was played by *Witentreu*/Chirbury before it was fortified in 915. We should also remind ourselves that however we dress up an interpretation of this landscape, a simple fact, emphasized in our 1982 report (and recognized by others long before), remains: what gave almost all of these major fortified places something in common was their proximity to the ford on the River Severn at Rhydwhyman, an important crossing point from the territory which (from a modern viewpoint) we might call 'English' into that which (similarly) we might call 'Welsh'.

It is also interesting to observe that settlement patterns of this sort have in recent years become topical subjects in rural settlement studies generally. Emphasis upon the important succession of fortified sites, with their more specialist defensive, social, political and ecclesiastical functions, should not disguise the fact that the rural framework of the Welsh borderlands as a whole was a dispersed settlement pattern of farms and hamlets but few villages. The agrarian history of the holdings which made up the Domesday *castellarium*, the marcher lordship and thirteenth-century parish would themselves be a subject worthy of enquiry within the wider context of rural studies established long ago by Dorothy Sylvester (1955 and 1969).

Fieldwork at Lymore Park and Sarkley

Field recording at Lymore Park and Sarkley was carried out by small survey teams during the annual seasons of our training excavations in the late 1970s and early 1980s. In both places, our attention was drawn by the survival of narrow ridge and furrow, of dimensions not dissimilar to that which excavation had earlier shown to be of pre-Norman date at Hen Domen itself (Barker & Lawson 1971). Lymore Park, an estate on the south-east side of the parish, also had a number of other interesting features, one of which we subjected to a small excavation. In neither place was it possible to date the surviving ridge and furrow: there were no stratigraphic relationships with adjacent features, no pieces of documentary or map evidence, no aerial photographs to provide complementary data to the ground observations. As a methodological comparison, it is notable that in a recent study of ridge and furrow adjacent to Offa's Dyke,

Fig. 6.5: The Montgomery area: reproduced from O.S. 1:25000 sheet Explorer 216, 1999 (reproduced from the Ordnance Survey map with the permission of Her Majesty's Stationery Office, Crown Copyright ED 187A)

for which several complementary forms of evidence *were* available, there was still no easy conclusion to be drawn about the date of the field system studied (Everson *et al.* 1991). Dating fields, through observation and recording alone, is an almost impossible task. Nevertheless, there is at least a possibility that the Sarkley and Lymore ridging, like that at Hen Domen, is of early date.

Sarkley

This property, whose name first appears in documentary record in the fifteenth century (above), lies to the south-east of Hen Domen and adjacent to the early road which runs across the parish to the ford across the River Severn

(fig. 6.3). In a field immediately to its south-east there survived (until the field was ploughed in 1981) clear, but low ridges, running down-slope. The best preserved area of ridging (traces of which also survived slightly north and south of the illustrated area) was surveyed in a series of profiles and the information processed in isometric projection with the vertical scale enhanced by a factor of ten (figs 6.6 and 6.7). They had an average width, ridge crest to crest, of up to 5.0m, occasionally wider. Their date cannot be demonstrated, since they were not at any point sealed by other landscape features. The featureless areas at the ends of groups of ridges (marked on the plan as 'x') may represent headlands. On the west they ran up to, but stopped short of, a hollow way and

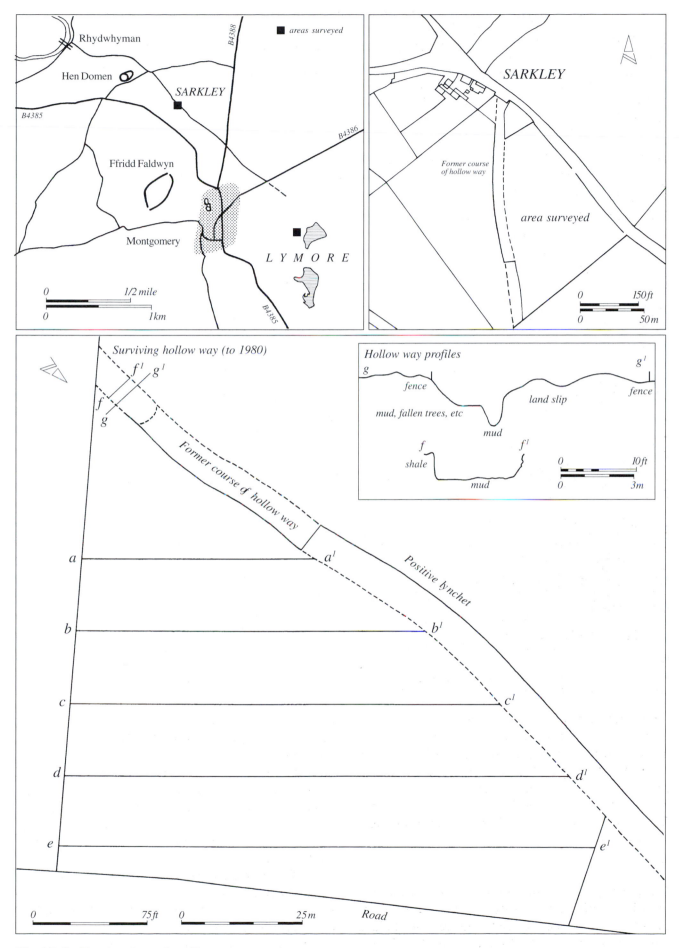

Fig. 6.6: Sarkley: location and profiles across survey area

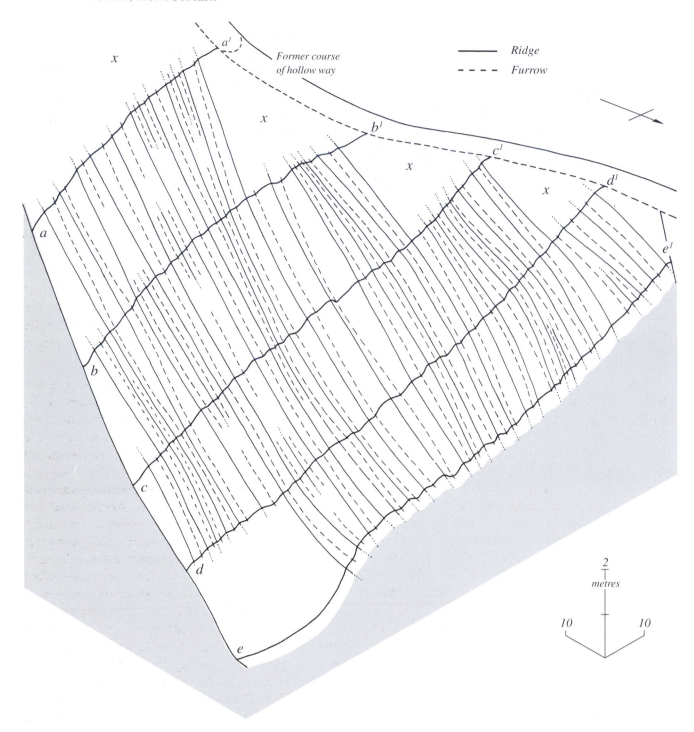

Fig. 6.7: Sarkley: isometric projection of surveyed profiles, showing ridging running north-east to south-west

were presumably later than it. This hollow way originally led from the existing road by Sarkley up the hill towards the northern end of the Iron Age hillfort at Ffridd Faldwyn. Much of this hollow way had been filled in at some time, though its overall shape had not entirely disappeared, and at the southern end of the field subjected to survey it still survived as a rock-cut trough. Its profile, between 1.0m and 2.0m in depth, is shown in fig. 6.6, which also illustrates its varied rate of survival even over a short length. A general view of it adjacent to the survey area is shown in fig. 6.8. Since the survey was carried

out, this feature, like the ridges in the field, has suffered further destruction. It was argued above that this hollow way was in origin a prehistoric road, with later phases of use into the medieval period. The ridged field itself may have been early medieval in date, like that at Hen Domen, and for some reason escaping destruction in subsequent centuries. Equally, it could have been ploughed in narrow ridges at some later date.

Fig. 6.8: Hollow way at Sarkley, looking towards Ffridd Faldwyn

Lymore Park

To the south-east of Montgomery, an extensive parkland was created not later than the seventeenth century, perhaps in an area used as a hunting chase in earlier centuries. Its name, Lymore, first occurs in documentary record in the fourteenth century (see above) but comprises two Old English elements, *leah* and *mor*, clearing/woodland and marsh (Smith 1956, II, 128, 42; Gelling 1984, 54, 198). Its seventeenth-century mansion was demolished in the 1920s and in the twentieth century the park has been an idyllic setting in which animals graze, cricket is played, fish are caught and pheasants shot. Like many parkland environments, it contains fossilized landscape features and deserves more archaeological attention than it has so far been given. Apart from the modest efforts described here, the centre of the park itself has been the subject of only one fieldwork exercise (Arnold & Reilly 1986), though fieldwork adjacent to Offa's Dyke has extended into the eastern fringe of the park (Everson *et al.* 1991). The survey conducted by Arnold and Reilly included an area of substantial ridge and furrow and other features including possible house sites. Despite (limited) excavation, this survey produced no dating evidence for any of these features.

Our attention was drawn in particular by two points of interest, an area of ridging and a linear bank (fig. 6.9). Immediately west of the lower pool is an area with narrow ridge and furrow which also survives further into the park. The former was surveyed in a series of profiles and the results are illustrated as an isometric projection with exaggerated vertical scale. As at Sarkley, there was no way of dating these narrow ridges, which, like those at Sarkley, measure up to 5.0m from ridge crest to crest. They may pre-date the emparkment, and may even be contemporary with the pre-Norman ridges at Hen Domen. Alternatively, since it is known that fields were sometimes ploughed in narrow ridges, often referred to as 'narrow rig' (Taylor 1975, Chapter 8), in the late eighteenth and early nineteenth centuries, they may

represent ploughing during the life of the park itself. This could perhaps have been during the Napoleonic wars when pasture was sometimes turned to arable to increase crop output. It may, however, simply have been a piece of land drainage and improvement, to which the creation of the pools in the centre of the park would also have contributed (though their primary function was presumably aesthetic). The relationship of the ridging with the adjacent (lower) pool did not emerge very clearly from the survey. The ridges seem simply to fade away and may have been eroded by water action at the pool edge. The lower pool seems to have been created *circa* 1800, since, although it is shown on the Tithe Map of 1839, it does not appear on a private map drawn up in 1785 ('A Survey and Valuation of the Several Estates belonging to the Earl of Powis in the parishes of Montgomery, Chirbury [and elsewhere]'; Shropshire Record Office, 4303/2). The upper pool, beyond the site of the former Lymore Hall, and an intermediate one (now drained) already existed in 1785.

Running through the western part of the park is a prominent, low, flat-topped bank, some 6.0 metres wide, whose course can be traced for approx. 250.0m from the northern side of the lower pool towards the Montgomery–Chirbury road (fig. 6.9). The eastern end of this bank seems to have been truncated by the digging of this pool and the building of its dam, suggesting that the bank is earlier than *circa* 1800. When considering the evolution of roads within the parish we speculated whether this bank might be the remains of a Roman road: it follows a course which continues the line of the early medieval route south-eastwards from the crossing of the River Severn and points in the direction of the Roman camps at Brompton. In order to test this hypothesis, a small excavation was carried out during a long weekend in May 1981. A section, 2.0m wide, was cut through the bank, in the hope of finding dating and constructional evidence (fig. 6.10). We are grateful to the then owner of the park, Major Herbert, for permission to excavate. Excavation (shown in progress on fig. 6.11) revealed a shallow ditch (4 on the section) flanking the north-east side of the bank. Since a fragment of the clay bank material (6) lay outside it, this ditch may have been a secondary feature with its upcast (2) on the inner side. The body of the bank (6) consisted of clay soil with some small stones. It was capped with a more consolidated layer of smoother small stones (3). On top of this, a humic soil and turf had developed since abandonment. From within and beneath the stony capping were recovered a handful of medieval and post-medieval sherds (the latter identified as from the seventeenth/ eighteenth century by Mike Watson, then of Shropshire Archaeology Service). Some brick fragments were also recovered. A shallow gulley and smaller bank (7 and 8)

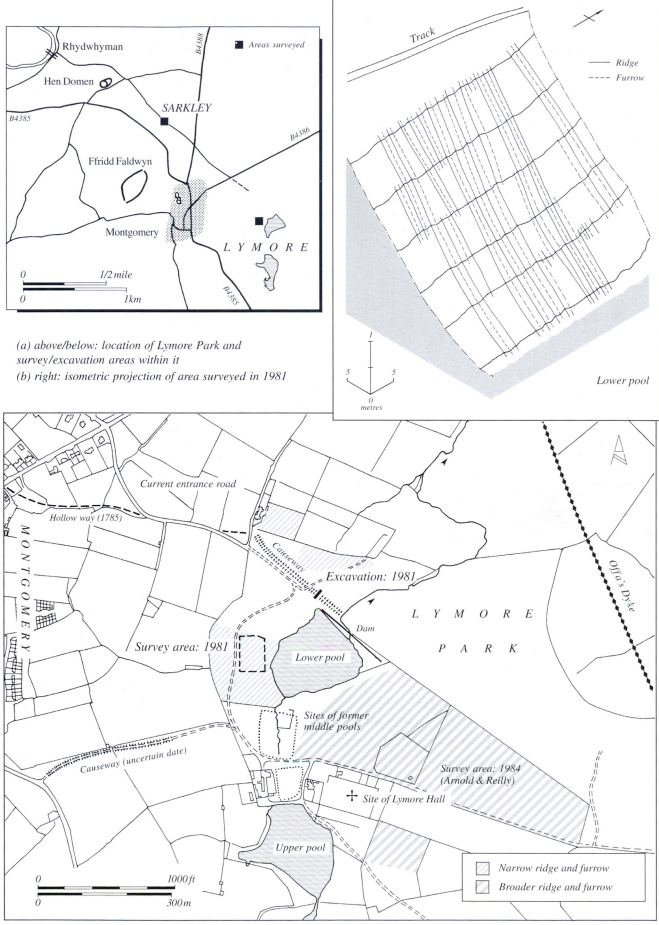

(a) *above/below: location of Lymore Park and survey/excavation areas within it*

(b) *right: isometric projection of area surveyed in 1981*

Fig. 6.9: Lymore Park

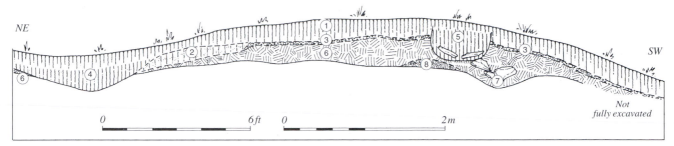

Fig. 6.10: Lymore Park: section through causeway north of Lower Pool, excavated in 1981

Fig. 6.11: Excavation in progress on causeway in Lymore Park

sealed near the south-west end of the excavated section may have been an earlier field boundary, and a hole in the very top perhaps a fairly recent fence-post position. Only a small sample of this bank was examined, so the possibility must be allowed that an excavation elsewhere along its course might have produced different information. Nevertheless, the available evidence suggests that the bank is a post-medieval feature, perhaps a carriageway leading through the park from the Chirbury road towards Lymore Hall. There presumably was an earlier road somewhere along this route, pre-dating the park, but this bank does not seem to have been it. It is perhaps also relevant that an embanked feature of similar appearance survives near the southern entrance to the park, by the road from Montgomery to Churchstoke.

CONCLUSION

In this chapter, consideration is given first to the dating evidence for the site, second to the general character of its building evidence and third to the overall impression of life here in the middle ages provided by all the categories of evidence recovered. Its structure therefore follows that of the concluding discussion to our 1982 report (Barker & Higham 1982, Chapter IX). The two may profitably be read in conjunction, although, as with other parts of this report, we have incorporated the major points of our 1982 publication in the present one so that the discussion is largely self-contained.

The Dating Evidence

In the first published report the archaeological dating evidence for the occupation at Hen Domen was separated from the historical framework in order to achieve critical application of both the documentary and physical evidence (Barker & Higham 1982, Chapters III and IX). The documentary framework suggests foundation of the site in the 1070s and provides a later thirteenth-century context for its decline. Roger de Montgomery, the founder named in Domesday Book, became earl of Shrewsbury in 1070 or 1071. From the 1270s, with Edward I's conquest of north Wales, the middle border was less important and even New Montgomery castle was past its military prime in the early fourteenth century. Within this approximate two hundred year period, the documentary evidence reveals two major changes of ownership context: from a son of Roger de Montgomery to the family of de Boulers, in the early twelfth century, and from the last of the de Boulers, with a brief interruption of Welsh possession, to the English crown in the early thirteenth century. Since a strong case was argued in the first published report for the identification of Hen Domen with Roger de Montgomery's castle, the historical framework inevitably influenced the interpretation of the successive excavated phases of archaeological evidence. It was assumed that the first castle structures encountered belonged to the 1070s and that the last were of the thirteenth century.

The archaeological dating evidence available when the first report was published, though limited in quantity, provided no difficulty with the historical correlation summarized above. Unfortunately, the only medieval coin discovered (an early thirteenth century cut halfpenny) was not found in a securely stratified context and was therefore of limited value. A sherd of Roman pottery from the pre-castle plough-soil provided a *terminus post quem* for the building of the castle rampart. There was also a C^{14} assessment, from the buried soil beneath the rampart, of 980 ± 290 (uncalibrated). A jug handle of late eleventh to early twelfth-century Stamford ware was discovered in the primary silt of the motte ditch. Sherds of 'developed' Stamford ware, of perhaps late twelfth-century date, came from the bailey. The latest (stratified) medieval pottery from the bailey, studied in the context of the region's pottery (Barker 1970), was of Shropshire origin and perhaps of late thirteenth or very early fourteenth-century date. The pottery in general did not include fourteenth century and later types identified in the region. The latest datable item of metalwork was a rowel spur, whose general use in England was thought at the time to have started in the later thirteenth century (as discussed in the London Museum Catalogue, 1954, 103). This came from the upper fill of the large pit 1/27, whose development spanned the latest stage of phase Y and the final structural phase (Z) of the site. Even without the historical evidence, therefore, excavation of the site would have suggested occupation from *circa* 1100 to *circa* 1300.

In the present volume, the account of the structural, artefactual and landscape evidence has been cast in the same chronological mould as that suggested in the 1982 report and in subsequent published interim discussions. Since 1982, no new historical evidence has come to light affecting either the identification of Hen Domen with Old Montgomery or the nature of its occupation between the late eleventh and late thirteenth-century limits derived from the documentary sources. But, from excavations in the subsequent decade, there is now a greater quantity of independently datable physical evidence with which to tackle the dating issue from an archaeological angle.

This new evidence (which also includes a few abraded fragments of Roman pottery from the pre-castle plough-soil) confirms the overall impression of a site occupied in the twelfth and thirteenth centuries, but also extends its occupation back into the eleventh century. It can be summarized as follows.

1. The pottery from the motte (above, Chapter 5) includes a small amount of 'developed' Stamford ware (whose circulation is thought to have ended in the early thirteenth century) as well as two sherds of French pottery of late twelfth to early thirteenth-century date. The latest local types are thirteenth-century, with one sherd perhaps slightly later.

2. Although the metalwork includes items of varying currency from the eleventh century onwards, the only distinctively datable object in a usefully stratified context remains the simple rowel spur, referred to above. The appearance of such spurs has, however, since been pushed back into the earlier thirteenth century, appearing in stained glass scenes in both England and France by *circa* 1220–1230. They were, nevertheless, increasingly used later in the century (Ellis 1982: Ellis in Clark 1995, 128).

3. The wooden tub from the bailey ditch: dendrochronological analysis suggests it was made from a tree felled in the later eleventh century (above, Chapter 5).

4. Four C^{14} assessments: the first three are from samples taken from excavated contexts in the early 1980s; the fourth is from a (bridge) timber which had been excavated in the early 1960s, put into storage, cut for dendrochronological study in 1969 (when its wide tree-ring pattern was deemed unsuitable for dendrochronology by the then specialists in the field) and subsequently subjected to C^{14} assessment with the other samples in the early 1980s. The following, which relate to contexts discussed in Chapter 3, are all English Heritage calibrations, made in 1995, of the original Birmingham University assessments made in the early 1980s:—

    a) a granary post-base (95% confidence range, AD 1010–1270);

    b) a granary post-base (95% confidence range, AD 970–1230);

    c) a charcoal sample from Building LIV (95% confidence range, AD 1170–1290);

    d) the preserved bridge timber found in the motte ditch (95% confidence range, AD 1040–1290).

Within the hundreds of archaeological contexts excavated, both common sense supposed and the study of the pottery and the metal slag has demonstrated (above, Chapter 5) much re-deposition and disturbance of clay and other building material, together with the artefact evidence within it, arising from successive building operations. For this reason, many artefacts must have been found in contexts different from those in which they were originally discarded, though in most cases this would not be independently demonstrable. However, we occasionally encountered artefact evidence which seemed quite out of place and which, on first impression, seemed to create dating difficulties. These instances were discussed at the appropriate points of the foregoing text. Three of the granary post-holes contained a sherd each of developed Stamford ware, three others contained sherds of local glazed wares, and a corner post-position of the primary motte tower contained three small sherds of local twelfth-century glazed pottery. Yet both buildings, we have argued, were earlier in date than this. Consideration of the stratigraphic data reminds us of the subtlety with which 'post-holes' and their contents must be interpreted. In each case, the finds came not from the pit (indeed no pit was discovered for the post on the motte—the top of the motte seems to have been laid around it) which was dug when the post was laid, but from the position which the post itself had occupied. They must therefore have got into place through one of two processes. One is the removal of the post, that is during the repair, rebuilding or demolition of the structures concerned. The other is during the rotting of the post *in situ* when the gradual replacement of timber by soft soil over a long period would have allowed the sinking of artefacts from above through progressively softer deposits (particularly if aided by worm action). In the case of the granary, the lack of association of the sherds with the erection of the structure is emphasized by the rather earlier trend of the C^{14} assessments from two surviving post-bases (one of which came from one of the features in question). One of the post-pits also contained a sherd of the earliest coarse fabric which occurs in the bailey. In the case of the motte tower the lack of association of the sherds with the erection of the structure is emphasized by the fact that they join exactly with similar sherds (from more than one vessel) found in later contexts on the motte (above, Chapter 5). The post-position also revealed signs of re-use during its life (above, Chapter 4). It is important to remember the potential for misleading 'dates' derived from the contents of post-pits and their post-holes if the possible sequences of events are not borne in mind. The issue has been discussed by one of us elsewhere (Barker 1977, 83–90: 'the life-history of a post-hole').

More important, however, is consideration of the general pattern of the dating evidence and its implications. All the new artefactual and dendrochronological evidence confirms the earlier archaeological dating of the site and this is true, broadly, of the C^{14} assessments. The general significance of the latter lies in their overall span, from the eleventh to thirteenth centuries, which is exactly the period covered by the historical evidence. It should also be remembered that the four sampled contexts represent a very tiny proportion of the total number of contexts in which timber was used on this site—almost all of which had disappeared. Nevertheless, the C^{14} assessments from Building LIV and, to a lesser extent, from the motte bridge timber would, if seen in isolation, suggest a later date for these structures than has been argued on the basis of their place in the overall stratigraphic sequence. The latter suggests that the bridge was an early feature of the site (though the timber was re-used from an earlier structure altogether since it had a redundant feature cut into its underside). The stratigraphic sequence in the bailey suggests that Building LIV followed fairly soon after the creation of the bailey rampart. The C^{14} assessments in isolation, however, would obviously place Building LIV later, and perhaps, by analogy, Buildings XXVI and XXVII, which overlay the tail of the rampart further west. They might also give an impression of a later date for the bridge timber (though its 95% confidence range does, in fact, include the late eleventh century, indicated by the historical and stratigraphic evidence).

Without wishing to enter into special pleading, it must, however, be allowed that C^{14} assessments are sometimes inaccurate, that they may be based upon samples which have become inadvertently contaminated, that their laboratory refinement progresses with time (these were processed in the early 1980s), and that, in any case, true 'dates' may lie at the extremes of, or even outside, a 95% confidence range. One of the four assessments under discussion (the bridge timber) was obtained from a sample which had been taken many years earlier. Another (from Building LIV) was from a charcoal hearth deposit where the possibility of intrusion from a higher deposit, through minor root action, cannot be ruled out (in which case, this C^{14} assessment would relate to the buildings of phase X or Y which overlay Building LIV). But, as a methodological principle, it should be admitted that, had these assessments been obtained in circumstances devoid of the other archaeological and historical data from the site, they would have had a major effect on the suggested dating sequence. In the bailey, the phases described (in the 1982 and 1988 reports) as X, Y and Z would all have to be put in the period *after* the life-span of Building LIV, that is from some time in the thirteenth century onwards to an unspecified but much later end-date. The proximity (and comparable size of foundations) of the first hall (Building LIa) in front of the motte ditch and the preserved bridge timber would have led us to suggest the hall itself was of perhaps mid-twelfth-century origin, rather than the earlier date which has been assumed. And, since the planning and construction of the hall, the bridge and the earliest motte tower encountered in excavation seem to have had much in common, we might have placed the start of our

recorded motte sequence in the twelfth century, too. Finally, since the massive timbers used in these various structures are paralleled in the earliest bailey palisade, we might, by extension, have argued that the latter was also later in date.

Contra these contentious, but interesting arguments, based on only part of a very limited quantity of C^{14} evidence, strong arguments are possible based not only on the general historical and archaeological framework but also on some specific observations. The lowest silting of the motte ditch, around the preserved bridge timber, contained only the sherd of early Stamford ware, not pottery of later date, nor were there any sherds in the immediately overlying layers (Barker 1970, 33). The early hall (LIa) was succeeded by another (LIb, phase X), after whose life-span a deep pit (1/27) was cut, adjacent to a structure of phase Y. This pit was later filled but its uppermost portion was floored, within a structure of phase Z. The layer beneath the floor contained pottery (including decorated 'face-jugs') of mid to late thirteenth-century date (*ibid.*, 34). This suggests the start of this long sequence, embracing at least three major periods of the site's development, was at a very much earlier date. Finally, since the general phases X, Y and Z have all to be dated after the life-span of Building LIV, which they overlie, if we postulate (on the basis of the C^{14} assessment) a date of *circa* 1200 for the start of Building LIV, then either the majority of the site's structural development has to be crammed into the thirteenth century, which seems most improbable, or, if occupation actually extended well beyond the late thirteenth-century horizon suggested by the historical context, then the site should have produced a considerable assemblage of pottery and other data from the late thirteenth century onwards deriving from phases X, Y and Z. In fact, the amount of specifically late material, even of the later thirteenth century, from the site is small (see Ratkai above, Chapter 5, and earlier pottery discussions by Barker 1970 and Clarke 1982). This pattern is much more in keeping with our suggestion of a phase of reduced occupation at Hen Domen during the life of New Montgomery castle. Excavations at New Montgomery castle (Knight 1990–91) revealed some overlap with the later pottery occurring at Hen Domen (already noted in Clarke 1982), but most of the medieval pottery was different (and there was also a substantial body of post-medieval material). It included a range of foreign imports and British wares, datable, both from documented contexts at New Montgomery castle itself and at a range of other sites, from the later thirteenth to fifteenth centuries. None of this material occurred at Hen Domen and its absence (as well as that of other post-1300 wares discussed in Barker 1970) is very telling. Had it been on the site it should have come to light given the sizeable areas excavated. It is also notable that whereas the Hen Domen metalwork bears general similarity to that from other eleventh–twelfth century castles, especially Goltho and Castle Acre (above, Chapter 5), it is on the whole different from the thirteenth century and later collection excavated at New Montgomery castle (Knight 1993). Moreover, finding a social or political context for occupation at Hen Domen later than the end of the thirteenth century is extremely difficult (see below). In retrospect, however, the captions for our main published phase plans (Barker & Higham 1982 and 1988) may have been slightly misleading: since the filling of pit 1/27 may have continued to the second half of the thirteenth century (see above), phase Y (of which it was part) may also have continued to that date, and phase Z, which followed, may have been late in the thirteenth century and not, as previously suggested, soon after New Montgomery's foundation in 1223. But certainty is impossible.

Thus, while it is theoretically possible that the whole of the structural sequence may be much later than argued in earlier publications, on the whole we prefer a chronology which, while perhaps extended a little in the late thirteenth century, takes overall account of the site's archaeology and history rather than allowing one C^{14} assessment in particular to create a wholly new interpretation. The two C^{14} assessments from the granary, it should be noted, create no difficulty with the interpretation of the early castle which we have suggested on stratigraphic grounds. The enigmatic C^{14} assessment from Building LIV, we suggest with due caution, is probably an aberrant result. Nevertheless, it is essential to acknowledge these problems, not only because they highlight an interesting methodological issue but also because they remind us of important points about the excavation itself. First, half the bailey remains undug and it may contain data crucial to understanding the site's overall chronology as well as the distribution of structures in different periods. Second, in the bailey, it was possible to remove all the archaeological deposits, including the massive rampart and the pre-castle plough-soil and underlying structures. With the exception of a short stretch of rampart left *in situ*, the archaeology of the northern half of the bailey was totally excavated (and thus destroyed). Third, on the motte, in contrast, the excavation, despite creating an imposing spoil-heap which had to be re-instated by machine, was able only to remove the upper levels. An operation comparable with that in the bailey, where the archaeology was removed down to the 'natural' boulder clay, was totally beyond our resources. We must therefore acknowledge that deeper within the motte, and perhaps underneath it, there may lie further evidence relating to the earliest castle mentioned in Domesday Book.

If it exists, such evidence probably lies very deep indeed: the material in which the earliest building (encountered) was constructed was very clean and the large section cut high up on the east face of the motte (above Chapter 4), where this material was extensively revealed, showed no sign of an earlier motte summit. The study of the pottery from the motte (above, Chapter 5) revealed, associated with the first tower identified, a few sherds of the pottery associated with the earliest levels in the bailey, as well as other types. But, as in the bailey, there was little pottery (of any sort) in the earliest phase encountered, but increasing amounts in subsequent phases, especially in the middle of the sequence excavated. Allowing for the problems of residuality and intrusion in the interpretation of the pottery, it may well be significant that both motte and bailey assemblages have this quantitative sequence in common. We also know that the motte was a primary feature of the castle, a fact revealed in 1967 by a section excavated across the north-east face of the motte which showed that it had not been added to a ringwork/bailey. It also revealed, however, a possible heightening of the motte, fairly low down its profile (Barker & Higham 1982, 72). This (thin and discontinuous) layer, which appeared to be a fragmentary turf-line within the motte, remains an enigma. Since it was seen only in section and not examined in the horizontal (or contoured) dimension, its true significance is not known. It may not have been an extensive horizon at all, but a localized deposit, within the construction of the motte (a problem which arises potentially in the case of any layer seen only in section and not examined horizontally). But, on the other hand, it may hint at an earlier phase of the motte and be relevant to the issue here under discussion. If there was an earlier, lower motte, however, it would have had a shallower ditch. During its life, this ditch might be expected to have accumulated occupational debris. This putative ditch must then have been replaced (and thus completely removed) by the digging of the deeper (excavated) ditch from which the present motte was constructed, perhaps in the twelfth century according to the arguments rehearsed above. If this was the case, it is odd that the bottom of this deeper ditch did not contain more occupational debris, both residual from the earlier phase and contemporary with its digging and early use. In fact, as explained above, the bottom layers of the ditch, where excavated, were devoid of artefactual evidence apart from the single sherd of early Stamford ware.

Nevertheless, a devil's advocate could argue that we have seen little of Roger de Montgomery's castle at all and that what we have revealed is essentially an enlarged castle, perhaps the work of his sons or re-created by the de Boulers in the twelfth century and a royal garrison in the thirteenth. Following this argument, and allowing for unknown evidence in the unexcavated (southern) half of the bailey, Roger's putative castle would have consisted of a low motte under the present one, a bridge represented (in the archaeological record) by only two features in the motte ditch, the structures represented by the features truncated by the foundations of Building LIa, and, finally, the building we have interpreted as a granary. The bailey may have been defended (though not demonstrably so) by a palisade and fighting platform whose front rested on a low bank. If this structure was framed and enclosed, we need not even assume that the massive rampart had yet been piled around it. This hypothetical earliest castle is unfortunately impossible to illustrate, even by a sketch plan, since the only structure whose shape could be shown is the 'granary'.

There is really no way of resolving this issue, though we prefer an interpretation based on overall stratigraphic and historical considerations. But, to be fair to the archaeological evidence, we have referred to the structures described in Chapter 3 simply as 'the early castle'. Whereas Buildings LIV, XXVI and XXVII are demonstrably 'early' in the relative sense that they pre-date the structures published as phase X, we have also indicated that they were, stratigraphically, secondary additions within the early castle, the time-span of whose development we do not know. Similarly, the general plans of subsequent phases have been labelled 'middle', 'later' and 'latest' to emphasize the relative chronology without burdening them with interpretative chronological labels. But, in preferring, on the basis of the history and the general stratigraphic story, an early castle of a fuller sort than that hypothetically suggested above, we may also recall the general circumstances surrounding the foundation and early history of the site. The castle mentioned in Domesday Book was built by a member of the most powerful circle of the Norman ruling class, had been given Roger de Montgomery's own name and was the centre of a newly created *castellarium*. It was the base from which considerable conquests to the west of the River Severn had been made by 1086. The killing of Hugh de Montgomery's garrison by the Welsh in 1095 so angered the Normans that a campaign was led into Wales by the king, William Rufus, in person. It was subsequently among the properties held by Robert of Bellême, a rich and eventually over-mighty subject with a formidable military reputation and numerous castles on both sides of the English Channel (see Thompson 1990 for a recent review of his career). It seems reasonable to assume that this castle was not only properly defended but also adequately provided with buildings.

We have also, throughout, reminded ourselves and our readers that the suggested overall 'phases' are

undoubtedly simplifications of reality. Isolating, for illustrative purpose, the 'early' from the 'middle' and 'later' castles may actually disguise a more gradual process of structural renewal which did not neatly correspond with changes of ownership and historically defined dates. This is not simply of general significance in our appreciation of the site but is also of relevance to the matter of dating when we consider the life-span of some of the 'early' structures under discussion. It has been suggested (see Beresford 1987, 75–77) that substantial earthfast oak posts, of dimensions approximately 12in square, could last up to 100 years. We have argued that many of the early timbers used at Hen Domen were of this approximate size and that some of those in the motte tower and bailey granary had a very long life (Chapter 4 and Barker & Higham 1982). In contrast, we have assumed that the primary palisade in the bailey was replaced at an earlier date by the structures described as phase UVW in the north-west and those equivalents further east (discussed in Chapter 3)—all of which pre-dated the defences belonging to the structures published as phase X. This may, in fact, have been the case, for whatever reason. Perhaps the defences were damaged, even slighted, after the successful attack by the Welsh in 1095 and needed replacing? Or perhaps the fact that they were buried so deeply influenced their effective life? Alternatively, our assumptions about the shorter life of the palisade may be wrong and, if so, the defences of our published phase X may not have been built until after the domestic buildings of that phase were complete and in use. Although 'phase plans' are an inevitable part of excavation reports, a more meaningful concept would be that of a 'building site' in a more or less continuous process of evolution.

Beyond this point, exploration of chronology, both relative and absolute, perhaps becomes pointless. We cannot expect the archaeological data to tell us more than it is capable of, and basic problems—the paucity of independently datable material and the small amount of pottery circulating during the castle's early occupation—remain. It is, nevertheless, a sobering thought that even where, as at Hen Domen, a considerable proportion of the whole site has been excavated, the evidence recovered may not necessarily (indeed, is perhaps unlikely to) lead to a single and simple set of conclusions. How much greater, therefore, is the danger of gaining (quite unknowingly) a distorted picture from an excavation of much smaller scale which might happen to produce some sorts of dating evidence but not others? It would be an interesting exercise to consider the dating (and other) evidence which might have been recovered from this site through a series of small excavations at varied locations.

The Structural Evidence

In the following discussion, three themes are explored: the building techniques employed; the planning of buildings; and the overall planning of the castle.

Building Techniques

The 1982 report included consideration of the various building techniques encountered in the excavated evidence (Barker & Higham 1982, 89–92). As well as post-built technique in a structure which pre-dated the castle, the evidence dealt with by that date indicated a number of distinct structural methods, suggesting buildings constructed in the following ways:—

1. with substantial ground-fast posts supporting walls which must have contained other timbers higher up, not visible in the ground evidence, and in which infill panels of wattle and daub may be presumed;

2. with slighter ground-fast posts and stakes, forming a skeleton around which more substantial clay walls were built;

3. with a completely framed technique, using no ground-fast posts, suggested by shallow post-depressions, by the extent of floor areas, or other tenuous but significant evidence such as lines of stones representing the edges of areas covered by structures; here it is assumed that sill-beams lay directly on the ground surface or that the bottoms of posts stood on the ground with horizontal timbers jointed in just above ground level;

4. with sill-beams laid in trenches, where the building was framed but nevertheless left clear ground evidence. In a limited number of cases, framing was also indicated by the preservation of timbers in waterlogged conditions. The motte bridge sole-plate (which lay in a shallow trench) revealed mortice and tenon jointing. The bailey palisade base revealed thick, pegged planking and probably lay directly on top of the rampart.

It was noted that these building methods were not uniformly distributed throughout the various phases of the site's development.

a) The early castle made much use of framing technique, in various ways: the bailey palisade, which, standing on the pre-castle surface, was buried within and rose from the bailey rampart; the early motte bridge and the hall in front of it, which were built on sill-beams laid in trenches; and smaller buildings behind the bailey rampart, represented only by their floors. The granary, in contrast, was supported by ground-fast posts.

b) The gradual rebuilding of the first castle, and its development through the twelfth century, made much use of ground-fast posts. These were sometimes substantial, as in the hall at the lower end of the bailey and in the re-constructed hall in front of the motte bridge. At other times, the timbers were much slighter, as in the various small buildings behind the rampart, and there was probably more use of clay as a walling material here. In one of these structures, part of the clay wall base was still *in situ*.

c) In the later phases of the castle's use, there was some mixing of techniques employed, from the reduced granary with big, ground-fast timbers (a building inherited from earlier phases), through structures with posts of various sizes, to others where framing on horizontal timbers is assumed. In the very last phase recorded, however, the evidence was exclusively of shallow post depressions and other features suggesting the use of framed techniques throughout.

By around 1980, when these building methods had been encountered, no direct evidence of roofing materials had been recovered. It was assumed that thatch, or more probably wooden shingles were employed. One or two preserved foundation timbers had been encountered (the motte bridge base-plate and a bailey palisade base-plate) but no evidence had been recovered of preserved superstructural details. There was an assumption that oak was the major material used when substantial timbers were needed: the two preserved pieces were oak and the large quantity of wood shavings preserved in deep pit 1/27 (Barker & Higham 1982, 63) and presumed to have come from the trimming of structural timbers was mainly oak. However, on the basis of medieval documentary and pictorial evidence, as well as surviving medieval timber buildings, it was suggested that the excavated structures may have been far more elaborate, even ornate, than the frequently simple ground evidence itself suggested. It is not impossible, for example, that timbers whose lowest extremities were crudely shaped, where they would stand within a post-hole, were squared, chamfered, or even decorated where they were to be visible in the building itself. These more general arguments about the nature and appearance of timber castles were subsequently developed at length (Higham & Barker 1992) using a variety of evidence. If the timber buildings at Hen Domen had any 'architectural' qualities, in doorways, windows or other details, they would, of course, have been of contemporary Romanesque style. In contrast, the successor castle at (New) Montgomery, built in the thirteenth century, was built in the Gothic style and mainly in stone.

The excavated evidence recovered since around 1980, discussed in detail in the present volume, has added to the earlier picture in various ways. The examination of the waterlogged area in the bailey ditch produced preserved wooden items (above, Chapters 3 & 5) including a wooden roofing shingle and fragments of building timber which add some life to our structures.

Additional ground evidence has come from the eastern half of the hall (LIa) in front of the motte bridges, from the Building (LIV) at the tail of the rampart in the north-eastern part of the bailey, from the primary bailey defences in the whole of the north-east sector, from a small portion of the outer rampart of the bailey, from the top of the motte and from a pre-castle phase in the extreme north-east corner of the site.

This new evidence, while adding greatly to our view of the castle as a whole, has not really extended the repertoire of building techniques already recognized. The eastern half of hall LIa was built, unsurprisingly, in a large foundation trench, as in the western half, which presumably carried a sill-beam. The evidence for Building LIV, a mixture of shallow post-positions, lines of stones and some carbonized wood, suggests a framed structure. The same was probably true of Buildings XXVI and XXVII, behind the rampart further west, represented only by approximate floor areas and building debris. Although the bailey defences were not of uniform dimensions throughout their length, they shared the same principle of standing on the pre-castle surface, leaving ground evidence which was sometimes difficult to detect but which sometimes took the form of shallow holes or pads of stone or clay. The palisade on the outer rampart had a skeleton of insubstantial timbers, irregularly set, suggesting that the wall they represented was heavily clad in clay. The pre-castle building, under what was to be the north-east corner of the bailey, was of simple construction with regularly spaced but slender ground-fast posts. The sequence of structures on the motte displayed more or less all the techniques encountered on the site: posts buried within the motte on its construction, major posts subsequently dug into the motte top during the evolution of the building, minor posts supporting areas of infill between larger ones, and, at the end of the sequence, a building platform without post-holes but with much degraded clay, suggesting a framed building with clad walls. The sequence on the motte also bears some comparison with that in much of the bailey, in that there was a progression from a (presumably framed) structure resting on buried posts (as in the bailey palisade), through a phase of post-hole construction (as in much of the bailey's middle life) to a final one of framed construction without post-holes (as in the last period of the bailey).

The Planning of Buildings

Defining, from ground evidence, the ways in which buildings were constructed is, of course, only part of the challenge of understanding them. How they were roofed and how they were internally organized are equally important questions to ask. It is an obvious but crucial point that, when dealing with timber buildings whose disappearance above ground has left us only with the 'ghost' evidence of post-holes and other features, the degree of certainty in our interpretation declines dramatically the further up the building's superstructure we venture. We can often (though not always) be certain about a building's ground plan and we can usually (as discussed above) observe the main method of its construction. But thereafter, interpretation rests on varying degrees of speculation and common-sense. We had hoped, at an earlier stage of the project, eventually to offer a considered and detailed reconstruction drawing for almost every building excavated, but this has not proved possible within the constraints of time, resources and opportunity available. Instead, we offer some further general observations as well as overall reconstruction views of the castle's main building periods. The latter, already discussed in the foregoing chapters, are here reproduced (figs 7.1 and 7.2) together at smaller scale for ease of comparison.

Ultimately, the critical purpose of any domestic building construction technique is to support a roof, which by its very nature is physically furthest from the excavated evidence in the ground and therefore most difficult to interpret. Nevertheless, hints about the nature of roofs were sometimes provided by our ground plans. In the case of framed buildings or buildings based on major ground-fast posts, we may observe the likely relationship of posts in walls with the roof construction if we can confidently identify where all the major posts stood. For example, it has been suggested (above, Chapter 4) that the early motte tower and the building which evolved from it was a square with corner posts, intermediate posts and corresponding posts in an internal dividing wall. It is possible, therefore, that these posts, which stood opposite each other, directly supported roof timbers above them, as in bay construction. In other cases, however, such as framed buildings which left an incomplete set of ground evidence, we cannot make this observation because we cannot know where all the uprights were situated. Nor can we know where the uprights sprang from the sill-beams which were the foundations for some structures, again limiting our view of roof structure. Where buildings depended on ground-fast posts we may sometimes observe where these do not occur in opposing pairs, indicating a roof resting on wall-plates rather than constructed in bays. A good example of the latter is the hall (XLVIII) in the lower half of the bailey (phase X) whose long walls contained different numbers of major posts (Barker & Higham 1982, 37, fig. 22).

Another interesting interpretational problem is the extent to which buildings had upper floors. In some cases, we presume this on common-sense grounds: it is impossible, for example, to imagine the square building

Fig. 7.1: Artist's reconstruction of early and middle periods (Peter Scholefield)

Fig. 7.2: Artist's reconstruction of later and last periods (Peter Scholefield)

on the motte being anything other than of two or more storeys, and we presume that the towers identified on the bailey rampart were of two storeys because their superstructures had to look out over the palisade and fighting platform. Another indicator of an upper storey may be massiveness of foundations, the obvious example of which is the large building (LIa etc) which stood for much of the castle's life in front of the motte bridges and which we have always envisaged as a first-floor hall. Where, in contrast, we encountered hearths at ground level, we assumed that the building was of a single storey only, as in the case of the lower bailey hall referred to above. But, overall, the presence or absence of hearths is a less than reliable source of inference, because they may have been removed by subsequent building operations and because fires could have been contained in braziers which kept them off the floor (as they must have been in upper storeys).

It is tempting, when observing the excavated evidence of timber buildings, to imagine that they were somehow simply 'built'. But, just as grand stone medieval buildings contain surveying, engineering and architectural issues for us to interpret, timber buildings must also be seen as products of decisions relating to layout and planning. Addressing this issue at Hen Domen involves the thorny problem of the 'metrication' of buildings, a matter which has been explored with success, for example in the Anglian royal palace at Yeavering (Hope-Taylor 1977) and other instances. In such studies, it has been possible to identify the 'building blocks' or common components of which houses were composed and even to suggest units of linear measurement which were employed.

Examination of the building plans at Hen Domen does not reveal, however, any fundamental and recurrent 'planning units'. There is perhaps a hint that the early castle was based on 6ft units (and here it is useful to think in imperial measurement, which brings us closer to medieval practice) but it can be no more than a hint. The first motte tower was an 18ft square. The bailey palisade in the north-west sector was based on approximately 12ft squares and that in the north-east sector had a rear line approximately 6ft behind the forward line. The bridge (to judge from the mortices cut in its base timber) was approximately 12ft wide. Building XXVI was also about 12ft wide and Building LIV about 18ft wide. But this point should not be over-played: the granary, for example, measured approximately 20ft × 14ft, and the large hall (LIa) was a very impressive 28ft wide. Little of even this limited observation carries over into the middle phase (X), though the lower hall (XLVIII) was 18ft wide. The overall impression in this phase is of greater irregularity all round. Arriving at even approximate measurements

in phases Y and Z is very difficult because, even where the sites of structures are evident, their extent is often less so.

In any case, the task of trying to identify recurrent measurements is made difficult by the varied nature of the foundation evidence which, in some cases, makes it impossible to know exactly where to measure 'from' and 'to' in such an exercise. We must also remember that, whatever measurements may seem apparent at foundation level, it was the usable space within buildings which mattered to their occupants and that this was influenced by wall thicknesses and other details. For example, the usable space within the large hall LIa was slightly narrower than the area revealed by simply measuring the overall area encompassed by its foundation trenches, and, conversely, if our interpretation of Building XXXVIII as a granary is correct, its raised floor area would have been slightly larger than the area encompassed by the post-holes discovered in excavation. Another variable, crucially important to the identification of building patterns, is the nature of the building materials employed. One aspect of this is the extent to which timbers were prepared specifically for the building in question and the extent to which they were re-used from earlier structures (in which case their existing size and character may have influenced the form of the new building erected). Another aspect of this issue is the changing nature of the social and economic background of the castle's builders. In the first phase and the latest phases these were immensely rich people, some of whose labour and materials were imported into the area: the Montgomery family and later Henry III. But in the middle phases, the de Boulers family depended on much more restricted resources and presumably a local building culture. It is perhaps not surprising to find the use of framed buildings, requiring better timber materials, more commonly in the early and later phases, whereas in the middle phases we find more use of clay-cladding over timbers of lesser quality. This distinction may have been a reflection not only of available materials but also of labour. The Montgomery family and those who acted on the king's behalf in the thirteenth century would have imported at least some of their craftsmen from Shropshire and adjacent areas, including men with varied experience of building. The de Boulers, in contrast, would have been more dependent on local labour most of the time, perhaps limiting the range or depth of skills available. Finally, as discussed below, there is the relationship of the castle's curvilinear outlines with its more rectilinear buildings. The compromise resulting from this relationship would have meant that many (particularly the smaller) buildings were sized to fit available spaces rather than to any pre-determined plans.

Despite these limitations, however, this exercise is not

entirely without value because it highlights the sorts of timber which must have been available to the castle's builders, particularly when vertical dimensions are taken into account as well as horizontal. To continue the analysis in terms of imperial measurement, if the construction of the first motte tower involved some timbers running the whole wall length then these were at least 18ft long. On the assumption that this building had a minimum of two storeys (though the ground floor may have been a rather low 'undercroft'), and since we know that the bottom 3ft of the main uprights was buried within the motte, the vertical timbers must have been 20ft minimum in length. The primary bailey palisade also consumed high-quality timbers which must have been of similar length to accommodate the 6ft of rampart clay which was piled around them and leave at least 12ft to protrude and provide both room beneath a wall-walk and a breast-work of at least man-height above that. Lateral timbers in the granary must have been of similar length both in the early and middle phases, and even though the evidence of the middle phase suggests a less sophisticated use of timber, the lower hall had roof trusses (on wall-plates rather than in bays, as argued above) spanning 18ft The most impressive structure was, in some ways, the large hall (LIa) at the foot of the motte bridges. We do not know how many bays it had nor, strictly speaking, whether its walls were of stave construction set in a sill-beam or spaced out major posts, similarly set, with panels between (though it had this style in its reconstructed form in phase X). But it was at least 40ft long and its width of 28ft raises interesting issues of roof construction. Excavation produced no evidence of aisle posts or a central row of posts: if these existed they must have stood on pads all trace of which had disappeared, which seems unlikely. The roofing issue is also linked to the interpretation of this building as either a ground-floor or first-floor hall. We have argued, above, that the massiveness of its foundations suggests two storeys, as well as a possible structural link with the motte bridge, and we feel this idea has much to commend it. A ground-floor hall might be expected to have had a lateral entrance, whereas this building's entrance was in its northern end. We have assumed, therefore, that this led into the undercroft and that entry at first-floor level was via an external stair (though no trace of this was ever discovered). But, if this was a first-floor hall, it makes the constructional challenge even greater because in addition to spanning its roof its builders would also need timbers long enough to create a horizontal first floor. Later, in phase X, this structure was rebuilt and extended eastwards by a further 10ft. In our discussion and published reconstruction drawing we have interpreted this as a portico added to a modified structure; another possibility would be that the building became a single-aisled hall at this time, the earlier eastern

external wall-line now becoming a line of aisle posts. But if the positions of the identified post-positions in this wall are any guide (they were irregularly spaced) the portico interpretation is preferable. The likelihood of the building connecting to the motte bridge is not affected by the first- or ground-floor alternative interpretations. In either event, the lack of space between the rear (west) of the building and the motte ditch makes connection likely.

The implications of access to the longer timbers required, particularly in the early castle, are considerable. Roger de Montgomery and his followers had access both to high-quality recyclable timber from at least one dismantled structure (as the redundant features on the bridge base reveal) as well as the products of a sophisticated industry of timber management. With the exception of Westminster Hall, whose original timber version of the mid-eleventh century must have been aisled to cope with its 60ft plus span, other available hall widths of the late Anglo-Saxon/early Norman period suggest that the example at Hen Domen was in the top rank. Halls with spans between 23ft and 33ft occur at the West Saxon royal palace of Cheddar (west halls I–II, Rahtz 1979), at the *burh* within the Roman fort at Portchester (Cunliffe 1976) and at the fortified house/castle at Goltho (Beresford 1987). At these sites, however, which were all ground-floor halls, the widest examples were either single- or double-aisled buildings, which emphasizes further the achievement of the Hen Domen hall. It was suggested that the successive Cheddar west halls (also unaisled) were roofed with substantial frames resting on massive horizontal (perhaps cambered) tie-beams and this is perhaps the simplest possibility for the Hen Domen hall. But the absence of detail about wall construction limits the interpretation. Nevertheless, the impression of the Hen Domen hall as a major, high-status building is confirmed by comparisons with other (unaisled or single-aisled) timber halls from castles, such as Sandal and Barnard (see Kenyon 1990, 98–110 for comparative data).

Finally, we must consider what range of functions the buildings identified actually performed. It has long been recognized that domestic buildings in castles, as in other medieval contexts, comprised not a random collection of structures for mixed and miscellaneous purposes, but units whose essential components were halls and chambers designed to accommodate households. These were supported by ancillary structures, a chapel sometimes being prominent, but the most obvious of which were the kitchens, so often, in medieval domestic planning, separate from the dwellings themselves. In castles, of course, some structures might have a purely defensive role, such as a gatehouse or mural tower, though it is obvious, from the study of stone castles, that the larger of these also provided valuable living space. In later medieval castles, the individual lodging also became an important element and some have argued that the daily use of halls declined and that of chambers and lodgings increased. To what extent, then, do the various plans of our timber castle at Hen Domen lend themselves to planning analysis? Observations are inevitably limited by lack of knowledge of the southern half of the bailey, whose evidence could theoretically change our overview dramatically. For example, we have no clear indication of a kitchen block nor of stables. Nevertheless, a few observations may be useful.

Phase Z gives little scope for archaeological interpretation and the historical framework suggests garrison rather than high-status social occupation.

Phase Y has a lower hall and a suggestion of an upper one next to a chapel but the nature of the motte top is problematic. A general problem is knowing how true is the impression of westward contraction of the built-up area. It is just possible that in phase Y the northern half was sparsely occupied but the southern half more fully, then the reverse in phase X.

Phase X gives the greatest scope for interpretation: there was a lower bailey hall and chamber, an upper bailey hall (with internal chamber division?) next to a chapel; the clay-walled house west of the cistern is more difficult, unless XIX and XVIII are a small hall and with XXII a chamber? Could this be an individual 'house', a precursor of the later 'lodging' tradition, perhaps specifically a priest's house for the nearby chapel? Or could a priest's house have been in the lower part of the mural tower (XVI) and adjacent substructure of the defences (16 and XV). The motte tower also offers more than one possibility: a vertically stacked hall/chamber arrangement (as in some stone keeps) or a horizontally planned arrangement, with two small units on either side of the dividing wall, one more public and the other more private. Or, could the motte tower in general be a chamber block for the upper bailey hall to which, we have argued, it was connected by the motte bridge? A general problem in this phase is knowing to what extent the subdivisions of the bailey palisade substructure created simply useful spaces, perhaps for storage, or occupiable spaces, perhaps for the use of local tenants, or hired men, carrying out their guard duty? The tower by the bailey entrance could well have contained the accommodation of the gatekeeper whose duty it would have been to manage it.

The primary features of the early castle suggest that the site was dominated by one large hall building, whose interpretation, in conjunction with the motte tower, parallels that of its successor in phase X. We have suggested a small hall may have crested the defences in the north-west corner. The spaces beneath the palisade could be storage or low-grade accommodation, as in phase X. The three buildings added at the rear of the rampart are problematical: rather small individually, but perhaps together a domestic range of some sort? But we do not know whether they were all exactly contemporary, which limits their interpretation.

The Planning of the Castle

In addition to the laying-out of individual buildings, any site with an enclosed perimeter, such as Hen Domen, also presented to its occupants a challenge of how best to employ the space available. In this site, as in countless others from prehistoric times onwards, there was, in one sense, a planning paradox. The overall internal shapes of the site, created by the line of the bailey rampart, the edge of the motte ditch and the perimeter of the motte top, were consistently curvilinear. The tradition of domestic and defensive building employed, however, was a rectilinear one. While this observation may seem so commonplace as to be almost superfluous, it is nevertheless a pertinent one. There was ample precedent for the planning of defended sites in rectilinear form: Roman works still littered the medieval landscape and some early medieval works, such as Anglo-Saxon *burhs*, had followed this tradition. While some castle plans adopted rectilinear form, it is notable how many did not—the majority allowed their shape to be determined more by topographical considerations and by their designer's personal wishes. In the case of a motte and bailey, we are also dealing with a design which, unlike some other medieval forms, owed nothing discernible to more ancient tradition other than the ubiquitous reliance on enclosure: the motte itself was a specifically medieval contribution to the history of domestic and defensive planning.

At Hen Domen, the builders harmonized their curvilinear framework with their rectilinear buildings in a number of simple ways, best seen in the early and middle periods of the castle (the less complete plans of later date making interpretation more difficult). First, they adapted the line of the bailey rampart so that it carried, to some extent, a series of relatively straight stretches of palisade. Three such stretches are apparent: first, from the north-west angle to the point of suggested division between the upper and lower halves of the bailey (at Building XXII); second, though here the straightening effect is less obvious, from the latter to a point adjacent to the corner of the lower hall and its annexe (XLVIII, XLIX, L); third, from the latter to the bailey entrance. Second, they laid out domestic buildings behind the defences in such a way as to reflect this. In the north-west corner of the bailey, some buildings run parallel to the back of the defences, while others run away from them (though not actually perpendicular to them). The space behind the middle section of the defences was occupied by the cistern (XLIII) and to its south-east lay another building line (the lower hall) parallel to the defences. In these ways, the effect of the overall curvilinear outlines of the site was modified: they would have been far less apparent to an occupant standing within the bailey than they are to the modern observer looking at a plan of the site. The final contribution of the rectilinear structures to the overall composition of the site comes, simply, from those buildings which occupied relatively central positions: notably the hall in front of the motte bridge and the tower on the motte. Although both stood by or on curvilinear earthworks (the motte ditch and upper motte perimeter respectively), their plans were totally uninfluenced by them. In any case, it is quite possible that the present shape of the upper motte perimeter is misleading. The large gullies around it, whose interpretation is so problematic (above) may have supported revetments which gave the top of the motte, in use, a different appearance.

Despite this degree of harmonization between the shape of the site in general and the buildings in particular, the outcome was still a compromise. Structures sometimes stood in apparently awkward juxtaposition to each other, as for example the granary (XXXVIII) and adjacent domestic building (LIV) in the early castle (and their successors in later periods). The spaces between buildings always remained irregular in shape and, particularly in the middle period, frequently rather small: the only open space of any size here was the courtyard between the upper and lower halls. In the early castle, in contrast, the equivalent courtyard was much bigger and there was also a sizeable space north of the upper hall. In the early and middle periods we also see indications of internal subdivisions or groupings of buildings. In the early castle, a fence (XXIX) separated the defences and the structures immediately behind them from the large hall in the centre of the site. In the middle period, the eastward extension of that hall seems to have been part of a general north/south subdivision of the bailey into upper and lower halves, with some social (and perhaps also defensive) significance (see above, Chapter 1, for a fuller discussion).

In this castle plan, we are clearly a long way from the greater integration of defences and domestic buildings which we see later in the middle ages. But Hen Domen was no less 'planned', following the simpler approaches of the eleventh to thirteenth centuries, than many contemporary castles whose stone remains enable us to see structures above the ground. We have an overall impression, as with most sites of the period, that the designers started with an outline dictated by defensive needs and then created within it the best possible distribution of domestic buildings: on the motte, free-standing within the bailey and behind the defences, and built into the back of the defences. We must, however, remember that the 'phases' whose overall plans it is tempting to analyse are only simplifications of what must, in reality, have been a more continuous process of evolution through repair and replacement of buildings. And although it is useful to consider the general evidence from the motte and the bailey together, we must also remember that we have no way of demonstrating that rebuildings in the bailey were contemporary with those on the motte, even though there are some attractive similarities between their evolutions.

General Discussion

It remains to consider the overall picture of life which is suggested by the various categories of archaeological evidence recovered in excavation, by the surrounding landscape and by the historical framework provided by the documentary sources. This is an important part, arguably the most important part, of a project of this sort even though all the evidence is deficient in some ways. We have excavated only parts of the site (though a very considerable proportion of the total) and it is possible that unexcavated areas hold information of wholly new character. Even within the excavated areas, important evidence may already have disappeared or been imperfectly understood by us. Our suggested reconstruction of the landscape surrounding the castle in the twelfth century is very general in nature and, were more evidence available, would no doubt bear refinement. The documentary sources, invaluable though they are, provide a selective view, reflecting the ownership of the castle and certain aspects of related political and tenurial matters. Nevertheless, despite the limitations of evidence, it should be possible to approach an overall interpretation on the basis of the variety of data available. Whatever their individual limitations, this historical, landscape, structural, artefactual and environmental data give us an overview of a type of site which, though extremely common, has remained generally less explored than other forms of medieval castle.

The Site's Development

In the conclusion to our 1982 report we discussed, in addition to matters of building construction, some issues of daily life in this timber castle and the overall development of the site's use. The structural theme has been dealt with earlier in this chapter. Overall development remains more or less as previously published, except that we can now add further details from the pre-castle, early castle and motte excavations. From beneath the castle, we have added evidence for the complexity of the immediately preceding setting: the castle was built on the junction of two parts of an agricultural landscape, one obviously ploughed in ridges, the other apparently not, whose settlement may lie to the west of the present motte, though this cannot be demonstrated with certainty. Domesday Book reveals that the area had been wasted before the Norman Conquest and used as a hunting ground rather than as a flourishing agricultural environment. The pollen analysis conducted at a much earlier stage of the excavation tended to confirm this impression (Barker & Lawson 1971). The recent excavations have also shown other features which pre-dated the development of this landscape, adding a further building (from beneath the eventual castle) and perhaps part of a field boundary (from beyond it, to the north). The cumulative effect of these tantalizing glimpses suggests that, for whatever reasons, this ridge of boulder clay overlooking the River Severn had been exploited by successive societies for a very long time, certainly from the early medieval period and probably from prehistoric times. Further excavation and fieldwork might well reveal more of this occupation.

The periods of the castle's use, as defined by the documentary evidence, remain unchanged, starting with a mainly military function in the time of Roger de Montgomery and his sons (though it is perfectly possible that they, too, and their representatives, used the area as an occasional hunting ground as their English predecessors had done). The twelfth century, when Baldwin de Boulers and his descendants ruled the marcher lordship of Montgomery, saw the development of a more residential and domestic character for the site, though still significantly defended within the frequently unstable society which separated England from Wales. In the early thirteenth century, a phase of English royal custody was succeeded by one of Welsh control (and

probably disuse), and finally, after 1223, by a period of subsidiary use to the new castle and town of Montgomery, probably lasting until late in the thirteenth century. Within this framework, there is still a general concordance of the historical periods and the main archaeological phases, if the already published dating scheme for the latter is maintained. Thus, the early castle structures are equated with the later eleventh century, the very full, compound phase of structures (published as phase X) equates with the twelfth century, the contracted building phase (Y) perhaps with the early thirteenth century and the final phase (Z) with the later thirteenth century. This concordance, allowing for the over-simplification involved in the portrayal of the main structural phases, was put forward for the bailey in our 1982 report. Allowing for the methodological difference (discussed earlier) between the excavations in the bailey and those which subsequently took place on the motte (the former reducing the northern half of the site to the underlying natural boulder clay, the latter being limited to the upper levels of the motte), it is also possible tentatively to place the sequence of motte structures encountered in parallel with those in the bailey. Thus, the first motte tower, with its large timbers, would equate to the early bailey structures, the development and gradual rebuilding of the tower would equate to the bailey's middle (X) period, its contraction into a smaller structure (admittedly its most difficult phase to interpret) might possibly equate to the bailey's phase Y, and its final (or, at least, last to survive in the archaeological record) replacement by a quite different structure might go with the bailey's phase Z. While it was argued above (Chapter 4) that equating the phases of the motte with those of the bailey was a hazardous process, there are sufficient similarities between the structural phases of

Fig. 7.3: The ruins of Henry III's castle at (New) Montgomery

Fig. 7.4: The site of the ford across the Severn at Rhydwhyman

the two areas to make this suggested scheme at least possible.

On the other hand, if certain archaeological dating issues, discussed in detail earlier, are pursued to their somewhat contentious, but theoretically possible conclusions, we would have to postulate (assuming our identification of Hen Domen with the first Montgomery castle to be correct) a different concordance of the historical framework and the archaeological phases. Here, the early castle would have fewer (known) structures, some structures previously argued to be early would become part of the twelfth-century development of the site, and full occupation in general would go on much longer than the postulated mid to late thirteenth-century phase of overlap with (New) Montgomery. This possibility raises more than an interesting issue of chronology. We have argued previously (Barker & Higham 1982, 4) that Hen Domen was of value to the occupants of (New) Montgomery castle because the latter had no visual command of the River Severn, whereas, allowing for the original heights of the tallest structures on their sites, the two castles were inter-visible. Thus, Hen Domen was part of (New) Montgomery's control of the important river crossing at Rhydwhyman, which was, throughout the middle of the thirteenth century, a critical meeting place for Welsh–English negotiations (figs 7.3 and 7.4). If a much later occupation of Hen Domen is postulated, finding a context for it is much more difficult. The onset of war in the 1270s saw renewed works at (New) Montgomery castle and town, and could, conceivably, be the context of the latest recognized occupation at Hen Domen. The development of the Welsh castle at Dolforwyn (Butler 1989, 1995), a few miles up the River Severn, also added to the

sensitivity of the central borderlands. However, the conquest of North Wales by Edward I, completed in the 1280s, reduced the political importance of the middle border for ever and (New) Montgomery castle itself was in disrepair by 1310, delapidation becoming a regular feature of fourteenth century surveys (Brown *et al.* 1963, II, 741–42). This, of course, adds to the case for the chronology for Hen Domen already published and, in general, favoured in the foregoing discussion. Had it still been a significant royal establishment in the later thirteenth and fourteenth centuries it would presumably have figured in the documented surveys of that period. Hen Domen, in the heart of a marcher lordship now in royal hands, can hardly have been occupied independently as a castle by some other lord. Even if we argue that the latest archaeological structures encountered (phase Z) reflected 'agricultural' occupation, being unrelated to the history of the 'castle' itself, we have still to explain a paucity of late occupation material (as well as the use of the motte top). The general circumstances suggest more obviously that it had gone out of use by *circa* 1300, as does the paucity of datable archaeological evidence of late date. It is also much easier to see the full archaeological picture of our published phase 'X' (which includes not only a lot of structures but also an enlargement of the main hall at the foot of the motte bridge) as a reflection of the twelfth-century de Boulers' lordship than as a reflection of a subsidiary role to New Montgomery castle, which is what it would become if the later chronology, discussed above, were preferred.

Daily Life

The impressions of daily life in the castle, provided by the structural, artefactual and environmental evidence, cannot, of course, be finely tuned either socially or chronologically. The evidence is bound to be distorted, though to what degree we cannot tell, by the largely dry nature of the site (to which our sampling of the wet part of the bailey ditch was a useful corrective) which has removed the organic evidence. It may well also be distorted by the incomplete nature of the excavation— the whole of the southern half of the bailey remains unexplored and may contain evidence which would alter our views. Having said that, the earliest levels of the castle, both on the motte and in the bailey, have very little occupation material of any sort strictly associated. This may well reflect a sparse and simple life for the garrison of the de Montgomery family, but without knowing more about the incidence of such data on other contemporary sites in the region, it is difficult to be sure. It is, however, interesting that two spindle whorls came from the early castle levels in the north-west sector (above, Chapter 5), though they might conceivably be residual finds of earlier date. Thereafter, the material becomes more plentiful, though with the added complication that some of it could be residual from the early period anyway. But it provides a general reflection of the twelfth and thirteenth centuries, when the castle's occupants enjoyed a more varied material existence. While revealing in some ways, the evidence also has limitations which must be borne in mind. The relatively short span of the castle's overall occupation, as well as the demonstrably residual or intrusive character of some of the artefactual data, makes it impossible to suggest chronological differences in the material culture enjoyed by its inhabitants: collectively, it creates an overall impression of the twelfth and thirteenth centuries, with (if the stratigraphic distribution of data is in any way meaningful) the emphasis on the twelfth. All individual categories of data have their interpretational problems. Our environmental sample (published in Barker & Higham 1982, 60–71), whose richness easily leads us to believe it was representative of its time, may in fact have been more selective: the uneroded sides of the deep pit from which it came suggest cover by a building (*ibid.*, 45), so that its contents were the result of particular processes of rubbish deposition (see fig. 7.5). Much of the plant and other remains (largely organic macro evidence together with some pollen), while useful in our reconstruction of the contemporary environment (above, Chapter 6), derived from material deliberately brought into the site and ending up as rubbish—they were not a general and representative sample from the local environment derived from wind-blown debris (though some wind-blown pollen presumably entered through the building's door and became part of the assemblage). This deep pit (from which much of the animal bone evidence also came) was also a middle and later period feature in

the site's occupation. Our view of organic data, other than from this deep pit, is confined to the small waterlogged areas excavated in the ditches: it is inherently unlikely that the wooden objects encountered are a representative sample of those originally in use, which must have been far greater in number and variety. Most important, our assemblage of discarded artefact data, of whatever sorts, represents scattered loss, not deliberate disposal in rubbish pits. Possibly there are pits in the unexcavated southern half of the bailey, but more probably much domestic rubbish was dumped on nearby fields (as was the case also with peasant communities) or in pits dug outside the castle. There is, strictly, no way of knowing how representative of the occupants' material culture are the artefacts encountered in excavation. In addition, it is clear from the study of the pottery, from both motte and bailey, and of the slag waste, that much movement, redeposition and intrusion of material took place during the fairly continuous re-building of the site. This is only to be expected, but prevents any meaningful differentiation of our data into discrete material cultures of different periods. Cleaning of the motte ditch and deposition of new material on its top during building operations there could even have resulted in artefacts originally discarded in the bailey ending up in the archaeological record of the motte (and conversely, material dropped over the shoulders of the motte may have ended up in the bailey). The study of the pottery showed no basic difference between the assemblages from motte and bailey and suggested that some cooking was also taking place on the motte. All in all, we are looking at a collection of data which reflects life in the castle as a whole, not at two assemblages of data one of which represents a discrete and higher-status style of life on the elevated motte—even though we may assume that this was the socially (as well as physically) elevated part of the site.

In our 1982 report, we ventured some provisional thoughts on life in the bailey of this little castle, whose ramparts afforded protection in a world where the possibility of violence, even warfare, was never far away. We argued that, within its confined spaces, its occupants lived in buildings whose appearance may have been more ornate than we suppose and that these occupants included households of men, women and children as well as, from time to time, members of a garrison. These people were accompanied by horses (attested by finds of numerous horse-shoe nails), presumably by dogs, and perhaps by other domesticated animals. Numbers of occupants would vary according to social and military need and the relatively simple material culture revealed in the archaeological evidence may have belied a more sophisticated lifestyle in which the enjoyment of poetry, music and social occasions, for example, may have been

Fig. 7.5: Pit 1/27 during excavation

more prominent than we can know. In our 1988 report we were able to extend interpretation by including the evidence of animal bones from the bailey. This data is published fully in the present volume (above, Chapter 5). Allowing for the generally poor bone preservation on site, the absence of an obvious kitchen site in the excavated area and the small number of contexts from which the studied bones came, this evidence makes a significant contribution to our view of lifestyle. The food remains included significant amounts of beef, and venison from red and roe deer, but pork was particularly common in the diet. Mutton, on the other hand, as well as fish, were scarcely represented in the data. Dog and cat bones, as well as carnivorous gnawing of many bones, attest the domestic animals we had hitherto guessed at, and bones of eight new-born piglets suggest a sow in the bailey. Fowl, goose, pheasant and woodcock added variety to the diet. Butchery marks on bones of many species suggest animals were brought live to the site for slaughter or as whole carcasses. But a complete pig, not subject to butchery, was buried in the rampart in circumstances which can only be guessed at (fig. 7.6).

At about the same time, we published a short essay (Barker 1987) critically examining the data from Hen Domen and questioning whether, apart from its defended character, there was anything in the archaeological (as opposed to historical) record to suggest high social status for its inhabitants. The repertoire of timber building techniques encountered had, for the most part, a long ancestry and was found on all sorts of archaeological sites. The artefact evidence was, on the whole, fairly simple and utilitarian in character. Life, it was argued, was simple and hardy. This was a useful exercise in encouraging close scrutiny of the data and was further

pursued in our discussion of Hen Domen in the wider context of timber castles generally (Higham and Barker 1992). But equally important observations, which enable an overall picture to be formed, are those arising either from the documentary sources (which certainly reveal a high-status castle-building class) or from common-sense arguments about the limitations of archaeological data. The latter cannot, by their very nature, reveal certain aspects of life which are critical to this issue, nor others (for example religion) which were crucial to the quality of people's lives. It cannot reveal the social hierarchy which may have existed except in very simple ways: here the defences of the site are of utmost importance, because their construction implies either control of resources by a powerful element of society or a society with sophisticated communal organization. Archaeology does not always reveal how people tied up their wealth: if this was in rich material culture it may be visible in the archaeological record, but if it was in some other form,

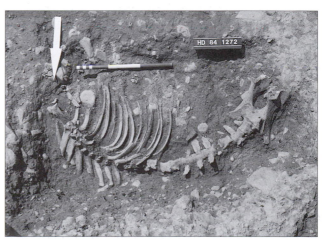

Fig 7.6: Pig burial in bailey rampart

Fig. 7.7: Metal-working debris in Building XV

for example livestock or land, it will not be.

In drawing the various strands of discussion together, in this final publication, we have not only the benefit of hindsight but also of more thorough analysis of data than was previously the case. Further study of the pottery suggests the range of types encountered to be no different from that encountered on a contemporary rural or urban site, to some extent supporting the argument explored in 1987. But, in retrospect, that argument underestimated the significance of the animal bone evidence (whose study was just beginning) and particularly the metalwork (whose study had hardly begun). The bone evidence included deer and boar, debris from two types of hunting, as well as goshawk bones stained green from contact with metal which may indicate it was a ringed hunting bird. Before the Norman Conquest, this area had been used as a hunting chase by three Mercian *thegns*, and the castle could have had a subsidiary role as a hunting centre in early Norman times. There is subsequently direct evidence for hunting in the de Boulers period, in the form of later references to provision of hunting attendants (Barker & Higham 1982, Chapter III). It is likely that all the medieval lords regarded these lands as a hunting preserve, regardless of the varied agriculture practised within them, with perhaps the most productive areas around the Ffridd and Lymore. Recent published discussions have emphasized the royal and aristocratic basis of medieval deer hunting as well as the preponderantly high-status character of the sites in whose excavation most deer bones are found. Where they are found on peasant sites, they are assumed to be an illegal food source derived from poaching (Stamper 1988; Grant 1988).

The metalwork is important in two respects, one general and one particular. First, although it is true that many of the items discovered are simple, their quantity is evidence of a community sufficiently wealthy to be able to own and discard them. In the middle ages, metal resources were highly valued and the more so the lower down society we descend. Broken or redundant items were a source of recyclable material: the classic example is the plough, which underpinned the whole of society but which is scarce in the archaeological record because its metal parts were melted down and re-worked. Analysis of the metal slags from Hen Domen has revealed that iron smithing (but not smelting) was taking place at the castle, but its occupants were sufficiently wealthy not only to possess but also to discard a significant number of metal objects. The floor of Building XV (Barker & Higham 1982, fig. 23) in the middle period was strewn with debris from metal working (fig. 7.7). And while there is some evidence for on-site manufacture of (presumably simple) iron objects, the similarity of the metalwork in general with that from castle sites in other regions reveals that the occupants of Hen Domen had access via market and personal links to items manufactured in possibly distant places.

Second, there is the nature of the items themselves. From the bailey, in addition to tools of many sorts there are weapons or related items including spurs, links from chain mail, knives and arrow heads which themselves contribute to a high-status interpretation of the site. Parts of padlocks and padlock keys suggest that domestic security was taken seriously. Other items from the bailey include decorative strips of bronze, perhaps from small household items of wood, as well as other high quality

Fig. 7.8: Wooden tub in situ during excavation

personal effects including decorated gilded buckles. From the motte, the iron objects include a padlock bolt, a pair of hair or cloth shears, buckles, a knife blade, a horse-shoe fragment and horse-shoe nails, a prick-spur, arrow-heads and a chain-mail link. A fascinating find, the circumstances of whose loss may have been an intriguing, though irretrievable episode, is the surgeon's cutting instrument. Non-ferrous items from the motte include parts of several copper alloy items, many of which were gilded. The analysis of the animal bones from the bailey reveals the use of saws and other heavy bladed tools, whose effects were visible in butchery marks. This is a useful reminder that the array of tools in use would have been wider than that which happens to survive in the physical record. Assessment of the artefactual and environmental evidence, *in toto*, suggests a distinctly high-status character for at least some of the occupants of this site. The impression of relative simplicity, which coloured our earlier published views, came perhaps from the slow accumulation of this data, over a period of many years in which the data was not addressed as a whole, which lessened its impact.

Other aspects of the material culture also shed light on life at old Montgomery, though not particularly on the 'status' issue. Woodworking was clearly practiced to a high level, reflected not just in general terms by the

wholly timber building tradition of the site but by the wooden artefacts recovered from the bailey ditch. However, while (from a twentieth-century perspective) being impressed by the manufacture of the wooden tub in particular (fig. 7.8), we should remember that, in their contemporary context, these were everyday objects of probably little note to their users. The same is true of the miscellaneous objects of bone, stone and leather which represent presumably humdrum items to medieval eyes, though some, to us, especially the two mortars/stoups, have a greater fascination. The evidence of wood shavings and leather offcuts (recovered from wet deposits), as well as the metallurgical evidence, also shows us that manufacturing activity was taking place in the castle itself.

We can never know the provenance of most of the items found on site. Some were probably made locally. Others may have come, via diverse contacts both economic and personal, from far afield. Of local marketing arrangements we are very ignorant. Shrewsbury was the nearest town of any size. Chirbury, the parochial centre before the creation of New Montgomery, may have had a local market. There is no reason why exchange should not have occurred with nearby Welsh centres, for example Welshpool, where the princes of Powys established a castle. At the end of the twelfth century, the de Boulers lords themselves seem to have been encouraging a market, perhaps even an incipient

Fig. 7.9: Reconstructed jug of (developed) Stamford ware

borough, at Old Montgomery itself (above, Chapter 6). With the pottery, through petrological and stylistic analysis, we are on slightly firmer ground. Most of it came from the neighbouring area, though we are ignorant of production sites. The rest came from the adjacent English shires—Shropshire, Herefordshire, Worcestershire and Staffordshire—though not necessarily as a result of direct marketing links with such places, and a re-distributive trade, perhaps through Shrewsbury, is likely. Occasional pieces from further afield, such as the Stamford ware and the French import, may have arrived as a result of indirect marketing links but could equally have resulted from the movement of personal baggage (the de Boulers had marriage links with a family in the Yorkshire/Lincolnshire area in the twelfth century, which might explain the developed Stamford ware). The accompanying photograph (fig. 7.9) of a reconstructed jug of this ware is a useful antidote to the fragmentary sherds from which our observations about pottery have to be made.

As well as exploring daily life through specific physical evidence, we can also approach it through slightly less tangible routes. One of these is to consider how past societies perceived the space around them. One mundane, but absolutely critical aspect of this issue was discussed earlier: that is how the occupants of Hen Domen organized the space within the castle for their buildings. Although the distribution of buildings was sparser in the early and late periods of the site's occupation, throughout the twelfth century it was a congested place whose interior must have been almost claustrophobic. In this context, the contemporary perception of overall space was probably very limited, though attention would certainly have been drawn by the hall in front of the motte bridge and the motte tower rising behind it. Whatever changes took place within the overall evolution of the site, the dominance of the motte and its building was a recurrent theme. Also fairly obvious is the fact that from within the site there would have been no view of the surrounding countryside: this would have been visible only from the bailey defences and from the top of the motte. This point requires us to make an important mental adjustment of our own, because the earthworks of timber castles now seem so open. In the late eleventh century, the castle was on the western fringe of the earldom of Shrewsbury but supported by its own *castellarium*. In the thirteenth century, it was largely a subsidiary fortification for New Montgomery castle. But in the twelfth century, from the building on the motte, the de Boulers would have seen much of their lordship: to the immediate west, where it ran with the Severn, to the north, where it ran with the lands of their Corbet neighbours, and to the east, where the lands around Chirbury adjoined the royal shire of Shropshire. Only

to the south was the view blocked, by the higher ground on which the Iron Age hillfort of Ffridd Faldwyn stood. With the motte tower at its full height, of course, the reverse is also true: from the more immediate parts of this marcher lordship the de Boulers' tenants would have seen the castle to whose lords they owed service. To our minds, such an observation fits nicely with the current trend for 'symbolic' interpretations of landscapes. In the twelfth century, of course, the importance of this fact was only partly symbolic: it also had crucial practical importance. We must not forget the social reality of medieval marcher areas. The de Boulers enjoyed, under the ultimate overlordship of the Norman and Angevin kings, self-governing authority and independence in financial, judicial, military and tenurial matters. Of this fact, both they and their tenants would have been constantly aware. Recently, the nature of medieval 'border' societies in Europe generally has become a subject of renewed interest (see, for example, Bartlett and MacKay 1989). In a modest way, our exploration of Old Montgomery makes a contribution to that wider study.

Another issue of perception of which we must be aware is our own cultural predilection for imbuing landscapes with aesthetic qualities. There would now be no doubt, in the mind of even the least visually educated observer, that the landscapes of the English–Welsh border are at the very least pleasant environments. For more visually attuned observers, including ourselves, these landscapes are outstandingly beautiful. But this appreciation is partly created by the traditions of recent centuries, in which rural landscapes have become, as well as the 'factory-floors' of agriculture, the subjects of art and literature, as well as places of leisure for visitors as much as for their inhabitants. Though we can never be certain, it is interesting to speculate whether the castle's occupants or their tenants shared this outlook or whether their attitude to their surroundings was purely functional, their notion of 'landscape' purely exploitational. It is hard, however, to imagine that they were not to some degree touched by the same spirit as ourselves.

It is, of course, the period of the de Boulers lordship in which this little castle gives us the best window on medieval society. The late eleventh and early thirteenth centuries were more dramatic, involving one of the most powerful families of the Anglo-Norman world and then an English king and his army. But here, despite the magnitude of the surrounding events, the personal involvement of the great men concerned was sporadic and the castle's daily life more the concern of delegates. But in the twelfth century, Old Montgomery was the only castle of modest marcher lords whose families would have been more regularly resident and whose social and economic network depended more on the castle and its lands. The bulk of the structural, artefactual and environmental evidence excavated comes from this period, and, among the various reconstruction drawings, the view depicting the twelfth-century castle has most to draw the eye. It was also the obvious subject matter for three-dimensional reconstruction. The model built by Peter Scholefield, exhibited permanently in Montgomery Civic Society's exhibition centre, 'The Bell', is not simply a fascinating exercise in turning excavated data into tangible form. It is also an inspired leap into the perception of the past: when viewed in close-up, from within, this model goes some way to creating the built environment of the castle's occupants, perhaps in a way impossible by any other means. And through this built environment (despite the errors of detailed interpretation which it may contain) we can enter, in some limited way, the lives of its inhabitants. The accompanying photographs (figs 7.10 and 7.11) show a general view and a more detailed internal view.

If more direct documentary evidence of the twelfth century had survived to accompany the archaeological data, reconstructing the overall social life of the de Boulers' castle would be a fascinating task, whether in

Fig. 7.10: General view of model of Hen Domen (model by Peter Scholefield)

the clinical manner of traditional scholarship or the more creative manner of Le Roy Ladurie's *Montaillou*. Administration of the lordship must have involved some record-keeping, but, like so much else from the world of secular archives, this has not survived. What we do have from the historical sources (largely royal and of later date—see Barker & Higham 1982, Chapter III, for a full discussion) are fascinating but selective glimpses: for example of the tenants' obligations to provide fighting men, hunting attendants and provisions, and of the steward's journeys from his (Shropshire) manor of Hodnet to carry out the financial business of the lordship at the castle. There must have been periods of intense activity here, for example when relations with neighbours were bad, whether they were the Welsh across the Severn or the Corbets (who sometimes had a violent reputation in later centuries) across the Camlad. Courts of the lordship, at which tenants would appear, or great hunting parties, would also have been high-spots of activity. At other times, daily life would be calmer, the numbers of castle residents very small and perhaps the lord or members of his family absent. Religious life was ever-present, with a private chapel served no doubt by a household chaplain who perhaps also provided some education for the lord's children. Deaths of tenants and lesser household members would involve journeys to the parochial centre at Chirbury, three miles away, whose church had burial rights and to which the castle chapel was presumably subordinate. Sometimes visitors would be present, perhaps from the de Boulers's lands in eastern England, which they held by marriage in the later twelfth century. The routine of life was no doubt sometimes interrupted by events of particular significance in personal terms. We know of only a handful of these, but they are all revealing. In the 1130s, Stephen de Boulers was killed in warfare against the Welsh. We do not know the circumstances, but the impact within the lordship must have been great (as, no doubt, it was also across the Severn, when members of Welsh princely families were killed in confrontations with the Anglo-Normans). It was a period when the customs of warfare and attitudes to enemies were evolving. Celtic attitudes remained traditional and harsh, whereas 'Norman' culture increasingly revealed restrained attitudes and mercy towards high-status opponents (Gillingham 1992). How this affected daily life and views in the always potentially turbulent marches we cannot know, but it may have been the Welsh massacre of the castle's garrison in 1095 which so offended Norman attitudes that the campaign in Wales which resulted was led by the king (William Rufus) in person. The incident is also a useful reminder of the martial rôle of timber castles, which, despite their undoubted social functions was very important. This theme has been recently emphasised to good effect in

Fig. 7.11: Detail of Hen Domen model

the wider context of medieval warfare (France 1999).

On the other hand, later in the century, the second Baldwin de Boulers married a woman who, to judge from her name, Gwenllian 'the fair', was a Welsh princess, perhaps from the neighbouring kingdom of Powys. Whether this was a love-match born of some social encounter, or whether it was an arranged marriage with political purpose, we do not know. But we can be sure it would have been the occasion not only of suitable celebration but also of much to-ing and fro-ing of personnel across the ford at Rhydwhyman. These contrasting sides of Anglo–Welsh relations reveal much about the nature of life on the medieval marches. Nor must we imagine that our marcher community was cut off from events well beyond its immediate neighbourhood. Even lords of modest means, as were the de Boulers, travelled, and the historical sources reveal mainly those individuals who represented direct descent in the male line. Others in the family may, for all we know, have gone on crusade, or entered the church. Alan de Boulers, a relative of Robert de Boulers, became a member of the priory of Augustinian canons which Robert founded at Chirbury (after an unsuccessful start at Snead) in the 1190s. Robert and his wife, Hilary Trussebut, chose however to be buried at Lilleshall Abbey in Shropshire, another religious house which they had also favoured (VCH, II, 59–60). A more distant member of the family unwittingly contributed to one of the most notorious events of the twelfth century. A daughter of the first Baldwin de Boulers and Sybil de Falaise married Richard fitzUrse, lord of Bulwick in Northamptonshire. Their son was Reginald fitzUrse, one of the murderers of Thomas Becket, archbishop of

Canterbury (Barlow 1986, 236). This event, news of which spread quickly, took place in 1170 when Robert, grandson of Baldwin de Boulers, was lord of Montgomery. The stir caused at the castle when Robert and his family learned their cousin was an infamous assassin can only be imagined!

Epilogue

At the start of his novel *The Go-Between*, published in 1953, L.P. Hartley wrote: 'The past is a foreign country: they do things differently there'. For many years of the excavation, in our main site-hut in the bailey at Hen Domen, we had this printed, in large letters, on a notice on the wall as a reminder of the difficulty of the task pursued. It is undoubtedly true that the separations of time, as well as of place, create barriers to understanding which are not easily overcome. Nevertheless, if we regard the passage of time as an insuperable obstacle to understanding the past, we confine ourselves to an appreciation of human experience which is extraordinarily short-term: the basis of historical and archaeological enquiry is that we *can*, however imperfectly, transcend this barrier. At the start of this volume we declared that this research project (a somewhat simplistic phrase doing little justice to the complexity of circumstance underlying its long life) was conducted in the belief that there exists some continuity of human thought and experience across the centuries. And it is in reinforcing that view that we draw this discussion to a close. The men and women who built and occupied this castle and its surrounding landscape in the middle ages were part of the same Judaeo-Christian culture as ourselves. Allowing for differences in dress

Fig. 7.12: View south-westwards towards Wales from Montgomery

and hairstyle, they looked physically the same as us (a fact underlined by the current vogue for facial reconstruction from old skulls). They had a written and spoken culture in languages which we can understand: we see the castle's owners through the written culture of Latin, but they would have spoken a version of old northern French. Baldwin de Boulers would presumably have been addressed as Bauduins in everyday parlance.

Although the political conditions of Roger de Montgomery's earldom may now seem somewhat strange to us and the marcher lordships have long disappeared, the 'border' character of this area (as of others) has endured. 'Welsh Wales' lies across the river Severn. 'English England' lies in Shropshire (figs 7.12 and 7.13). The marcher lordship of Montgomery has, however, left a cultural legacy, because, while influenced by English and Welsh migration in later times and administratively located in Wales since the sixteenth century, the area still contains a 'border society' with roots in the Celtic, English and Anglo-Norman past. The most obvious man-made symbols of 'border' in the present landscape are Offa's Dyke and the castle established by Henry III. But Old Montgomery castle, at Hen Domen, though now a less spectacular monument, was of no less importance in the history of this borderland and the development of its culture.

Fig. 7.13: View north-eastwards towards England from Montgomery

A PHOTOGRAPHIC MEMOIR

It is inevitably the case that excavation reports, while communicating the essential academic results of research, cannot convey the daily reality of the excavations themselves. This is even more true when, as at Hen Domen, excavations continue over many years and acquire their own 'culture'. Excavation, on whatever scale, is inevitably a slow process. A photograph or plan of excavated evidence rarely even hints at the painstaking effort which has made it possible. Nor, in the case of excavations such at Hen Domen, where everyone lived together on, or close to, the site itself, can the published record provide a sense of the communal domestic life which underpinned the archaeological effort. These points have been explained, and illustrated, in numerous public lectures given in many places over many years.

As a brief gesture towards a more holistic account of the project described in this volume we offer the following montage of photographs. It is a reminder that, not only is archaeological evidence hard won from the ground, but that the process of excavation itself is a rewarding experience in its own right. While this may seem an obvious point to make, it is worth making at a time when the numbers of traditional large scale volunteer-based excavations have declined.

REFERENCES

Arnold, C.J. & Reilly, P. 1986: 'Archaeological investigations at Lymore Park, Montgomery', *Montgomery Collections* 74, 73–78

Arnold, C.J. 1990: *The Archaeology of Montgomeryshire* (Welshpool)

Astill, G. & Grant, A. 1988: *The Countryside of Medieval England* (Oxford)

Baillie, M.G.L. 1977: 'Dublin medieval chronology', *Tree-Ring Bulletin* 37, 13–20

Baillie, M.G.L. 1982: *Tree-Ring Dating and Archaeology* (London)

Baillie, M.G.L. & Pilcher, J.R. 1973: 'A simple cross-dating program for tree-ring research', *Tree-Ring Bulletin* 33, 7–14

Barker, P.A. 1970: *The Medieval Pottery of Shropshire from the Conquest to 1400* (Shropshire Archaeological Society)

Barker, P.A. 1977: *Techniques of Archaeological Excavation* (London)

Barker, P.A. 1986: *Understanding Archaeological Excavation* (London)

Barker, P.A. 1987: 'Hen Domen revisited', in Kenyon & Avent 1987, 51–54

Barker, P.A. 1988: 'Hen Domen', *Current Archaeology* 111, vol. 10, no. 4 (September 1988), 137–42

Barker, P.A. & Higham, R.A. 1982: *Hen Domen, Montgomery. A Timber Castle on the English–Welsh border* (Royal Archaeological Institute)

Barker, P.A. & Higham, R.A. 1988: *Hen Domen Montgomery. A Timber Castle on the English–Welsh Border. Excavations 1960–1988. A Summary Report* (Hen Domen Archaeological Project, Exeter & Worcester)

Barker, P.A. & Lawson, J. 1971: 'A pre-Norman field system at Hen Domen, Montgomery', *Medieval Archaeology* 5, 58–72

Barlow, F. 1986: *Thomas Becket* (London)

Bartlett, R. & Mackay, A. (eds) 1989: *Medieval Frontier Societies* (Oxford)

Barton, P.G. 1997: 'Medieval windmills in Montgomeryshire and the Marches', *Montgomery Collections* 85, 51–61

Basset, S. (ed.) 1989: *The Origins of Anglo-Saxon Kingdoms* (Leicester)

Bauch, J., Eckstein, D. & Brauner, G. 1974: 'Dendrochronologische Untersuchungen an Gemäldetafeln und Plastiken', *Maltechnik Restauro* 80, 32–40

Bedwin, O. & Holgate, R. 1985: 'Excavations at Copse Farm, Oving, West Sussex', *Proceedings of the Prehistoric Society* 51, 215–45

Beresford, G. 1987: *Goltho: The development of an Early Medieval Manor c.850–1150* (English Heritage Archaeological Report, no. 4)

Biddle, Martin 1990: *Object and economy in Medieval Winchester. Winchester Studies 7.ii. Artefacts from Medieval Winchester* (Oxford)

Blockley, K. et al 1990: 'Excavations in the vicinity of Forden Gaer Roman Fort, Powys 1987', *Montgomery Collections* 78, 17–46

Brothwell, D. & Higgs, E. (eds) 1969: *Science in Archaeology* (London)

Brown, R.A., Colvin H.M. & Taylor, A.J. 1963: *A History of the King's Works: The Middle Ages,* 2 vols & plans (London)

Browne, S. 1985: 'Report on the bone from Oving, West Sussex', in Bedwin & Holgate 1985, 232–39

Buteux, V. 1998: 'Pottery from the Queen Anne House site', in Baker, N.J. (ed.) *Shrewsbury Abbey: Studies in the Archaeology and History of an Urban Abbey* (Shropshire Archaeological and Historical Society)

Butler, L. 1989: 'Dolforwyn castle, Montgomery, Powys. First report: the excavations 1981–1986', *Archaeologia Cambrensis* 138, 78–98

Butler, L. 1995: 'Dolforwyn castle, Montgomery, Powys. Second report', *Archaeologia Cambrensis* 144, 133–203

Charles, B.G. 1938: *Non-Celtic Place-Names of Wales* (London)

Clark, John (ed) 1995: *The medieval horse and its equipment c.1150–c.1450. Medieval finds from excavations in London: 5* (London)

Clarke, P.V. 1982: 'The pottery' in Barker & Higham 1982, 73–86

Coad, J.G. & Streeten, A.D.F. 1982: 'Excavations at Castle Acre Castle, Norfolk, 1972–1977: country house and castle of the Norman earls of Surrey', *Archaeological Journal* 139, 138–301

Cowgill, J. et al. 1987: *Knives and Scabbards. Medieval finds from excavations in London: 1* (London)

Crew, P. 1980: 'Forden Gaer, Montgomery', *Bulletin of the Board of Celtic Studies* 28, iv, 730–742

Cunliffe, B. & Poole, C. 1991: *Danebury: An Iron Age Hillfort in Hampshire. Vol. 5, The Excavations 1979–1988: The Finds* (Council for British Archaeology Research Report no. 73)

Cunliffe, B. 1976: *Excavations at Portchester Castle. Vol. II: Saxon* (Society of Antiquaries of London Research Report no. XXXIII)

Davies, R.R. 1987: *Conquest, Co-existence and Change in Wales 1063–1415* (Oxford)

Egan, G. & Pritchard, F. 1991: *Dress Accessories c.1150–c.1450: Medieval Finds from Excavations in London 3* (London)

Ekwall, E. 1960: *The Concise Oxford Dictionary of English Place-Names* (4th edition. Oxford)

Ellis, B. 1982: 'Spurs', in Coad & Streeten 1982, 230–35

Everson, P., Barker, P.A. & Musson, C.R. 1991: 'Three case studies of ridge and furrow: 1. Offa's Dyke at Dudston in Chirbury, Shropshire. A pre-Offan field system?', *Landscape History* 13, 53–63

Fletcher, J.M. 1976: 'Oak antiques. Tree-ring analysis', *Antique Collecting and Antique Finder* (Oct), 9–13

Fletcher, J.M. 1977: 'Tree-ring chronologies for the 6th and 16th centuries for oaks of southern and eastern England', *Journal of Archaeological Science* 4, 335–52

Fletcher, J.M. (ed.) 1978: *Dendrochronology in Europe* (British Archaeological Reports, no. 51)

Fox, C. 1955: *Offa's Dyke: A Field Survey of the Western Frontier-Works of Mercia in the Seventh and Eighth Centuries AD* (Oxford and London)

Foxall, H.D.G. 1980: *Shropshire Field Names* (Shrewsbury)

France, J. 1999: *Western warfare in the age of the Crusades, 1000–1300* (London)

Gelling, M. 1984: *Place-Names in the Landscape* (London)

Gelling, M. 1989: 'The early history of western Mercia', in Basset 1989, 184–201

Gelling, M. 1990: *The Place-Names of Shropshire. Part One: The Major Names of Shropshire* (English Place-Name Society)

Gibson, A. 1992: 'Ffridd Faldwyn, Montgomery', *Archaeology in Wales* 32, 92

Gillingham, J. 1992: 'Conquering the barbarians: war and chivalry in twelfth-century Britain', *Haskins Society Journal* 4, 67–84

Goodall, A.R. 1982: 'Objects of copper alloy', in Coad & Streeten 1982, 235–40

Goodall, A.R. 1987: 'Objects of copper alloy and lead', in Beresford 1987, 173–76

Grant, A. 1982: 'The use of tooth wear as a guide to the age of domestic ungulates' in Wilson, Grigson, & Payne 1982, 91–108

Grant, A. 1988: 'Animal resources', in Astill & Grant 1988, 149–87

Griffiths 1989: 'The emergence of the modern settlement pattern, 1450–1700', in Owen 1989, 225–48

Gwynne, T.A. 1971–72: 'Domesday society in Shropshire', *Transactions of the Shropshire Archaeological Society* 59, 91–103

Higham, R.A. 1977: 'Excavations at Okehampton Castle, Devon. Part I: The motte and keep', *Proceedings of the Devon Archaeological Society* 35, 3–42

Higham, R.A., Allan, J.P. & Blaylock, S.R. 1982: 'Excavations at Okehampton Castle, Devon. Part II: The bailey', *Proceedings of the Devon Archaeological Society* 40, 19–151

Higham, R.A. & Barker P.A. 1992: *Timber Castles* (London)

Hillam, J. 1981: 'An English tree-ring chronology AD 404–1216', *Medieval Archaeology* 25, 31–44

Hillam, J. 1983: 'Tree-ring dates for buildings with oak timber', *Vernacular Architecture* 14, 61

Hillam. J., Morgan, R.A. & Tyers, I. 1987: 'Sapwood estimates and the dating of short ring sequences', in Ward 1987, 165–85

Hollstein, E. 1980: *Mitteleuropäische Eichenchronologie* (Mainz)

Hope-Taylor, B. 1977: *Yeavering: An Anglo-British Centre of Early Northumbria* (London)

Jessop, O. 1996: 'A new artefact typology for the study of medieval arrowheads', *Medieval Archaeology* 40, 192–205

Jones, G. 1960: 'The pattern of settlement on the Welsh border', *Agricultural History Review* 8, 66–81

Jones, G. 1989: 'The Dark Ages', in Owen 1989, 177–197

Jones, N. & Britnell, W. 1998: 'Montgomery town wall: excavation and recording at Plas Du, 1995–1997', *Montgomery Collections* 86, 5–15

Kenyon, J.R. 1990: *Medieval Fortifications* (Leicester)

Kenyon, J.R. & Avent, R. (eds) 1987: *Castles in Wales and the Marches: Essays in Honour of D.J. Cathcart King* (Cardiff)

Kilby, K. 1971: *The Cooper and his Trade* (London)

Kilmurry, K. 1980: *The Pottery Industry of Stamford, Lincolnshire, c.AD 850–1250* (British Archaeological Reports, no. 84)

King, D.J.C. & Spurgeon, C.J. 1965: 'The mottes in the vale of Montgomery', *Archaeologia Cambrensis* 114, 69–86

Knight, J.K. 1990–91: 'The pottery from Montgomery castle', *Medieval and Later Pottery in Wales* 12, 1–100

Knight, J.K. 1992: 'Excavations at Montgomery Castle. Part I: The documentary evidence, structures and excavated features', *Archaeologia Cambrensis* 141, 97–180

Knight, J.K. 1993: 'Excavations at New Montgomery castle. Part II: The finds. Metalwork', *Archaeologia Cambrensis* 142, 182–242

Knight, J.K. 1994: 'Excavations at New Montgomery castle. Part III: the finds—other than metalwork', *Archaeologia Cambrensis* 143, 139–203

Laxton, R.R., Litton, C.D. & Simpson, W.G. 1983: 'Tree-ring dates for some East Midlands buildings: 2', *Transactions of the Thoroton Society of Nottingham* 87, 40–45

Lewis, J.M. 1993: 'Excavations at Loughor Castle, West Glamorgan, 1969–1973', *Archaeologia Cambrensis* 142, 99–181

Maltby, M., 1982, 'Animal and bird bones' in Higham, Allan & Blaylock 1982, 114–18

Morgan, R. 1981: 'The territorial divisions of medieval Montgomeryshire', *Montgomery Collections* 69, 9–44

Morgan, R. 1997: *Welsh Place-Names in Shropshire* (Cardiff)

Morgan. R.A., Hillam, J., Coles, J.M. & McGrail, S. 1981: 'Reconciling tree-ring sampling with conservation', *Antiquity* 55, 90–95

Morris, C. 1980: 'A group of early medieval spades,' *Medieval Archaeology* 24, 205–10

Noble, F. 1983: *Offa's Dyke Reviewed* (British Archaeological Reports, no. 114; ed. M. Gelling)

O'Neil, B.H. St J. 1942–43: 'Excavations at Ffridd Faldwyn Camp, Montgomery, 1937–39', *Archaeologia Cambrensis* 97, 1–57

Owen, D. H. (ed.) 1989: *Settlement and Society in Wales* (Cardiff)

Owen, D. H. 1989: 'The Middle Ages', in Owen 1989, 199–223

Powis Schedule 1971: Schedule of Powis Castle Deeds and Documents, 5 vols, National Library of Wales, Aberystwyth

Pryce, C.S. 1912: 'The Flos lands', *Montgomery Collections* 36, 53–78

Rahtz, P. 1979: *The Saxon and Medieval Palaces at Cheddar* (British Archaeological Reports, no. 65)

Ratkai, S. forthcoming: 'The pottery', in Palmer, N. & West, G., *Excavations at Haughmond Abbey*

Rees, W. 1932: *South Wales and the Border in the Fourteenth Century,* four sheets (Ordnance Survey)

Rees, W. 1972: *An Historical Atlas of Wales from Early to Modern Times* (2nd edition Cardiff)

Rhodes, M. 1980: 'Wood and woody tissue', in 'Excavations at Billingsgate Buildings, Lower Thames St., London, 1974)', *London & Middlesex Archaeological Society,* Special Paper no. 4, 144–46

Salzman, L.F. 1952: *Building in England down to 1540* (Oxford)

Saunders, P.& E. (eds) 1991: *Salisbury Museum Mediaeval Catalogue* (Part I) (Salisbury and South Wiltshire Museum)

Siebenlist-Kerner, V. 1978: 'The chronology, 1341–1636, for certain hillside oaks from western England and Wales', in Fletcher 1978, 157–61

Silver, I.A. 1969: 'The ageing of domestic animals' in Brothwell & Higgs 1969, 283–302

Smith, A.H. 1956: *English Place-Name Elements* (2 vols, English Place-Name Society)

Smith, W.J. (ed.) 1963: *Herbert Correspondence,* (Board of Celtic Studies, University of Wales, History & Law Series, 21)

Stamper, P. 1988: 'Woods and parks', in Astill & Grant 1988, 128–48

Sylvester, D. 1955: 'The rural landscape of eastern Montgomeryshire', *Montgomery Collections* 54, 3–26

Sylvester, D. 1969: *The Rural Landscape of the Welsh Borderland* (London)

Taylor, C.C. 1975: *Fields in the English Landscape* (London)

Thompson, K. 1990: 'Robert of Bellême reconsidered', *Anglo-Norman Studies* 13, 263–86

van Houts, E. 1987: 'The ship-list of William the Conqueror', *Anglo-Norman Studies* 10, 157–183

VCH Shropshire II 1973: *Victoria History of the County of Shropshire,* vol. II (ed. A.T. Gaydon, Oxford)

von den Driesch, A. 1976: *A Guide to the Measurement of Animal Bones from Archaeological Sites,* Peabody Museum Bulletin 1

Ward, R.G. (ed.) 1987: *Applications of Tree-Ring Studies* (British Archaeological Reports, International series no. S.333)

Warlop, H.E. 1975–76: *The Flemish Nobility before 1300* (Eng. trans. by J.B. Ross, 4 vols, Kortrijk)

Whitfield, J. 1951–53: 'The lordship of Cause, 1540–41', *Transactions of the Shropshire Archaeological Society* 54, 45–68, 327–37

Wilson, B., Grigson, C. & Payne, S. (eds) 1982: *Ageing and Sexing Animal Bones from Archaeological Sites* (British Archaeological Reports, no. 109)